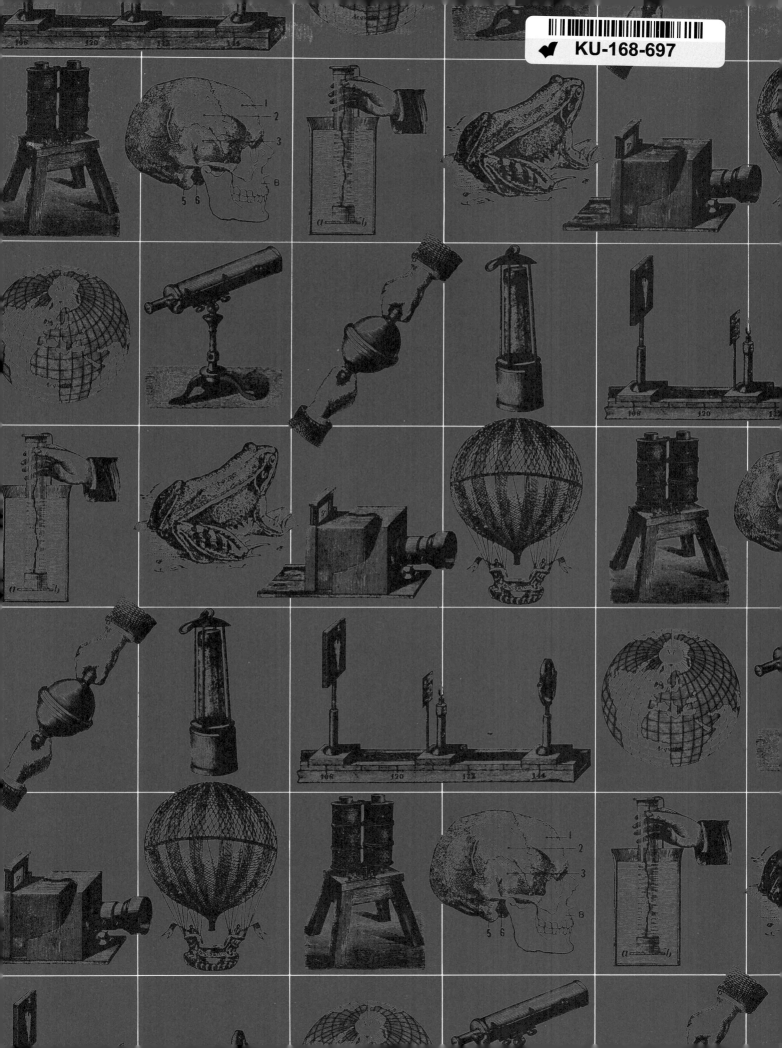

THE
FAMILY
SCIENTIST

THE
FAMILY
SCIENTIST

JUDITH HANN

MACDONALD GENERAL BOOKS
MACDONALD & JANE'S · LONDON & SYDNEY

First published in 1979 by
Macdonald and Jane's Publishers Limited
Paulton House, 8 Shepherdess Walk,
London, N1 7LW

Made by Roxby Press Productions Limited
98 Clapham Common Northside,
London, SW4 9SG
Editorial Director Michael Leitch
Editors Jana Gough, Louisa McDonnell, Ann Ridley
Art Director David Pocknell
Designer Michael Cavers
Picture Research Ikon
Production Reynolds Clark Associates Limited
Printed and bound in Belgium by
Henri Proost & Cie, Turnhout

CONTENTS

ABOUT THE BOOK

Studying and understanding the world around us should be one of the most compelling and satisfying things to do. But, unfortunately, science is often shunned because it has a reputation for being rather dull and grey – a reputation which is not always helped by existing methods of teaching or by science books.
I have therefore tried to achieve something different with **The Family Scientist.** Many of you will have read books at school about the principles behind science, and you may have found ideas for practical projects and magical scientific tricks in your local library.
But **The Family Scientist** is unusual in combining those facts and experiments in a simple, colourful way which I hope will stimulate a deeper interest in all areas of science. Each of the eleven sections starts with an outline of the principles involved in chemistry, astronomy, etc., and then goes on to related projects and experiments which are illuminating, and often amusing, to carry out.
I tried to avoid making them too complicated or daunting, so that the youngest and most inexperienced scientists can cope with them in and around their own homes. They do not need fancy, expensive equipment. Almost everything necessary is already there in your house.
So have fun with the book, and I hope that it will lead you to new areas of interest, so that an ardent biologist, for example, will become fascinated by chemical reactions, while the amateur astronomers amongst you will want to learn more about the goings-on in your own bodies.

Judith Hann

PART ONE
SCIENCE
IN THE HOME

When you imagine a scientist at work, you perhaps think of him or her in a laboratory surrounded by mysterious-looking equipment. You think of experiments involving lots of intricate flasks and tubes carrying bubbling, coloured liquids or vapours. You probably think of electron microscopes, sophisticated magnets and electrical gadgetry.

But you must not assume that science is limited to the laboratory. Chemical and other changes are going on around us all the time, in a growing flower, in a rusting nail, and on the kitchen stove. Cooking, in fact, is a chemical process, and the salt, vinegar, bicarbonate of soda and alcohol used in recipes are no less chemicals than the suspicious-looking substances contained in the glass-stoppered bottles of laboratories.

Your home is really a perfect place to learn more about science. The kitchen, the bathroom and the garden contain all you need to help you in your experiments. The kitchen is ideal for most demonstrations in this book. If compounds like water, salt and vinegar are accidentally spilled, there are no carpets and cushions to be damaged. There is always a good water supply, and most kitchens today contain a refrigerator for cooling substances and providing ice. And if there is a kitchen table, spread it with several layers of newspaper to absorb any spilled liquids. It will be a perfect home laboratory bench.

THE HOME LABORATORY

Kitchen cupboards
These contain such ingredients as soap flakes, mothballs, bleach and cleaning fluid which, although they may not sound very scientific, all play an important part in experiments.

Refrigerator
Your fridge cools equipment and ingredients, and produces ice for experiments, eg to show how water increases in volume when it freezes.

Food store
The larder is also essential to the home laboratory. Eggs, potatoes, vinegar, salt, beans and yeast are in regular demand. Eggs demonstrate principles as different as osmosis and the Bernouilli effect.

The sink
Filled with water, this is your reservoir, the place for such floating experiments as making jet-propelled boats and magnetic ducks. Running taps demonstrate water's surface tension.

The window
Here you get the natural light you need for growing everything from small seeds to a long potato shoot that finds its way through a dark maze to the light.

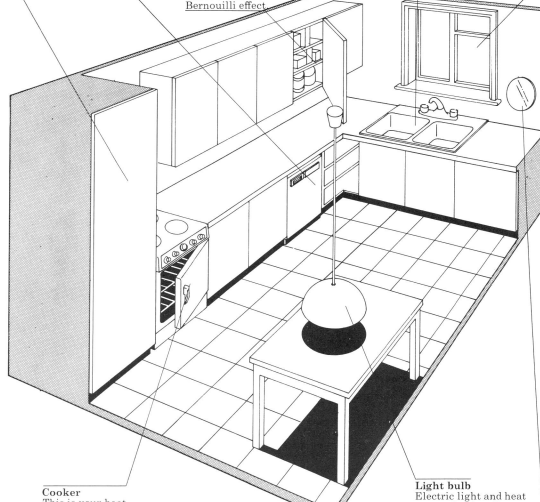

Cooker
This is your heat source – for boiling liquids during chemistry experiments, for lighting tapers to test for oxygen and for demonstrating heat conduction or the principle of the hovercraft.

Light bulb
Electric light and heat are needed for all sorts of experiments – with shadows, to show radiation, and the differences between hard and soft light.

Mirror
Would-be astronomers need a mirror to make an image of the Sun, while biologists can use it to make a simple microscope, and magicians to produce a mirror cabinet.

EQUIPMENT AND STORES

When you look around your home you will be amazed at just how many of the ingredients and equipment it already contains for the experiments in this book. The kitchen food cupboards will provide the following items, which turn up in experiments again and again:
Vinegar
Yeast
Sugar
Sodium bicarbonate
Potatoes
Butter

Dried peas
Food colouring
Salt
Eggs
    The household equipment which you will find useful includes:

Kitchen scales
Electric drill
Alarm clock
Vacuum flask
Room thermometer
Fan heater or electric fan
Mirror.

The garden shed will provide:
Flower pots
Trowel
Garden hose.
    Buy the following seeds as and when you need them:
Broad bean
Mung bean
Mustard and cress
Nasturtium
Pumpkin
Sunflower
Tomato
Parsley.
    Buy a collection of bulbs some seed potatoes

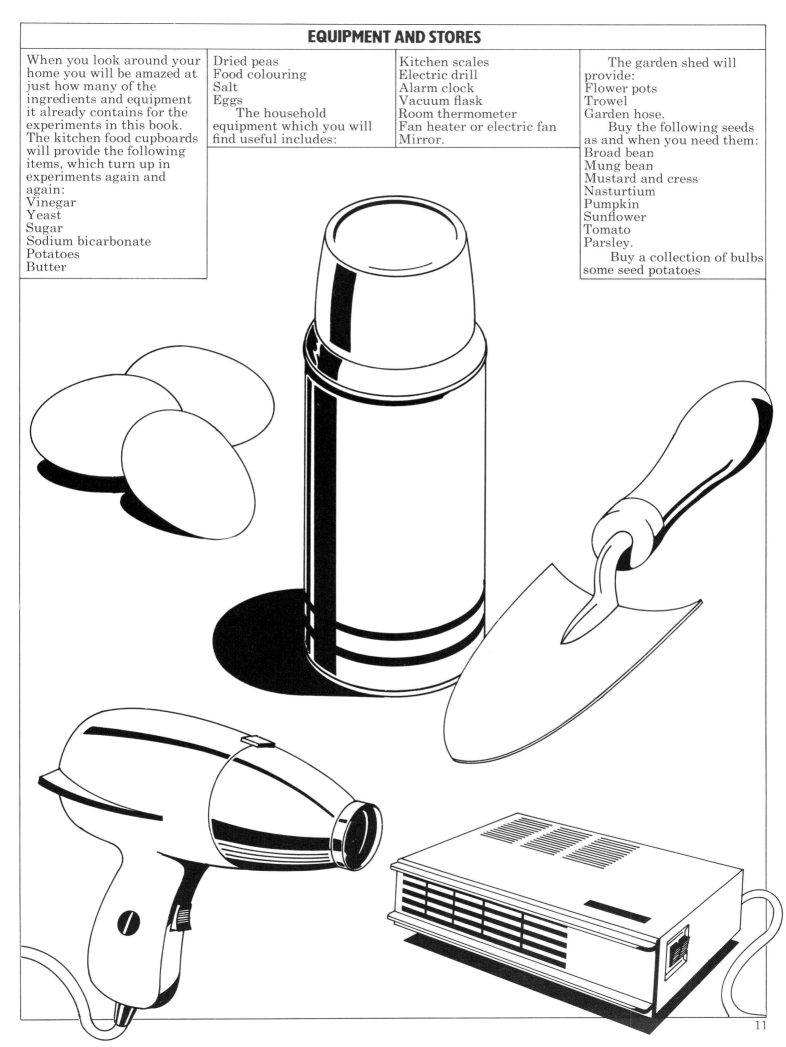

Beg, borrow or buy the following specialist items:
Magnifying glass
Glass prism
Convex and concave lenses
Batteries for electricity experiments
Magnets and iron filings
Access to a microscope would be interesting but not essential.

The majority of the experiments in this book can be done using the sort of things thrown away in the normal household, like empty yoghurt pots, glass jars and old corks. The following list covers virtually all the experiments in the book. Few things will have to be specially bought.
Sticking plaster
Torch
Coloured tissue paper
Coloured sheets of plastic
Crayons
Glass bottles
Sand
Piece of asbestos
Table-tennis balls
Old metal plate
Tin lids

Glass tumblers
Old glass jars of all shapes and sizes
Plastic bags
Old enamel pan
Paper napkins
Modelling clay
Paper towels
Old spoons
Small glass test-tube
Small bottle with stopper
Thread
String
Pencil
Sieve
Aluminium baking foil
Feather

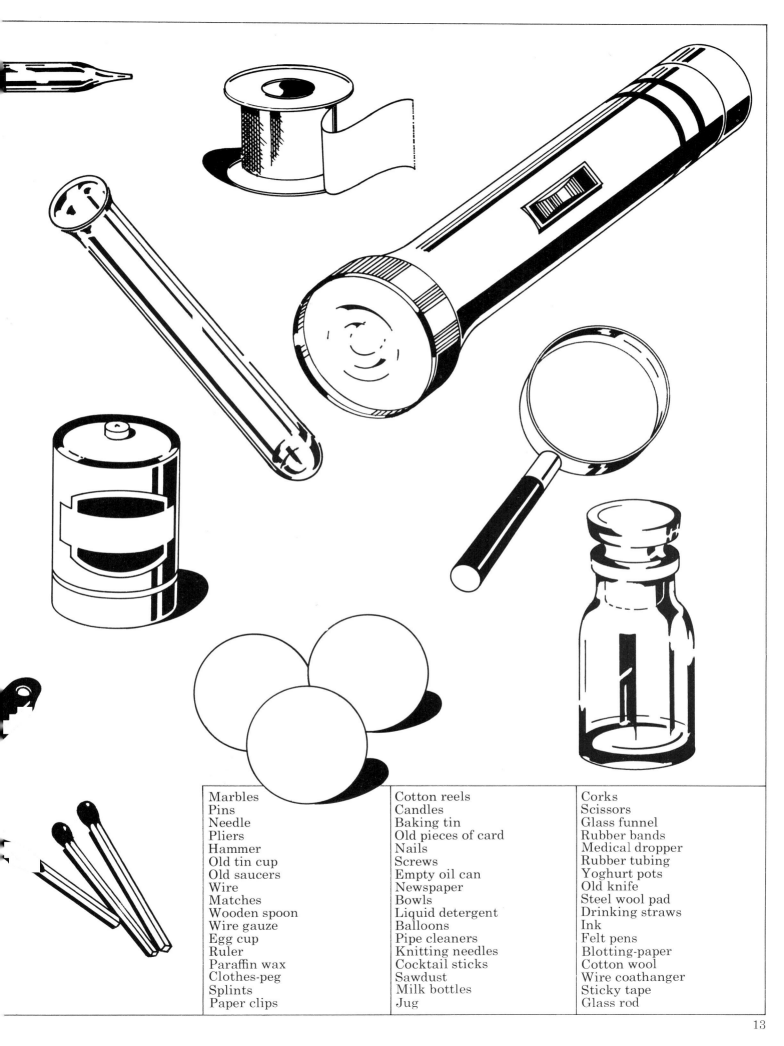

Marbles	Cotton reels	Corks
Pins	Candles	Scissors
Needle	Baking tin	Glass funnel
Pliers	Old pieces of card	Rubber bands
Hammer	Nails	Medical dropper
Old tin cup	Screws	Rubber tubing
Old saucers	Empty oil can	Yoghurt pots
Wire	Newspaper	Old knife
Matches	Bowls	Steel wool pad
Wooden spoon	Liquid detergent	Drinking straws
Wire gauze	Balloons	Ink
Egg cup	Pipe cleaners	Felt pens
Ruler	Knitting needles	Blotting-paper
Paraffin wax	Cocktail sticks	Cotton wool
Clothes-peg	Sawdust	Wire coathanger
Splints	Milk bottles	Sticky tape
Paper clips	Jug	Glass rod

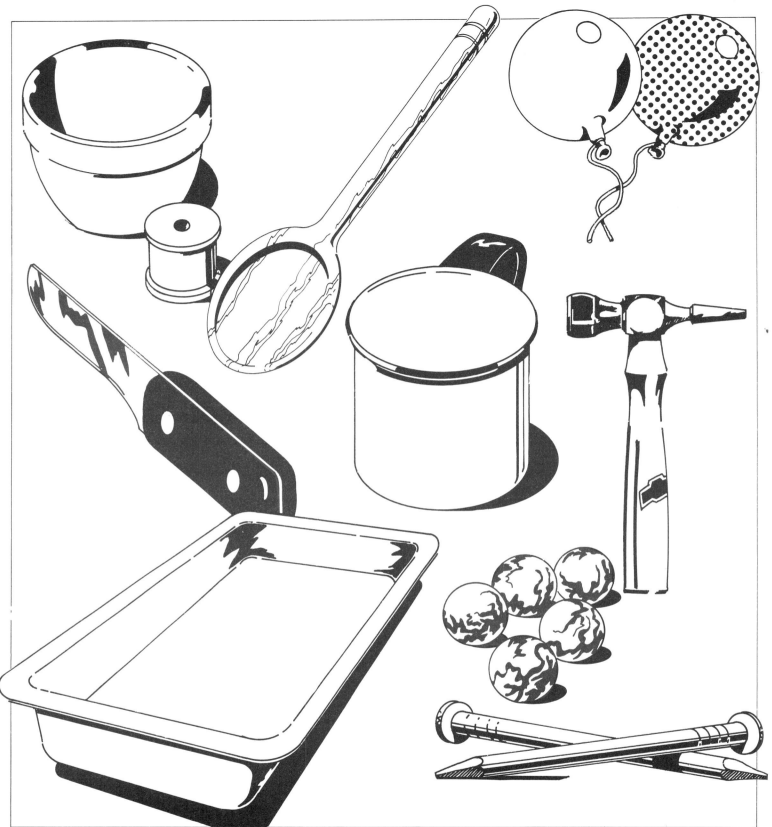

Chemicals
These can be found around you in the bathroom cupboard, the garden shed and the kitchen. You will have to buy a few special items at your local pharmacist. Do keep them in old glass jars with tight-fitting lids. Label them always. Whenever chemicals and heat are used, an adult should be present. Hot liquids scald and chemicals can behave strangely if you do not follow the instructions for the experiment closely.

You may already have some of the following chemicals, but you will probably have to buy those towards the end of the list:

Bleach
Surgical spirit

Mothballs
Iodine
Camphor
Methylated spirit
Hydrogen peroxide
Limewater
Universal Indicator Paper
Hydrochloric acid
Sulphuric acid
Dry ice
Acetone
Turpentine
Carbon tetrachloride

Ferrous sulphate
Copper sulphate
Nickel sulphate
Calcium nitrate
Manganese sulphate
Iron alum
Potash alum
Cobalt chloride
Ferric chloride
Zinc sulphate
Boric acid
Cream of tartar
Chloride of lime.

THINGS TO MAKE

To carry out some of the more interesting experiments you have to provide heat. In many instances you will be able to use the ring on the kitchen cooker, plus an old enamel pan. In a few instances the heat of a candle flame will be enough. But there are times when you will need a small heater of your own, which you can make in the following way:

Spirit burner

You will need:
Small tin like a tobacco tin, or an ink bottle
Piece of wood
Hammer
Screwdriver
Wick, or if that is not possible, some cotton wool
Methylated spirit.

Take the lid off the small tin, or the cap off the bottle if you are using this instead. Put it on the piece of wood and, using the hammer and screwdriver, make a hole through the middle. Put a wick through the hole and into the tin or bottle. If you are using cotton wool instead, pack the tin or bottle with it and, as you replace the lid, thread a tuft of cotton wool through the hole to act as a wick.

When you want to use the burner, pour in methylated spirit until the wick is well soaked. Replace the lid and light the wick. Stand the burner on a plate for safety. The fuel for the burner is alcohol and it is passing up the wick by capillary action. It is the alcohol vapour which burns.

Electric heater

Using a transformer and rectifier from an electric train set you can make an electric heater with a piece of resistance wire. Get it from an old electric heater element. Take a length that will get very hot, but not red hot, when it is joined to the output terminals of the power unit. Wind the wire round the outside of a test-tube and keep it by you for heating liquids.

Test-tube holder

You can make your own test-tube holder by using a wire coathanger and shaping it with a pair of pliers into the holder shown here.

Tripod stand

Thick strong wire bent as shown will make a sturdy stand to go over your spirit burner. Stand a circular piece of gauze on the top, with a tin lid above it to hold any glass container being used in the experiment. Use a wooden clothes-peg to remove hot lids and metal plates from your tripod stand.

To make your filter, which will be so useful in chemical experiments, stand the yoghurt pot on a paper towel, draw a circle around the bottom of the pot with a pencil and then cut out the circle of paper. This is your filter paper. Use a nail to punch five holes in the bottom of a yoghurt pot. Push the filter paper into the pot so that it fits inside the bottom over the holes. Put the pot on top of a jar, so that it just fits in the neck. Stir up the chemical mixture in the cup and pour it slowly into the yoghurt pot. Any solid left in the filter paper is called the residue, while the clear liquid passing through is called the filtrate.

Test-tube holder

Tripod stand

STORAGE AND SCIENCE MUSEUM

After you have been doing experiments for a while, you will start to accumulate objects which you have made in order to demonstrate certain scientific principles. These can be usefully placed in a Family Science Museum for future reference. Try and get hold of a pair of bookshelves or, better still, an old bookcase, preferably glass-fronted to keep out the dust. Divide it into two distinct areas. One can contain the various stores and equipment you need, and the other can house your museum.

Stand the various exhibits – plants, telescope, rain gauge, pinhole camera, musical instruments, etc., in appropriate rows. Get some postcards and label each object with its name and the date you made it, and write out a brief description of the scientific principles involved. This description will not only be a useful reminder for you, it will also help your friends and other visitors to understand what you have been doing.

Set aside one shelf or section for the various documents that you are likely to amass: transects of vegetation, weather charts, and so on. Alternatively, you may find that a folder or ring binder is adequate for storing your documents. Again, don't forget to label everything clearly. It's surprising how quickly you can forget the details of an experiment only days after you did it.

PART TWO SCIENCE IN ACTION

THE SCIENCE OF PLANTS AND ANIMALS

Since primeval times plants have been used by man to cure or kill, and they have also been worshipped as a gift from the gods. The Egyptians were particularly famous for their 'green fingers', and they grew shrubs, flowers and herbs successfully, despite their dry soil, which needed irrigation. They recorded the healing properties of herbs on papyrus with an accuracy that would surprise many herbalists today.

It was one of Aristotle's pupils, Theophrastus (3rd century BC), who was the first to separate the study of plants from the kitchen and medicine. He compared hundreds of plants scientifically, establishing an early, although rather inadequate, classification system. Aristotle did the same for animals, studying 500 species, particularly fish, and comparing their anatomy after dissection. The science of biology had begun.

It was no accident that the men who began to create a more realistic biology were scientists in other fields. The fuchsia in our gardens is named after the German professor of medicine, Leonhart Fuchs (1501–66), who dissected plants and wrote about his findings so that ordinary people would become more aware of the useful and poisonous plants around them.

When the early European explorers found their way to America and Asia, biologists were able to describe, and eventually classify, new plants and animals according to their structure. The work of Linnaeus (1707–78) was the most famous. Pupils of this Swedish naturalist travelled with explorers, bringing back thousands of specimens which were classified in his *Systema Naturae* in 1735.

The early plant hunters were true pioneers who had to overcome severe natural obstacles in their search for new specimens. Journey times to places like Canada, the Himalayas and China had to be estimated in terms of years rather than weeks. Specimens had to be specially labelled on the spot, field notes written up, and seed collected later in the year. The plants were carefully packed, and sent home with small chance of surviving the journey – not least because indifferent sea captains did not hesitate to jettison such unlikely cargo if it got in their way.

One important invention was the Wardian case, a kind of miniature greenhouse in which plants could be sealed off from the dangers of hostile weather and sea water. The first national herbarium was set up to house the incoming plants by Professor Chini of Bologna, and the first directions for preparing herbarium specimens were published in 1606 by Adrian Spieghel in *Isagorges*.

The English country parson, Stephen Hales (1677–1761), was another great scientist amongst the many amateur botanists of his time. He did experiments with plants like the sunflower to find out more about their nutrition. He covered up the sunflower's pot with lead and the leaves with pigs' bladders, checking the weight of water taken in by the roots and the amount of evaporation from the leaves. He also dug holes by the roots of trees and measured the suction force of roots, discovering that capillary action in the root overcomes the laws of gravity. He realized that plants were using more than the goodness of the soil to grow, but he did not understand the whole process of nutrition.

This became much clearer in the late 18th century, when the results of Jean Senebier's experiments in Geneva were published. To find out how plants breathe he put them in a vessel, which was partly filled with water and partly a vacuum. A scale measured the gases produced. When he pumped carbon dioxide into the vessel, he found more oxygen was given off. At night this experiment did not work. So he concluded that the fleshy green parts of a plant use carbon dioxide in daylight to produce oxygen. The green colouring matter in plants was later given the name chlorophyll.

Plants were also being used more scientifically for healing. An English doctor, William Withering, made an important discovery in 1775, when he found an old woman in Shropshire curing

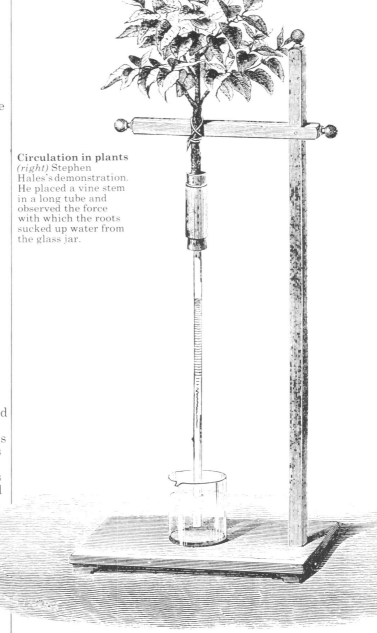

Circulation in plants *(right)* Stephen Hales's demonstration. He placed a vine stem in a long tube and observed the force with which the roots sucked up water from the glass jar.

sufferers from dropsy with the foxglove plant. He used the same methods in his daily surgery for poor people, drying the leaves of the foxglove, and using the product to help patients with many types of heart complaint.

The improvement of microscopes in the 19th century led to the new science of cell research. Matthias Schleiden (1804–81), a German solicitor who gave up his career to concentrate on botany, was one of the pioneers of this method. He scoffed at other scientists 'whose entire wisdom is spent determining and classifying this artificially collected hay'.

But, despite the great advances that he and other cell biologists made, he did make one big mistake. A drawing by him, depicting three cells of the hair of a potato plant, shows a smaller body inside each nucleus, which today we call the nucleolus. Schleiden thought that it was the germ of a new cell, proving that he was a long way from understanding plant reproduction.

Microscopes also enabled zoologists to study animals at the cellular level and to discover single-celled animals and the bacteria that cause disease. But the majority of scientists were still more interested in anatomy. It was Pierre Belon (1517–64) who made a start with comparative anatomy. 'We tried to dissect every bird that came into our hands,' he said. He compared the skeletons of birds and man, realizing that there were many similarities. For example, the wing structure of the bird is like the hand of man. Scientists began to suspect that higher animals developed from lower ones.

Charles Darwin (1809–82) confirmed this, after his voyage

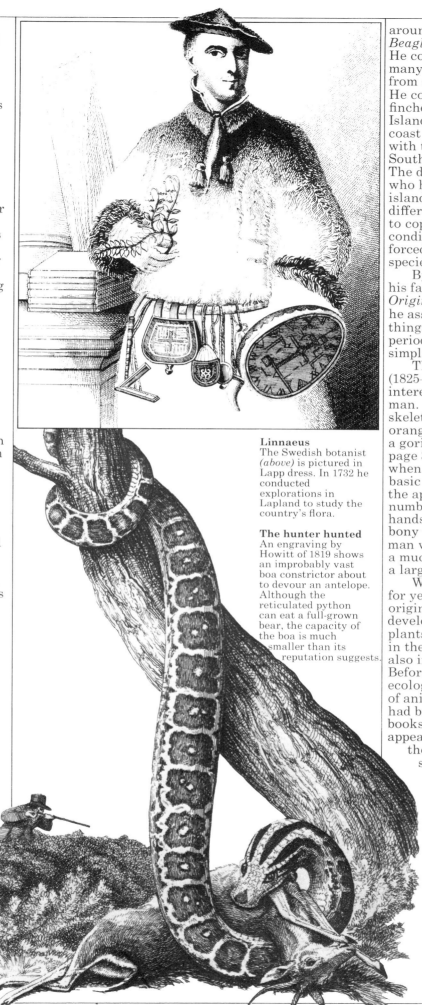

Linnaeus
The Swedish botanist *(above)* is pictured in Lapp dress. In 1732 he conducted explorations in Lapland to study the country's flora.

The hunter hunted
An engraving by Howitt of 1819 shows an improbably vast boa constrictor about to devour an antelope. Although the reticulated python can eat a full-grown bear, the capacity of the boa is much smaller than its reputation suggests.

around the world on HMS *Beagle* from 1831 to 1836. He collected and studied many plants and animals from all over the world. He compared species of finches on the Galapagos Islands, 600 miles from the coast of South America, with those living on the South American continent. The descendants of birds who had strayed off to the islands had developed different-shaped beaks to cope with varying conditions. Darwin was forced to conclude that species were variable.

By 1859 he had written his famous book, *On the Origin of Species*, in which he asserted that living things developed over long periods of time from lower, simple forms to higher ones.

Thomas Huxley (1825–95) was particularly interested in evolution and man. He compared five skeletons of a gibbon, an orang-utan, a chimpanzee, a gorilla and a man (see page 39). He found that when he compared their basic structure and organs, the apes had the same number of teeth, similar hands and the lack of a bony tail, as did man. But man was upright, and had a much heavier brain inside a larger skull.

While scientists argued for years about man's origins, a new science was developing. Animals and plants were studied not just in the laboratory but also in their environment. Before this new interest in ecology, accurate drawings of animals in their habitats had been made for hunting books, an example of which appears below left. But in the late 19th century, scientists themselves were studying out in the field. Biology had come a long way since the early systems of classification and the obsession with anatomy.

Plants of all sizes, from single cells to gigantic trees, grow all around us almost everywhere in the world. They do not grow just in well-watered gardens, but thrive in the sea, in rivers, on rocks, on old tree trunks, in swamps and even in the most unlikely places, like the top of Arctic snow or on an old crust of bread.

It is far easier to ignore plants than it is to remain oblivious of animals that move around and often make a lot of noise. But plants are just as much alive as animals, and they have to cope with similar problems. They must find the right place to live, and they need food. They fight enemies to maintain their position, and they produce young so that the next generation of plants will grow.

By taking films of plants at hourly intervals, then running off the pictures one after another, scientists have been able to show just how active plants really are. They twist their stems, grow new buds, flowers and seeds, move towards the Sun and give off water through their leaves.

Unlike animals, plants stay in one place to obtain their food, making it from raw materials. They use water and a few minerals from the soil, plus carbon dioxide from the air. Only green plants can make food in this way, because they contain the substance called chlorophyll, which uses sunlight to produce food for the plant. This process is called photosynthesis.

By doing the experiments described on these pages, you can prove that the plants growing in your own home can move in various different ways. They do so because they are attracted by gravity (geotropism), and because they need water (hydrotropism) and sunlight (phototropism). This last requirement can induce quite extraordinary patterns of growth, as the plant maze (opposite) shows. Here also we look at ways of measuring plant growth.

Geotropism

Fill a large glass jar with wet cotton wool and slip bean seeds between it and the sides of the jar. After a few days roots will begin to grow downwards from the beans. If you turn the jar upside down and leave it for another few days, the roots will change direction and begin to grow downwards again. Roots are attracted towards the earth because of the force of gravity. This is known as geotropism. In their search for water, however, roots do not always grow downwards.

Hydrotropism

You can show how roots grow towards water. Fill a large tin with sawdust and push a porous pot down into the centre. Fill the pot with water. Use the bean seeds from the last experiment and plant the roots into the sawdust round the pot, leaving the beans on the surface. After a few days, carefully brush away the sawdust around the beans and you will see that the roots have begun to grow sideways towards the water. This movement is called hydrotropism.

Phototropism

Unlike roots, shoots grow towards the light they need for photosynthesis. You can prove this by standing a large cardboard box upright and cutting a hole in one side almost at the top. Put a pot plant inside the box and replace the lid. Stand the box in a sunny spot with the hole pointing towards the Sun. The plant will soon begin to lean towards the hole to get sunlight. If you turn the plant round in the box the same thing will happen. It will change its position and lean towards the Sun again. This movement of plants towards light is called phototropism.

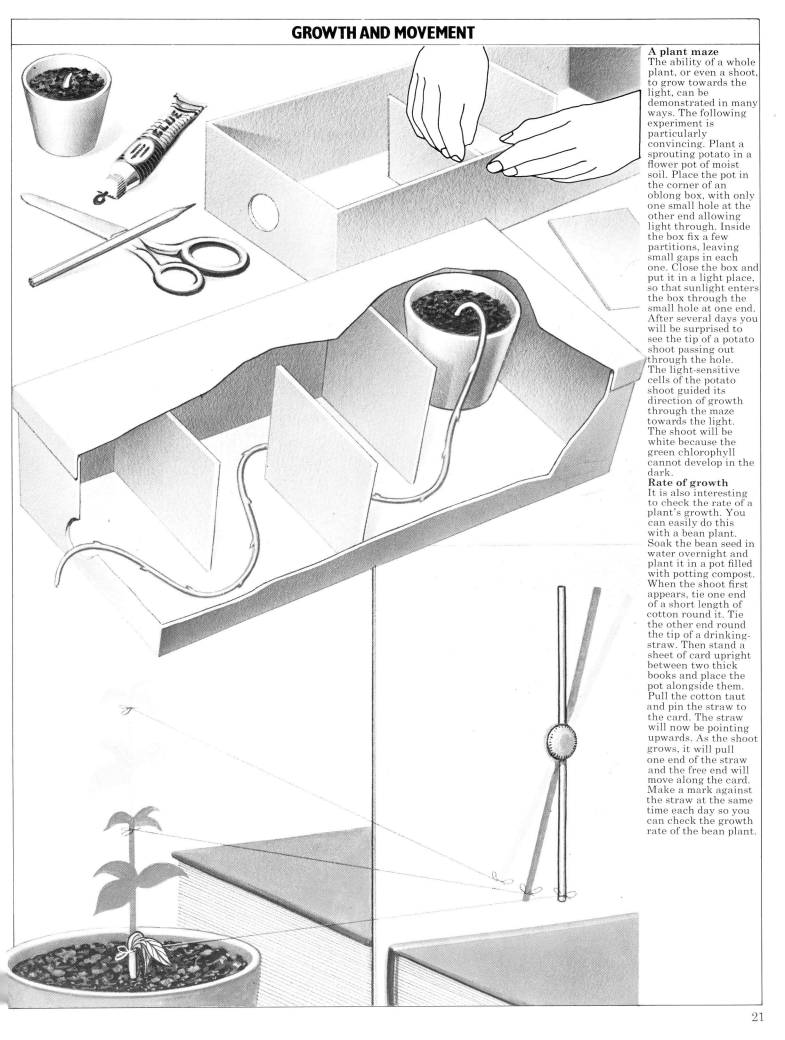

A plant maze

The ability of a whole plant, or even a shoot, to grow towards the light, can be demonstrated in many ways. The following experiment is particularly convincing. Plant a sprouting potato in a flower pot of moist soil. Place the pot in the corner of an oblong box, with only one small hole at the other end allowing light through. Inside the box fix a few partitions, leaving small gaps in each one. Close the box and put it in a light place, so that sunlight enters the box through the small hole at one end. After several days you will be surprised to see the tip of a potato shoot passing out through the hole. The light-sensitive cells of the potato shoot guided its direction of growth through the maze towards the light. The shoot will be white because the green chlorophyll cannot develop in the dark.

Rate of growth

It is also interesting to check the rate of a plant's growth. You can easily do this with a bean plant. Soak the bean seed in water overnight and plant it in a pot filled with potting compost. When the shoot first appears, tie one end of a short length of cotton round it. Tie the other end round the tip of a drinking-straw. Then stand a sheet of card upright between two thick books and place the pot alongside them. Pull the cotton taut and pin the straw to the card. The straw will now be pointing upwards. As the shoot grows, it will pull one end of the straw and the free end will move along the card. Make a mark against the straw at the same time each day so you can check the growth rate of the bean plant.

PHOTOSYNTHESIS

Plants and oxygen

When you get the chance, take a close look at an aquarium which is standing in sunlight. In any area where green plants are growing in the aquarium, you will see small bubbles of gas collecting on the leaves and rising to the surface.

Do this experiment to see what is happening. You will need a large glass jar, a glass funnel, a test-tube, water weed, matches and a taper. The funnel should be heavy enough not to float upwards when you fill the jar with water. The water weed can be taken from the aquarium, or else you can buy some from a pet shop. Put it at the bottom of the jar and position the funnel so that it covers most of the weed. It is best to keep a gap between the bottom of the jar and the funnel, and trapped pieces of weed will do this. Pour water into the jar until it is almost full, and then completely fill a test-tube with water. It must not have any air inside it.

Now put the filled test-tube over the stem of the funnel. Stand the jar and its contents in strong sunlight and leave it for an hour. When you look at it again, you will see bubbles of gas rising out of the plant.

These bubbles will rise up the stem of the funnel, pushing out the water in the test-tube. Leave the jar until the test-tube is full of gas. This will probably take several hours. Now take the test-tube out of the water, keeping your thumb tightly over the end. Try to keep the test-tube upside down to prevent the gas escaping.

You may need to enlist the help of a friend for the next part of the experiment, because unless you are really well organized in your home laboratory you will need another pair of hands to assist you with the flame test. Pick up your taper or splint, light it, blow out the flame and push the still-glowing taper into the test-tube. It will relight, because the gas is oxygen (scientists

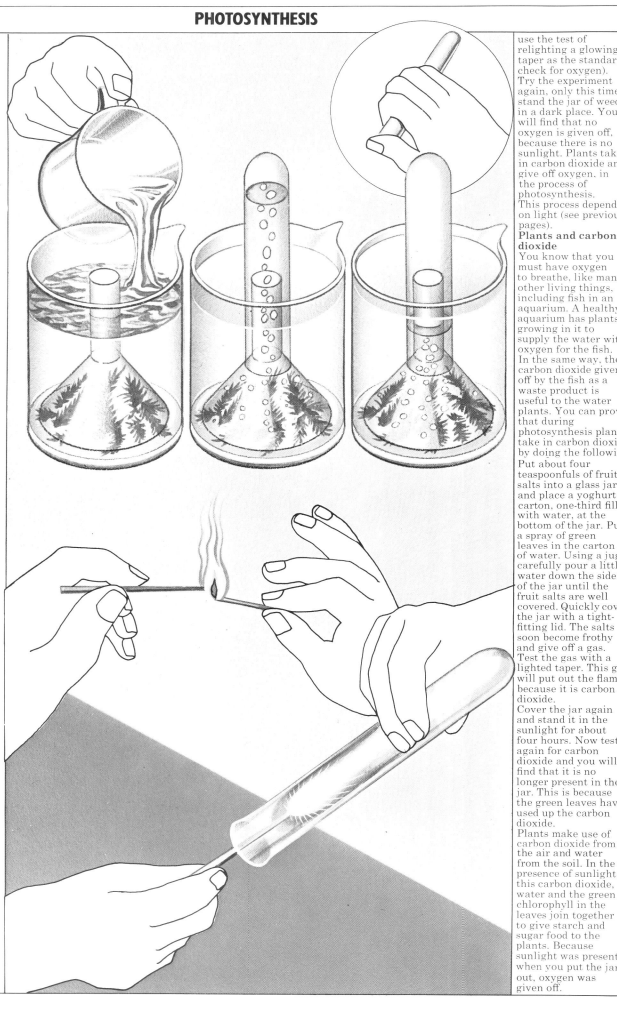

use the test of relighting a glowing taper as the standard check for oxygen). Try the experiment again, only this time stand the jar of weed in a dark place. You will find that no oxygen is given off, because there is no sunlight. Plants take in carbon dioxide and give off oxygen, in the process of photosynthesis. This process depends on light (see previous pages).

Plants and carbon dioxide

You know that you must have oxygen to breathe, like many other living things, including fish in an aquarium. A healthy aquarium has plants growing in it to supply the water with oxygen for the fish. In the same way, the carbon dioxide given off by the fish as a waste product is useful to the water plants. You can prove that during photosynthesis plants take in carbon dioxide by doing the following.

Put about four teaspoonfuls of fruit salts into a glass jar and place a yoghurt carton, one-third filled with water, at the bottom of the jar. Put a spray of green leaves in the carton of water. Using a jug, carefully pour a little water down the side of the jar until the fruit salts are well covered. Quickly cover the jar with a tight-fitting lid. The salts soon become frothy and give off a gas. Test the gas with a lighted taper. This gas will put out the flame because it is carbon dioxide.

Cover the jar again and stand it in the sunlight for about four hours. Now test again for carbon dioxide and you will find that it is no longer present in the jar. This is because the green leaves have used up the carbon dioxide.

Plants make use of carbon dioxide from the air and water from the soil. In the presence of sunlight, this carbon dioxide, water and the green chlorophyll in the leaves join together to give starch and sugar food to the plants. Because sunlight was present when you put the jar out, oxygen was given off.

Starch test

You can test leaves to check that they do contain this starch food. But first the green colouring, or chlorophyll, must be removed from a leaf. Take a freshly-cut leaf from a plant – a geranium will be suitable. Plunge it into boiling water for about 20 seconds. This kills the leaf. Then put the leaf into an old saucer and add enough surgical spirit to cover it. The green colouring will leave the leaf, passing into the spirit. When this has happened, rinse the leaf in cold water and put it in the cleaned saucer. Add a few drops of iodine solution using a dropper. You will find that a blue-black stain appears when the iodine touches the leaf, which is the positive test for starch.

Leaf patterns

Choose two green plants and try some tricks with silver foil. Choose a leaf on one plant and completely cover it, front and back, keeping the foil in place with paper clips. Now cut out some foil shapes. Strips and small circles would be ideal. Put the strips across another leaf, front and back, and use the circular shapes on a leaf of the second plant. Now put both plants in sunlight for about three days. Remove the three leaves with foil attached. Take off the foil and take the chlorophyll from these leaves as described above. Add the iodine solution and you will see definite patterns of circles and stripes on a blue-black background on two leaves, while the leaf completely covered in foil does not go dark because it contains no starch. The other two leaves contained starch only at those places which the Sun could reach.

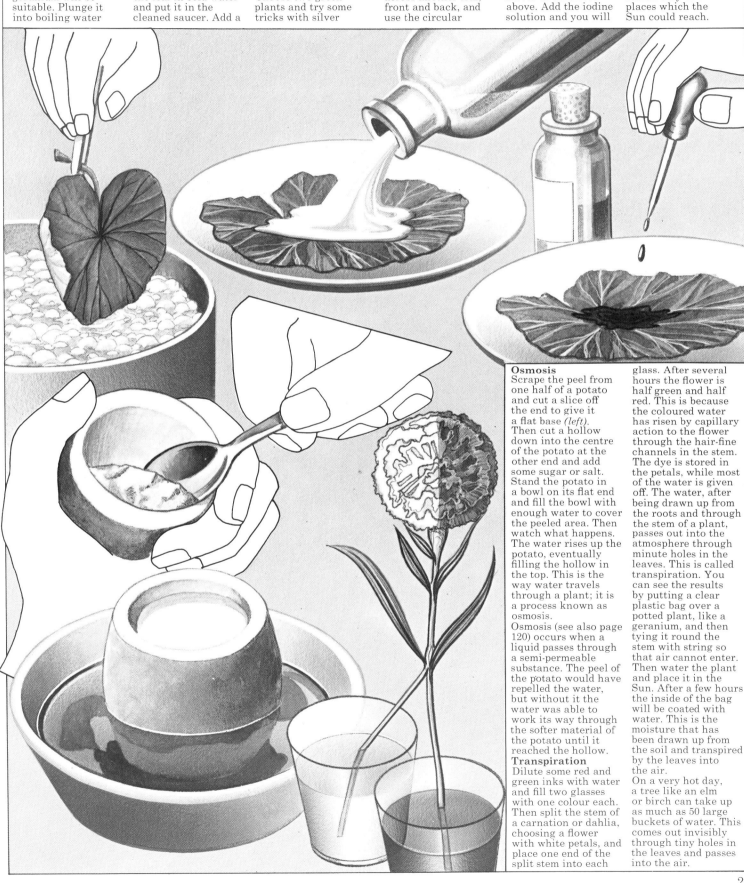

Osmosis

Scrape the peel from one half of a potato and cut a slice off the end to give it a flat base *(left)*. Then cut a hollow down into the centre of the potato at the other end and add some sugar or salt. Stand the potato in a bowl on its flat end and fill the bowl with enough water to cover the peeled area. Then watch what happens. The water rises up the potato, eventually filling the hollow in the top. This is the way water travels through a plant; it is a process known as osmosis.

Osmosis (see also page 120) occurs when a liquid passes through a semi-permeable substance. The peel of the potato would have repelled the water, but without it the water was able to work its way through the softer material of the potato until it reached the hollow.

Transpiration

Dilute some red and green inks with water and fill two glasses with one colour each. Then split the stem of a carnation or dahlia, choosing a flower with white petals, and place one end of the split stem into each glass. After several hours the flower is half green and half red. This is because the coloured water has risen by capillary action to the flower through the hair-fine channels in the stem. The dye is stored in the petals, while most of the water is given off. The water, after being drawn up from the roots and through the stem of a plant, passes out into the atmosphere through minute holes in the leaves. This is called transpiration. You can see the results by putting a clear plastic bag over a potted plant, like a geranium, and then tying it round the stem with string so that air cannot enter. Then water the plant and place it in the Sun. After a few hours the inside of the bag will be coated with water. This is the moisture that has been drawn up from the soil and transpired by the leaves into the air.

On a very hot day, a tree like an elm or birch can take up as much as 50 large buckets of water. This comes out invisibly through tiny holes in the leaves and passes into the air.

If you start your own garden, you will find that you and your plants work together with the soil. Plants need water and food from the soil, plus lots of sunshine, to thrive.

If you are lucky enough to have room for a garden plot, choose a place where your plants will get sun for at least half the day. If you only have space for gardening in pots or window-boxes, try to place them in a sunny position. There are some plants which prefer shade, but there are many more which depend on the Sun.

If you have no outside space at all, do not give up plans to try gardening experiments. Many projects in this section can succeed indoors. But do remember that plants grown in small pots need special soil. They quickly use up the goodness in the small amount of soil they have. Potting soil needs to be light and crumbly to let plant roots and water spread through it easily. The best thing is to buy a bag of professional potting-soil mix from a garden shop. This is rich in everything that growing plants need.

Anyone without a garden of their own can try to see if there are elderly neighbours about who find it hard to keep their gardens tidy. They might be happy to hand over part of their ground, particularly if you offer to share some of the produce you grow. The local allotment society may also be prepared to make small plots available to people who prove that they take gardening seriously.

Wherever you do your gardening, success depends on the condition of the soil. If you are starting a plot where no garden has been before, your soil will need a lot of attention. Turn it over with a garden spade to break it up and let in light and air. Pick out any stones and remove grass and weeds. Use a rake to break the clods into fine, crumbly soil. You can make your own small rake by hammering long nails through a piece of wood.

This all helps to improve the soil, but to be really successful it is important to convert whatever soil you happen to have into loam. All soil is a natural mixture of four basic ingredients – sand, clay, chalk and humus. When the balance between them is just right the soil is loam, a fertile, free-draining mixture, ideal for plants.

But perfect loam is rare, so it is important to improve the balance of your soil. It will contain all the ingredients which make up loam, but they are likely to be present in the wrong proportions.

The first thing to do is to identify the type of soil in your garden. The tables below show how to put a name to your soil, and then how to improve it.

The properties of soil

You can find out a lot about your garden's soil by separating it out in water, and by growing seeds in soil dug from different levels. First take a large screw-topped jar, half fill it with garden soil, and then fill it to the top with water. Replace the cap and shake it well.

After letting the jar stand for an hour or two, you will see that the soil separates into different layers. The heavy particles, like gravel and sand, sink to the bottom. Next comes a layer of clay and perhaps chalk. The water itself stays cloudy because very fine particles of clay are floating in it. And on the surface you will see small floating particles – the humus made up of plant and animal matter decayed by bacteria in the soil. The humus provides valuable minerals for feeding growing plants. So the

Putting a name to your soil
Stony
Scores of stones in a square metre of soil.
Peaty
Dark brown or black, very rich in plant remains, and spongy in texture.
Chalky
Dark surface soil, with white sub-soil.
Sandy
Light-coloured, gritty to touch.
Loam
Light-coloured, smooth and unsticky to touch.
Clay
Light-coloured, smooth and sticky to touch.

Ways to improve soil
Stony
Remove larger stones from the surface. Use plenty of fertilizer. Keep digging shallow.
Peaty
Good drainage and generous liming are essential. You can add a loamy topsoil.
Chalky
Keep digging shallow and use plenty of fertilizers and green manure. Liming may be necessary.
Sandy
Use as much humus-making material as possible. Fertilizers are also essential.
Loam
The perfect soil. Keep it as it is with lime, manure and fertilizers.
Clay
Artificial drainage may be necessary. Dig thoroughly and manure.

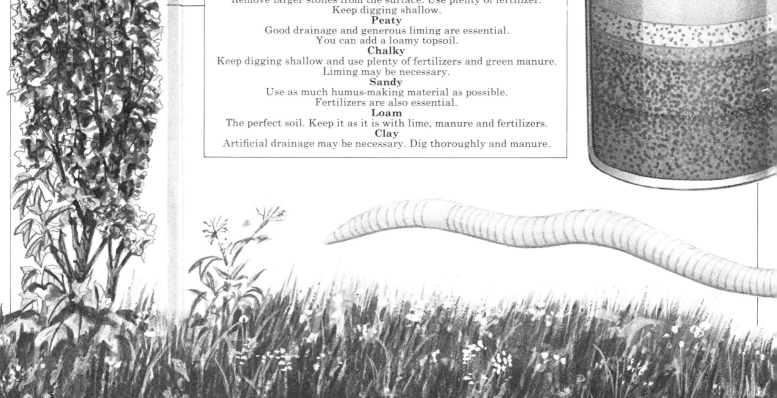

four basic ingredients of soil form themselves in layers for you to see.

Topsoil

The soil used for this experiment is called topsoil because you dig it up from near the surface of the garden. So now do another experiment by putting a sample of this topsoil in one of two metal cans, perforated with drainage holes. Then dig about 45 cm (1½ ft) below the surface and put some of the subsoil from the same area into the second can. Soak two bean seeds overnight in water and plant one in each can. Keep both moist.

When the bean seeds grow, the plant grown in topsoil will look much healthier than the one grown in the subsoil. This is because the subsoil is less fertile, and contains smaller amounts of humus.

Earthworms

Earthworms do much to improve the fertility of a garden. Although they live near the surface of the soil in damp and rainy weather, in cold or hot weather they plug the openings of their burrows and retreat into the deepest parts down in the subsoil.

The worms swallow earth, not only while digging their burrows, but also because they need the decaying plants and parts of small animals in the soil as food. These are digested, while the bulk of the soil passes through the worm. When there are a lot of leaves on the surface, worms pull them into their burrows, which increases a soil's fertility.

But when there are fewer leaves, worms make more soil casts on the surface. This soil is exposed to the air and broken up, while the burrows themselves improve drainage because they allow air to get into the soil. The passage of soil through worms is one of the very best ways of cultivating soil, and waste material from worms increases the organic material in soil, which improves the growth of plants. An average of 18 tonnes of earth per ½ hectare (1 acre) per year is brought up by earthworms and deposited on the soil's surface.

Earthworms are so essential to healthy soil that in some countries they are being introduced to wormless areas to improve fertility. You can check whether soil fertility in your garden is linked to the number of worms living in the area. Make a transect by marking a straight line across the garden. Then study the distribution of earthworms by counting the number found in samples of soil of the same volume at points along the transect. See if there are more worms in areas where plants grow well.

The same transect can be used for recording many other measurements. You could list the names of all the species found along the line: or you could make quantitative measurements like the height of plants. You could also make a profile of the shape of the ground along the line taken by the transect. This is done by stretching a string horizontally between two pegs and recording the distance from the string to the ground at particular intervals. The measurements can be used to make a scale drawing of the profile.

It is important to keep your main string level. Use a spirit level to check this. A smaller, hand-held version of the line transect is the point frame. This consists of a piece of wood with long nails driven through it at regular intervals of about 5 cm (2 in). Push your point frame lightly into the ground and count the number of plants growing in particular habitats in your garden. Note which plants succeed best in, say, the lawn, the compost heap or under a hedge.

YOUR GARDEN YEAR

Spring
Sow seeds:
nasturtium
pumpkin
sunflower

Summer
Harvest nasturtium leaves and flowers for salads.
Nip off new pumpkin tendrils.
Pollinate the female pumpkin flowers with male pollen.
Stake tall sunflowers.
Water garden every day.
Plant bean seeds.
Plant a tree.

Autumn
In early autumn pick nasturtium seeds when the flowers have died.
Keep them to sow next year for another crop of nasturtiums.
Harvest pumpkin for pie and Hallowe'en lantern.
Harvest and dry sunflower seeds.
Plant bulbs.
Plant your bucket potato.

Winter
Plant seeds in pots indoors.
Make your garden plot. Fertilize it ready for spring.
Feed birds with sunflower seeds.
Plant a tree.

(See pages 26–29 for growing instructions.)

The pH of soil

The degree of acidity or alkalinity of soil is also important to flowers and vegetables. This can be estimated very simply. Take a small sample of soil and put it in a glass jar. Add a few drops of hydrochloric acid and, if it fizzes, the soil contains a lot of lime and is alkaline. If it does not react to the test, the soil is neutral or acid.

There are also simple kits which you can buy from gardening shops to test your soil. They give a more sensitive estimate of the alkalinity or acidity in terms of its pH number.

In Britain most soils cover a range of pH from 4 to 8.5. A neutral soil has a pH of 7, while acid soils have a pH lower than 7, and alkaline soils a higher number.

Many soils become too acid because rain steadily washes lime out of the soil, at an average yearly rate of 28 g (1 oz) per 1.7 m² (2 sq yd). You can add lime to improve the soil's condition and allow a greater variety of plants to grow. The tests already mentioned will tell you if your soil needs lime. But you can also use Universal Indicator Paper, as described in the test on the right.

Soil test

Turn over the top 5 cm (2 in) of soil with a trowel. Mix 1 level teaspoonful of this moist soil with 1 teaspoonful of tap water in a saucer. After about 30 minutes, place a strip of Universal Indicator Paper so that one half lies on the wet soil and the other half against the side of the saucer. After five minutes check its colour.

If it remains pink, the soil is very acid or sour. It is essential to add lime unless you are going to grow acid-loving plants like heather. If it changes to orange, the soil needs some lime, unless it is to be used for potatoes, or other plants which like a

SEEDS

Seeds are rather like packets of plant food with a tiny plant inside each one. The new plant begins to grow when all the conditions are just right. This usually happens under the ground, although certain types of seed need only water to get the message to begin sprouting.

It is very interesting to watch seeds sprouting or germinating. Start with large seeds, like sunflowers, beans and nasturtiums, so that it is easier to see the root appear and the first leaves unfurl. Soak the seeds overnight in water before scattering them on a bed of damp cotton-wool or tissue. Keep them damp and within a matter of days you will see first the roots, and then the stems emerging. When they begin to germinate, do remember to put them near a window to get plenty of Sun. The store of food in each seed will nourish the plant until the roots and leaves have grown big enough to support it. On the right you will find instructions for producing seedlings and growing them on until they are ready to be planted in their final position in the garden.

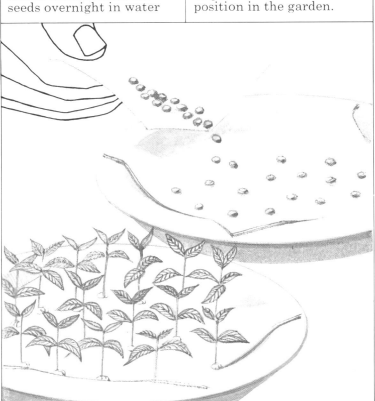

Mustard and cress

Good plants to begin with are mustard and cress, which are simple to grow indoors. Scatter the cress seeds on wet blotting-paper in a saucer. Do the same with the mustard seeds in a second saucer. After 10 to 14 days you will have fresh mustard and cress to put in sandwiches. Use the same method to grow the bean shoots that you eat in Chinese food. These Mung beans are sold by most gardening shops. Full of protein and Vitamin E, the shoots can be eaten raw in salads and sandwiches, as well as cooked in chow mein.

Where to sow seeds

Different containers can be used for germinating seeds. Large individual seeds can be grown in small yoghurt pots, or you can raise seeds communally in foil trays left over from pies or frozen foods. You can also try eggshells placed in an egg-box. Remember to punch holes in the bottom of plastic or foil containers with a knitting needle for drainage. Fill each container to

little acid.
If the paper turns green, the soil is neutral and the amount of lime present is perfect for normal gardening.
If it changes to blue-green, there is too much lime, and plants that like an alkaline soil should be grown.
Soil temperature
The heat-conducting property of your soil is also important. During the day, the soil surface is heated by the Sun. If your soil is a poor conductor of heat, little of this heat energy will be conducted to the lower layers of the soil, where it is needed to help the plants grow. Likewise, at night, when heat is lost from the surface, little heat will be conducted from the lower layers to compensate. Poor conducting soils have a much colder surface than normal soils. It is easy to compare the relative conducting properties of different soils. Pack two different samples of soil into identical cardboard containers. Put them on a warm hot plate. As cardboard is a poor heat conductor, conduction will take place through the soil to the surface. Then measure the temperature at both surfaces with a thermometer. The soil with the higher, final steady temperature will be the better conductor.

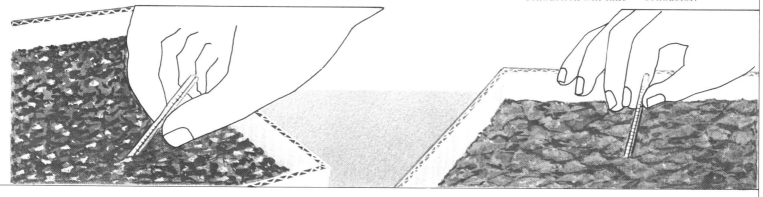

the top with potting compost and press down lightly. Lay single large seeds in place, or sprinkle smaller seeds on the surface. Cover with a very thin layer of compost. Again press down lightly.
Soak the compost with water, punch holes in plastic bags and use them to cover the seed containers. Keep the compost moist, but not wet, while the seeds are growing. Once germination has begun, put the seeds in a sunny window. When the seeds have grown into seedlings, they must be replanted. To do this, turn the yoghurt pots or eggshell upside down, holding the stem of the seedling lightly between the fingers of one hand, and tap the container rim against the edge of a table. The plant should then slide out, still firmly rooted in the compost. With the foil tray of seeds, use an old spoon and carefully lift out each seedling with soil still around its roots. Put the seedlings either into bigger pots with extra compost, or dig a small hole in the garden, pour in some water, put in the seedling and compost, press the soil around it, and finally add plenty of water.
Nasturtium flowers
Nasturtiums are good for beginner gardeners, because the seeds are large and easy to handle. The plants will grow almost anywhere, although they do prefer Sun. Start the seeds off in the house in the spring, as described, or make a hole in the ground for each seed and cover up lightly.
Experiment by growing nasturtium seeds in poor and good soil. They act as good indicators of soil fertility because there are more flowers produced on the plants grown in poor soil. In rich soil, you will end up with a jungle of nasturtium leaves, but very few flowers.
In the summer, pick both nasturtium leaves and flowers to eat in salads or sandwiches. In August or September, when the flowers have died, collect the seeds. Dry them indoors and put them in a labelled envelope for another good show of nasturtiums next year.

Pumpkins and pollination

Pumpkins should be planted in spring or early summer. Buy a packet of seeds and give some to your friends. You can then see who grows the largest pumpkin. Or you could dry four or five fat pumpkin seeds to use for planting. This is one plant which you cannot grow in pots because it needs plenty of food to develop well. So prepare the garden and dig in a lot of manure. This is the secret of growing large pumpkins. Make a low mound and poke four or five seeds around the edge, making holes for them with your finger. The seeds should germinate after about two weeks. Water them daily and once the vine begins to spread, it will grow very fast indeed. When the flowers appear, nip off new tendrils to stop the vine spreading further. This strengthens the plant and encourages new flowers.

Most of the flowers will be male. The female flowers have the beginnings of pumpkins below their petals. These must be fertilized with the male pollen to develop. You should see bees visiting the male flowers and carrying pollen to the females. To be sure of fertilization, transfer the pollen yourself. Break off a male flower and rub its pollen-covered stamen into the centre of the female flower.

The petals of the female wither as the small pumpkin grows. Break off the other flowers, so that all the plant's strength goes into producing a few big pumpkins. Water well and pick at the end of the summer when the strong stalk begins to wither.

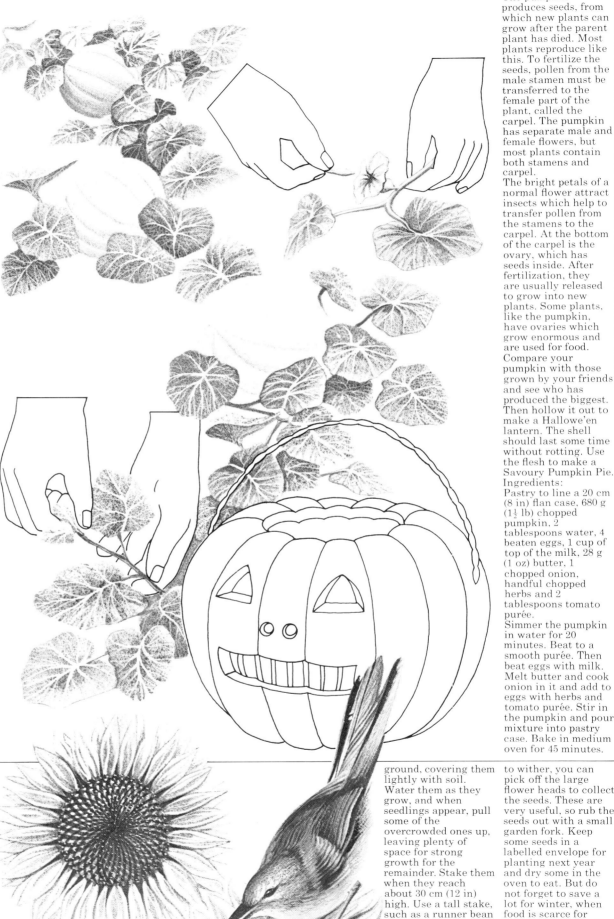

The pumpkin produces seeds, from which new plants can grow after the parent plant has died. Most plants reproduce like this. To fertilize the seeds, pollen from the male stamen must be transferred to the female part of the plant, called the carpel. The pumpkin has separate male and female flowers, but most plants contain both stamens and carpel.

The bright petals of a normal flower attract insects which help to transfer pollen from the stamens to the carpel. At the bottom of the carpel is the ovary, which has seeds inside. After fertilization, they are usually released to grow into new plants. Some plants, like the pumpkin, have ovaries which grow enormous and are used for food.

Compare your pumpkin with those grown by your friends and see who has produced the biggest. Then hollow it out to make a Hallowe'en lantern. The shell should last some time without rotting. Use the flesh to make a Savoury Pumpkin Pie. Ingredients:

Pastry to line a 20 cm (8 in) flan case, 680 g (1½ lb) chopped pumpkin, 2 tablespoons water, 4 beaten eggs, 1 cup of top of the milk, 28 g (1 oz) butter, 1 chopped onion, handful chopped herbs and 2 tablespoons tomato purée.

Simmer the pumpkin in water for 20 minutes. Beat to a smooth purée. Then beat eggs with milk. Melt butter and cook onion in it and add to eggs with herbs and tomato purée. Stir in the pumpkin and pour mixture into pastry case. Bake in medium oven for 45 minutes.

Sunflowers and winter birds

Sunflowers, as the name suggests, need Sun to grow. Plant them in the spring and many of them should grow taller than you. Ask your friends to grow some too and then keep a chart of the varying growth rates in different gardens and positions.

The large seeds can be started off indoors for faster growth, or you can scatter them directly on the ground, covering them lightly with soil. Water them as they grow, and when seedlings appear, pull some of the overcrowded ones up, leaving plenty of space for strong growth for the remainder. Stake them when they reach about 30 cm (12 in) high. Use a tall stake, such as a runner bean pole, to encourage them to grow straight as well as tall. When the plant has flowered and begins to wither, you can pick off the large flower heads to collect the seeds. These are very useful, so rub the seeds out with a small garden fork. Keep some seeds in a labelled envelope for planting next year and dry some in the oven to eat. But do not forget to save a lot for winter, when food is scarce for birds. It is a way of spreading summer sunshine, because hungry birds love sunflower seeds.

Bulbs

Not all plants start as seeds from flowers. Some start as bulbs or corms that look rather like onions and grow near the roots of the parent plant. They are really stores of sugar and starch foods which allow the plant to grow. As an onion is a bulb, you can cut it in half to see the normal arrangement of the new flower bud surrounded by scale leaves. When the fleshy scale leaves have fed the plant, they wither and turn into the brown, thin covering that surrounds the onion. Corms, like the crocus, are similar to bulbs. They are a store of food for the growing plants, but when you cut one in half you see that it does not have scale leaves. It is really part of the stem that grows fat with its reserves of food. Try growing bulbs such as daffodils, snowdrops and tulips, or corms such as crocuses, gladioli and freesias. The good thing about these plants is that they

flower in winter or spring when the garden is bare, and they also come up again year after year. As new bulbs form next to the originals under the ground, you will have more flowers each year. When they do flower, never pick the leaves. These die after they have finished making the food the buried bulbs need. You can also grow bulbs and corms indoors in pots or bowls, using a special bulb fibre. First put the fibre into a bucket and fill it

with water. Leave it to soak overnight. Squeeze the water out of the fibre and half-fill the pots you are using for the bulbs. Set the bulbs on the fibre, with the pointed end of the bulb facing upwards. Fill up the pots with fibre, leaving the bulb tops sticking out above the surface. Place the bulbs in a dark place for two months, then bring them out into the light to grow. You can also grow bulbs with just pebbles, charcoal and water in the pots.

Grow potatoes in a bucket

You can plant a potato in a large bucket and with any luck you should have grown a whole bucketful of potatoes within four months. You should plant the potato in early or late spring. Make sure your bucket has some drainage holes. Choose a potato with lots of eyes, because these are the buds. Before you plant the potato, leave it in a light place for two or three weeks so that the eyes begin to sprout.
When you are ready to plant, leave only the two strongest shoots on the potato, and rub off the remaining ones. Then half-fill the bucket with soil and a little compost. Make a hole in the soil for the potato and cover it over. Within a month green shoots will show above the ground. Then add just enough soil to cover them again, because this forces the stem to keep pushing upwards while the small potatoes are forming along it below ground. Continue to cover the plant until the bucket is full, remembering always to keep the soil moist.
When the plant flowers, you should stop watering, because otherwise the potatoes may rot. When the whole plant dies, tip out the bucket and count the number of potatoes you have produced. You can go one better and produce four or more potato plants from only one potato. Do this by pushing four cocktail sticks into a potato, so that they form a cross in the middle of it. Fill a glass jar with water and place the lower half of the potato, supported by the sticks, in the water. Keep the jar filled with water and after several days shoots will grow from the eyes.
When they have grown a little, remove the potato from the water and cut it into pieces, each with its own shoot. Plant each piece in a separate pot, well covered with compost. Soon you will have a collection of healthy potato plants – and eventually, you should have plenty of potatoes.
If you have sufficient room you can always grow a row or two of potatoes in the open ground. Potatoes fare well in rough ground that has not been dug for a while, but they will do even better in ground containing manure or compost. The method of growing is much the same as before. Rub out all but the two strongest shoots and plant in a row 10–12 cm (4–5 in) deep and 60–100 cm (2–3 ft) apart. Earth up the row with a fork to encourage growth beneath the ground. Remove any weeds that appear in the row.

SEEDS

Sowing seeds in wallpaper paste

There are two special challenges for the gardener. The first is to get his plants to mature as early in the season as possible, and the second is to have success with seeds which are difficult to germinate. Amazingly enough, a method of sowing pre-germinated seeds in a gel made from wallpaper paste is answering both challenges.

Scientists at the National Vegetable Research Station in Britain are still developing techniques for doing this on a commercial scale. But you can try it yourself at home. It is a simple way of producing seedlings earlier, as well as establishing plants from difficult seeds such as parsley and celery. It also allows you to watch the process of germination.

1 First take a sandwich box and line it with several layers of soft paper tissue. Then cover this with a sheet of paper towel.

2 Gently pour water over the paper and when most of it has been absorbed, tip any excess away.

3 Sprinkle the seeds evenly and thinly over the paper. Wet the top of the seeds with a fine spray of water.

4 Cover the box with the lid or a plastic bag, and keep it fairly warm. A temperature of about 22 C (70 F) is ideal.

5 Watch the seeds every day, and within one to four days the roots will usually appear. Smaller seeds like lettuce are ready for sowing when their roots are about 5 mm ($\frac{1}{4}$ in) long, but larger seeds can be left till their roots are about 9 mm ($\frac{3}{8}$ in) in length.

6 When the majority of the seeds have rooted, they are ready for sowing. If conditions are bad, they can be stored for up to two days in the refrigerator. The best way of removing the seeds from the box is gently to wash them out, collecting them in a fine sieve.

7 Make the gel by mixing a regular wallpaper paste at half the normal strength. The most suitable type of paste does not contain fungicides which would harm the seeds. Mix the seeds gently in the gel until they are evenly distributed. If they sink to the bottom, it means that the mixture needs to be thicker.

8 Fill a clear plastic bag with the gel, close the top and snip off one corner. Squeeze the mixture out onto damp soil, or into a seed box of potting soil. It should be squeezed out at a rate of about 150 ml ($\frac{1}{4}$ pint) to 9 m (30 ft) of row. Some people find it easier to use a wide-nozzled cake-icing syringe instead of the clear plastic bag.

9 Cover the seeds with soil, and water as usual.

Your seeds, given this advantageous start, will germinate more quickly and you will therefore have vegetables and flowers earlier in the season. It is possible to prove this by setting up a control group for comparison. Sow half a packet of parsley seeds by the gel method. At the same time sow the other half outside in the same soil which will be used for the pre-germinated seeds, once they are transferred to the garden. Keep a chart of how many plants you get from each method and the dates when they mature. You will be surprised how much the seeds benefit from a start in the gel.

This idea of setting up a control group as a standard for comparison is common practice in biological and other scientific experiments.

Parts of a tree

Trees have three main parts. The root is important to fix the tree firmly into the earth. The root type varies with each species. Cone-bearing trees, for example, often have shallow roots and are more easily blown down. The second part of the tree, the trunk, carries liquid food from the roots to the leaves. The shape of the trunk depends on the third part, the crown. This consists of the branches, twigs, buds and leaves.

How trees grow

A tree grows by using liquid food, taken in through the roots, and added minerals to form new wood. The diameter of the trunk increases by extra layers of cells forming between the older wood and the bark. The thin layer of living cells between the wood and the bark, known as the cambium, obtains foods from the sugary sap, and continues to increase in size. The cells on the inner layer produce further wood and those on the outer surface develop more layers of bark. This continuous process causes the outer bark to stretch and crack. These cracks vary in different species of trees and help us to recognize them, especially in winter when there are no leaves.

Make bark rubbings using thin white paper and brown wax crayon. Use the results to decide which types of tree grow in your neighbourhood.

You can also check the age of any trees which have been felled by examining the circles of alternate darker and lighter colour in the wood. Known as annual rings, they are formed by the differing rates of growth in spring and summer. In spring when growth is greatest, a tree uses a lot of water, so the cells and tubes are enlarged. In summer, when there is less growth, the wood is denser and therefore darker. You can find the age of the tree by counting the rings from the centre to the bark.

Tree seeds

Trees are flowering plants which produce seeds. It is interesting to collect different types and attempt to germinate them. Try acorns from oak trees and nuts from hazel, walnut and chestnut. These are the big, heavy seeds, weighing as much as 50 – 500 g (2 oz – 1 lb). At the other end of the scale, the birch produces minute seeds. The wind disperses lighter seeds, while birds and squirrels help to spread the heavier types. Other seeds have wings to encourage their flight, such as pines, sycamore, maple, elm and ash. Seeds such as willow and alder prefer wet soils, and often travel in rivers and streams. Collect as many seeds as possible, soak overnight and attempt to germinate them indoors. Extract seeds from cones by putting them in a warm place. Collect your seeds during the following months.

January: Scots pine, Corsican pine.
August: birch.
September: Japanese larch, Douglas fir, Sitka spruce, Noble fir and sycamore.
October: Norway spruce, oak, beech, ash, sweet chestnut and horse chestnut.
November: European larch.

You can plant any successful seedlings outside after a few months. If you plant a flowering native tree in your garden, you will find that native birds visit it. This is a good thing to do in cities where many native trees have been cut down. Remember that trees grow very tall and take on a broad spread, so make sure that you have enough space. When you have chosen the right tree for your garden site or tub, water it very well and add a lot of fertilizer.

You could also start a tree from fruit pips. Soft pips like orange are easier than hard ones like cherry. But try several types, first soaking them overnight. Put several pips in one pot because some will not grow. Once a fruit tree has settled in the garden, you can watch the changes throughout the year as the tree blossoms, the fruits develop and birds and bees arrive.

Oak

Birch

Sycamore

Beech

Ash

Horse chestnut

Scots pine

European larch

Norway spruce

ANIMALS IN YOUR GARDEN

If you have a garden, however small, it will contain millions of inhabitants for you to study. And if you live in a flat or house without any grass, soil and plants to act as home for small animals, your local park will make an ideal area for study.

You only have to lift a stone or look under a few plants to find dozens of different animal species. Watch and examine carefully everything you find, because amateur naturalists have an important contribution to make, and often discover previously unknown facts about the behaviour or breeding habits of quite common animals.

Keep an ecology notebook, with details of every animal you see, where you see it, what it was doing, and how it looked. Try to draw characteristic markings, because these will be a great help when you want to name the animal from a reference book.

You will soon discover that there is a constant struggle going on between the animals living in your garden. Animals fight among themselves for many reasons, for food, for territory, to protect a mate and to protect their young. A bumble-bee blundering into a strange nest is instantly stung to death, because an intruder could mean danger to the bees living there.

Overcrowding also leads to warfare. Some species make a habit of over-producing, and if there are not enough predators to deal with the regular population explosion, cannibalism results.

As you watch all the warfare that goes on in your garden, you may think that insects come off worst. But they take care to maintain their position by prolific breeding. Many of them, like aphids, produce family after family in quick succession, large numbers of which are then eaten by other insects and animals.

Flies

Let's start with flies. These very common animals are always found around buildings and people. Although they have a bad reputation for causing damage, they do also have more positive roles to play, for example as pollinators of flowers and destroyers of harmful pests. Flies belong to the order Diptera, the fourth largest group of insects, which contains 5,000 British species, plus many others in different parts of the world. They can be recognized by their *one* pair of wings, with two small organs called halteres, which take the place of hind wings and help the fly to keep its balance. The larvae, or maggots, are legless, so they can only move by wriggling. When the maggot pupates, its coat hardens and forms a capsule, inside which the maggot is changed into an ordinary pupa. It does not cast off its larval skin like most insects. Collect as many different types of these larvae as possible.

Hover-flies

The hover-fly is one of our most useful flies. It works hard to pollinate flowers. It can also destroy pests such as aphids at a rate of about 1,000 in its short life. It looks rather like a wasp because of its black and yellow striped body. Look out for it on a sunny summer day, hovering apparently motionless in the air by focusing its large eyes on an object below so that it can take its bearings. Although it seems still, its wings are in fact moving so fast that they are invisible. There are almost 250 species in the hover-fly's family, the Syrphidae. Most of the larvae live in decaying vegetable or animal matter, although some hover-flies lay their tiny yellow eggs on leaves near the aphids they attack.

The hover-fly looks like a wasp or bee, presumably as a method of protecting itself against attack. One species looks so like a bee, that it gave rise to the myth that it was able to produce honey.

Mosquitoes

The most harmful flies are probably mosquitoes, which in some parts of the world carry deadly diseases like malaria. Scientists have studied them in great detail because of their danger. It is only the female that sucks blood. She lays her eggs on the surface of water and the larvae hang head down with their breathing apparatus protuding. Scientists have tried to prevent the larvae breathing by spreading oil on the surface of water where mosquitoes breed. Despite attempts to wipe them out, mosquitoes are still a major problem, and new species unfortunately continue to be discovered. There are 29 different types in Britain. When you have studied a mosquito, do not think twice about killing it, because although it may not spread disease in your country, it still bites very painfully.

The type you are most likely to find in your garden is *Culex pipiens.*

Daddy-long-legs

The amazingly long legs of this insect, also known as the crane-fly, are not used for walking. The fly clings with them to whatever it is resting on. The most common type of daddy-long-legs is *Tipula paludose*. Its larva is called the leather-jacket and damages potatoes, oats and various types of root crop. The leatherjacket has a hard skin and its 'head' is equipped with biting mouth-parts and antennae.

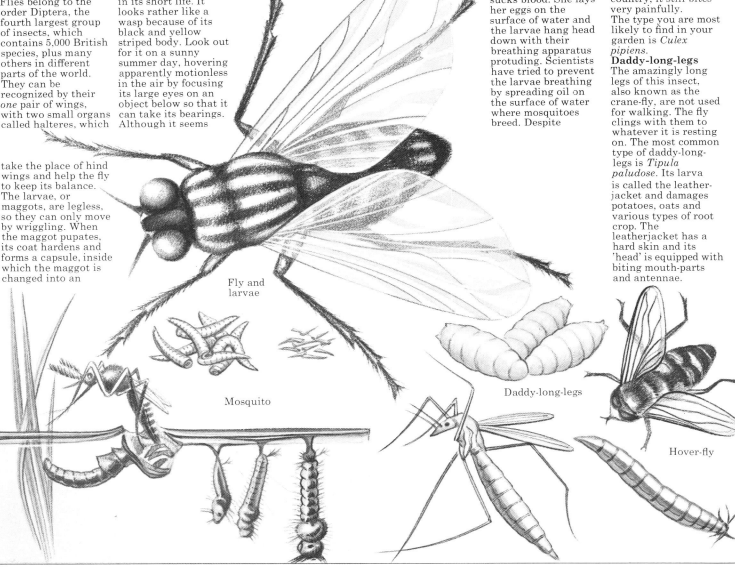

Fly and larvae

Mosquito

Daddy-long-legs

Hover-fly

Bumble-bees

Bumble-bees are far more popular than flies because of the efficient job they perform in pollinating crops and flowers. Unfortunately their numbers are declining, because nesting sites are harder to find now that so much vegetation has been cleared. The death of a queen bee in spring means the loss of hundreds of workers, so if you see a queen searching for a nesting-place, try not to frighten her. And if you ever find a nest, leave it undisturbed. The queen looks for a safe, weather-proof place to build her nest. An old fieldmouse's or bird's nest will do. She then collects moss, old leaves and grass to make her own hollow, spherical nest. She builds a wax, cup-shaped, egg cell, fills it with pollen and nectar, and lays about 12 eggs on top, sealing the cup with more wax. She stores honey in a second cup for herself.

The workers hatch first, so that they can help the queen with the chores, leaving her time to lay more eggs. An average nest rears about 400 workers, plus the lazy males and the important queens. The nest temperature is very high because of the body heat of the males, but if it becomes too hot they fan the surface of the comb with their wings. Bumble-bees work longer hours than the honey-bee, and are unusual because they go out in all weathers. Plants have evolved to compete for the attention of bees, attracting them towards their pollen and nectar by their colour, their shape and scent.

Beetles

There will be plenty of beetles in your garden, but you will have to work hard to find them because they prefer an unobtrusive night life. There are 3,600 species in Britain, which belong to the order Coleoptera, living almost everywhere – under stones, in rotting wood and in water. You will recognize them because their wings are encased in a hard, protective cover called the elytra, which is useful for burrowing into crevices. Watch beetles fly, and you will see the elytra being raised to allow the wings to move. You are most likely to find black ground beetles in your garden, where they are useful to the gardener because they prey on insects. They rarely fly, although they can move quickly on their strong legs. The largest beetle in your garden is the male stag-beetle, which has long jaws, branched and toothed like a stag's antlers. Be careful, though; they bite! Because they are clumsy fliers you may see one crash-landing in your garden at dusk, when it is looking for food. Both the male and the female are shown above. Another common beetle is the ladybird. Do count the spots to see if the ladybird is a common species, like the two-spot or seven-spot, or if it is a rarer type, like the ten-spot. You may find a large number hibernating in a dry, sheltered corner of a shed or attic. Once you have found the site, look again each year because new generations go back to the place where their parents hibernated. Ladybirds perform a useful service for gardeners in that they devour large quantities of aphids.

33

MORE SMALL GARDEN ANIMALS

Earwigs

Earwigs are insects belonging to the order Dermoptera. The most common earwig is *Forficula auricularia*, with a thin, flat, dark reddish-brown body. The large wings, which are rarely used, are pleated in tiny folds under the wing covers. The insect has a pair of pincers on the end of its body, used to frighten off predators.

You will have to search for the earwigs in your garden because they are nocturnal animals. Look in any dry spot, eg under bark or in hollow sticks. They also like to hide in flowers; their particular favourites are dahlias and zinnias.

Earwigs are pests in the garden because they can do a lot of damage to young plants. Look for their hibernation home.

They usually choose a dry, sheltered corner, and the female then gets to work, first digging a hole in the soil as a shelter for herself and her mate. She lays about two dozen pale eggs in late January or February.

Wood-lice

Most crustaceans such as lobsters, crabs and shrimps live in the sea. Wood-lice are one of the few crustaceans to live on the land. They are very common in gardens, where they are unpopular because they eat all kinds of vegetable matter. If you lift up a few damp stones you will see these dumpy animals scurrying about on six pairs of short legs under their protective many-jointed shell. This shell causes the wood-louse a lot of problems. As it grows, the shell becomes too tight and has to be

cast off. This moulting occurs about ten times in a lifetime. After the first moult, an extra pair of legs is grown. But if you are lucky enough to see a wood-louse after a moult, you will see how defenceless it is until its new shell is grown. Also look out for the female after mating, when she grows a pouch between her front legs, where first the eggs and then the young stay until the pouch splits. About 20 small white youngsters emerge from the pouch one by one.

Spiders

Spiders were amongst the earliest animals, living 400 million years ago, long before birds or mammals appeared. They ate primitive insects, and later turned to flies, which are now their favourite food, and which appeared 100

million years later. Spiders belong to the class Arachnida, named after a Greek girl in a legend. She was so proud of her skill as a weaver that she challenged the goddess Athene to a contest. The goddess punished her cheek by turning her into a spider, so that she could weave silk from her own body for ever. Spiders' webs are beautiful, particularly on a frosty morning. Look out for the common garden spider, *Araneus diadematus*, which has a white cross on its back, and watch how it constructs its complex web. Draw the final result. Look out for different types of webs, including the funnel shapes woven by some spiders, which fit into a crevice to catch unsuspecting flies. You should also find

the crab spider, *Misumena calycina*, in your garden. See the way it can run sideways as well as backwards and forwards. Find and draw the striped zebra spider, *Salticus scenicus*, which has a poisonous bite to kill its prey. You will often find it moving about on walls in search of further prey. Look at the different types of insects caught in a web. Spiders have a huge appetite, and each one is said to eat at least 500 insects every day. They do not like aphids, ants and wood-lice, but eat most of the other insects they kill. They do not eat the whole victim, but suck out the contents of the skin, discarding the empty shell.

In May and June you should be able to find a spider's nest in your garden. The female

first spins a sheet, laying hundreds of eggs in it, which are then wrapped in another sheet. A thicker web is finally spun around both. The completed nest may be found attached to plants, or it may be more sheltered – under bark or a stone. The eggs hatch quickly, and once the young spiders can spin silk, they leave the nest in a most fascinating way. They often climb up a plant stem, turn to face the wind and spin a long thread. They are then carried away to new pastures by the wind. You will have noticed grass covered with fine threads in the autumn. These belong to young spiders preparing to leave their mother's nest. In the illustration below are the garden spider in its web and, bottom, the zebra spider.

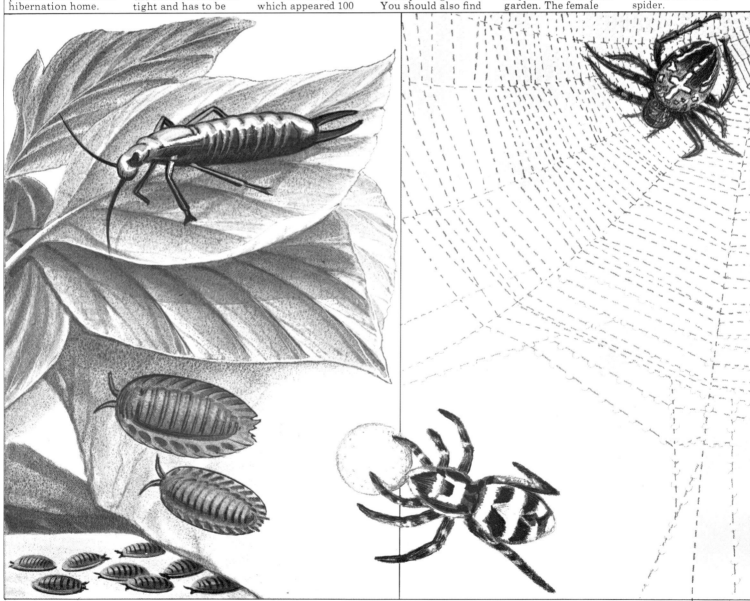

The toad

Most people see a toad in their garden at some time or other. If you do, you can make it feel at home and encourage it to stay by putting out a shallow dish of water, sunk into the ground. Every toad needs water, because although they never actually drink, they absorb water through their skin. They like to sit in water, but if they cannot find any in hot weather they often surround themselves with cold damp soil to avoid getting too dry.

If you watch a toad carefully, you will see that it changes colour to match its surroundings – brown when it is on soil and a dull green when it is hiding in grass. If you are lucky, a toad will decide to make a home in your garden. It will choose somewhere damp and peaceful, like a hole in the rockery or a leafy corner.

It will come out for food in the evenings, and you may see it looking for beetles, wood-lice, caterpillars or ants. In fact it will eat almost anything small, with the exception of slugs and worms. Listen to the smacking sound of the toad's tongue as it catches an insect. Try leaving different types of food out for the toad. Meal-worms will never be refused.

If you live near a pond, look for toad-spawn after March when toads breed. Unlike frog-spawn, the eggs are laid in long strings, and then twisted around underwater plants. For this reason it is more difficult to find toad-spawn than frog-spawn, which floats on the surface. If you collect the eggs, expect them to hatch in about two weeks. You will recognize the toad tadpole because he is brown and much lighter in colour than the black frog tadpole.

Tiny legs and arms appear after about four weeks, and lungs soon develop so that the young toads can start to breathe air. They have many enemies, both in the water and on land. But any young toads that do survive will return to that same pond every year to breed. Their sense of direction is impressive, and toads have been known to travel as much as 6.4 km (4 miles) to and from the breeding pond. This is remarkable, when you realize that toads can only move at about 183 metres (200 yd) per hour.

Although toads are slow creatures, they have for their defence a set of glands under the skin which secrete an unpleasant substance. This often causes predators to spit out a toad which they had hoped to eat. If you are lucky, you may see your toad changing its skin, which happens every 10 days. The skin first splits down the back, then the toad rubs its head and wriggles out of the old skin, which he proceeds to eat. Although the new skin looks wet and shiny at first, it soon turns into the dry, old skin which has just been shed.

Toads are the gardener's friend, because in their long life of about 30 years they eat vast quantities of garden pests like ants and wood-lice.

Mice

Although mice are timid creatures, you may be lucky enough to find the grey-brown fieldmouse or the longer-tailed woodmouse in your garden. The fieldmouse is about 12 cm (5 in) long, with a tail which is only 3 cm (1¼ in). It has a blunt nose, small ears and a plump body.

Look for its dome-shaped nest, made of moss and grass, and hidden away in places like the roots of a tree or shrub. It will use the nest several times a year to rear half-a-dozen blind, hairless young.

You may see the fieldmouse by day or night, all round the year. It does not hibernate, although when the weather is very cold it often sleeps in the nest for several days.

It is harder to catch sight of the woodmouse because of its night-time habits. But it does leave plenty of evidence behind in the form of hoards of nuts and seeds, which it tries to hide in old birds' nests or holes in the ground. It is about 9 cm (3½ in) long, with a tail of the same length, and has brown skin on its back and white underparts. Its ears are larger than the fieldmouse's, and it has very prominent eyes. Despite their size, the woodmouse is short-sighted, so if you are quiet, you may be able to get very near the animal and even pick it up. Woodmice live in the ground, and like company, and you may come across a large group of them. Sometimes they can be seen climbing up trees to store their food in holes or old birds' nests. They are also noted for their ability to swim.

Hedgehogs

Regular guests to suburban gardens are hedgehogs, particularly if there is a rough piece of ground or a shrubbery. They belong to the order Insectivora, so called because they are insect-eaters. Like their relatives the shrews and moles, they belong to a very old family, Erinaceidae.

A hedgehog is useful in the garden, because apart from insects it will also dispose of snails, slugs, earwigs and wood-lice. Hedgehogs come out mainly at dusk or during the night, hunting by sound. Even the slightest rustle of a wood-louse is enough for the alert hedgehog.

Put out a bowl of water for any hedgehog which appears. It will come back again and again for a drink. It will also appreciate bread and milk, raisins, and even cat food.

If a hedgehog is disturbed, it will probably leap into the air, and turn its body into a tight ball. Hedgehogs have few enemies; the main hazard is road traffic, but, barring accidents, hedgehogs often live for about six years.

A hedgehog mates for life, and builds a nest of grass, moss and leaves. The female has four babies about 1 cm ($\frac{1}{2}$ in) long, and they stay with their parents for some time. They get ready to hibernate in mid-October,

usually reappearing in early April. It is said that this animal can predict the weather. If a hedgehog leaves his nest in February, but then goes back into hibernation, there are said to be six more weeks of cold weather. If, however, he stays out, the rest of the winter will be mild.

Birds

You can attract birds to your garden if you put out food in winter, and a shallow container of water in summer. String up a coconut, a ball of fat, or leave out seeds. Berries are important to birds in winter, and they in turn are just as important to the berry-bearing plants. They scatter the seeds widely, either immediately after eating the soft part of the berry, or after the food has been swallowed, when the seeds are passed out later as droppings. Identify all the plants with berries in your garden and then keep a notebook, entering details of which birds ate which berries on which date. Count the number of berries eaten by a bird at one time. Check if certain birds **prefer** particular berries, and if they prefer them ripe or unripe.

Look for droppings containing seeds under trees; pick them up using an old spoon, and plant them in pots. Water regularly, and identify the plants when they have grown.

Birds enjoy the following berries: hawthorn, yew, cotoneaster, blackberries, rowan, firethorn and holly. The berry-eating birds in your garden will include waxwings, redwings, fieldfares, blackbirds and greenfinches.

Birds such as blue-tits and starlings turn to fruits and berries when their normal insect diet is sparse. The mistle-thrush is one of the few birds to eat mistletoe berries. Bullfinches feed on tree seeds like ash, but if these are scarce, they turn to garden **berries**. They sometimes damage orchards by stripping off the early buds.

Fieldfare

Greenfinch

Blackbird

Redwing

Blue-tit

Goldfinch

Waxwing

Garden favourites
Use a notebook to record which birds like which berries and how they take them. Above, some typical garden visitors are making the most of a variety of berry-bearing plants. The fieldfare is shown on a holly branch, for example, and the redwing on a cotoneaster.

37

The average lifespan of our early ancestors was only between 30 and 40 years, half what it is today. This is because poor living conditions caused many diseases, and battles with other tribes and fatal attacks by wild animals were common. It is therefore not surprising that early man gave a lot of thought to his body, and how lives could be saved. At first, magic and medicine were closely connected. Blood, for example was thought of as a magical 'life-spirit', because it was known that when a

Opening the skull
In the primitive operation known as trepanning, a piece of the cranial bone was cut out to allow evil spirits to escape. Woodcut from van Gersdorff's *Book of Surgery* (1517).

in good condition in museums.

The Greeks were excellent students of the human body. Probably the most famous of the Greek medical men was Hippocrates. We remember him for the 'Hippocratic Oath', a code of practice which doctors still vow to follow before they qualify. Hippocrates taught a thorough, scientific approach to treating the

the veins. He carried out a lot of work on the nerves, and concluded for the first time that the brain, and not the heart, controls the working of the body.

The most influential figures after those men were Galen (c130–c200) and Avicenna (980–1037), the Persian 'prince of physicians'. Avicenna's *Canon of Medicine* and Galen's account of the human body were accepted by the majority of medieval physicians.

Surgery was a dubious profession in the Middle Ages. It was considered a sin to study a dead body, and the Church banned clerics from practising it because 'men vowed to religion should not touch those things which cannot be honourably mentioned in speech'. By the late 13th century the ban on dissection was relaxed in Italy, and scientists travelled there to study in anatomical theatres.

There was very little dramatic progress in understanding the body, however, until the early 17th century, when William Harvey (1578–1657), an Englishman, made one of the most important medical discoveries. He proved that the blood is circulated round the body in one

person stops breathing, the flow of blood also stops, and death follows.

Operations were performed even in those early days. One popular practice, thought to release evil spirits, was called trepanning. This involved cutting a hole in the patient's skull, and was practised in civilizations as far apart as ancient Peru and medieval Europe. Fortunately, by the time of the Egyptians medical knowledge among the more advanced peoples had developed to the point where people knew that damage to the brain could cause other parts of the body to become paralyzed. The Egyptians also became experts at preserving the bodies of the dead by embalming them with special lotions. Today, after 3,000 years, these 'mummies' can still be seen

body, which helped to bring an end to the religious and magical aspects of medicine.

During the 4th century BC, Alexander the Great conquered nearly all the countries of the Middle East, and Alexandria became a centre for the development of medicine. One man, an anatomist and surgeon called Herophilus, was outstanding, inventing medical terms which continue in use today. He made a detailed study of the human body, discovering how the human eye works and how its optic nerves are joined to the brain. He is thought to have carried out experiments on animals, and even on condemned criminals. But, however he did it, he ended his career understanding the workings of the lungs and differences between the arteries and

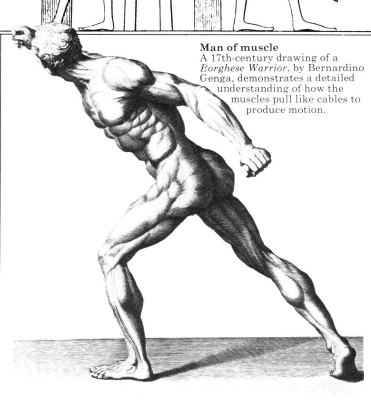

Man of muscle
A 17th-century drawing of a *Borghese Warrior*, by Bernardino Genga, demonstrates a detailed understanding of how the muscles pull like cables to produce motion.

direction only by the pumping action of the heart. Now doctors knew for the first time that the blood did not flow in a forward-then-backward motion.

At about the same time a quite different study opened up a whole new area of medical research. The first microscope was built. Anton van Leeuwenhoek (1632–1723), a Dutch naturalist, developed a small, single lens which was held up to the eye, with the object to be examined fixed on a small pin (see also page 131). With this type of microscope, which could magnify up to 400 times, he discovered the existence of red blood cells and bacteria.

The importance of bacteria, however, was not established until the 19th century, when the French

person to another. The new science of bacteriology had begun.

Pasteur decided to adopt an idea, first used by Dr Edward Jenner in the treatment of smallpox, in which a less deadly substance was used to vaccinate the patient against a more dangerous disease. He found that some bacteria became inactive when cultivated outside the body, and was able to use the inactive bacteria of a disease to produce vaccines. Before Pasteur's discovery of airborne bacteria, many people died from unknown causes and after minor operations from which they should have recovered. With the knowledge that bacteria in the air could cause infection, hospitals and operating theatres were

Anatomical theatre
A corpse lies ready for surgeon and student-audience in the world's first anatomical theatre, set up in the 1590s at Padua University.

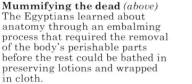

Mummifying the dead *(above)*
The Egyptians learned about anatomy through an embalming process that required the removal of the body's perishable parts before the rest could be bathed in preserving lotions and wrapped in cloth.

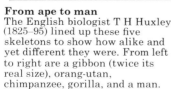

From ape to man
The English biologist T H Huxley (1825–95) lined up these five skeletons to show how alike and yet different they were. From left to right are a gibbon (twice its real size), orang-utan, chimpanzee, gorilla, and a man.

chemist Louis Pasteur (1822–95) was asked by brewers to find out why beer and wine can turn sour. He discovered that micro-organisms were the cause, and then went on to establish that they are always present in air, and that diseases are often due to bacteria carried from one

cleaned up. Pasteur's work greatly influenced Joseph Lister (1827–1912). After studying inflammation and the suppuration of wounds, he invented a carbolic-acid spray for use in operating theatres to kill bacteria. This device opened the new field on antiseptic surgery.

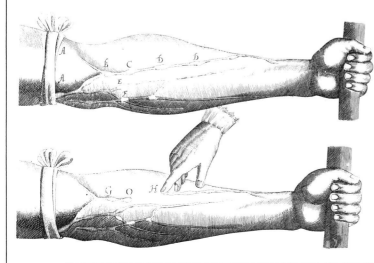

How blood circulates
This illustration from William Harvey's *Essay on the Motion of the Heart and Blood* shows that there are valves in our veins. They appear when a tourniquet is applied above the subject's elbow *(upper picture)*. In the lower picture the vein disappears when the supply is stopped at H. From such experiments Harvey concluded that the blood 'is forced into a circular course and that it is in constant motion'. His revolutionary findings were first published in 1628.

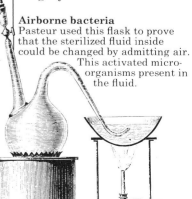

Airborne bacteria
Pasteur used this flask to prove that the sterilized fluid inside could be changed by admitting air. This activated micro-organisms present in the fluid.

Your body is just like a machine, but the most complex machine ever devised. It is built on a framework of bones – the skeleton – which is beautifully designed for its purpose, giving your body shape and protecting the soft and sensitive interior parts. The main parts of the skeleton are the skull, the spine and the limbs, and there is an intricate system of joints that allows you to move.

To understand your bones a little better, examine a skeleton. Many school science departments have one, or alternatively you should be able to find an example in a local museum.

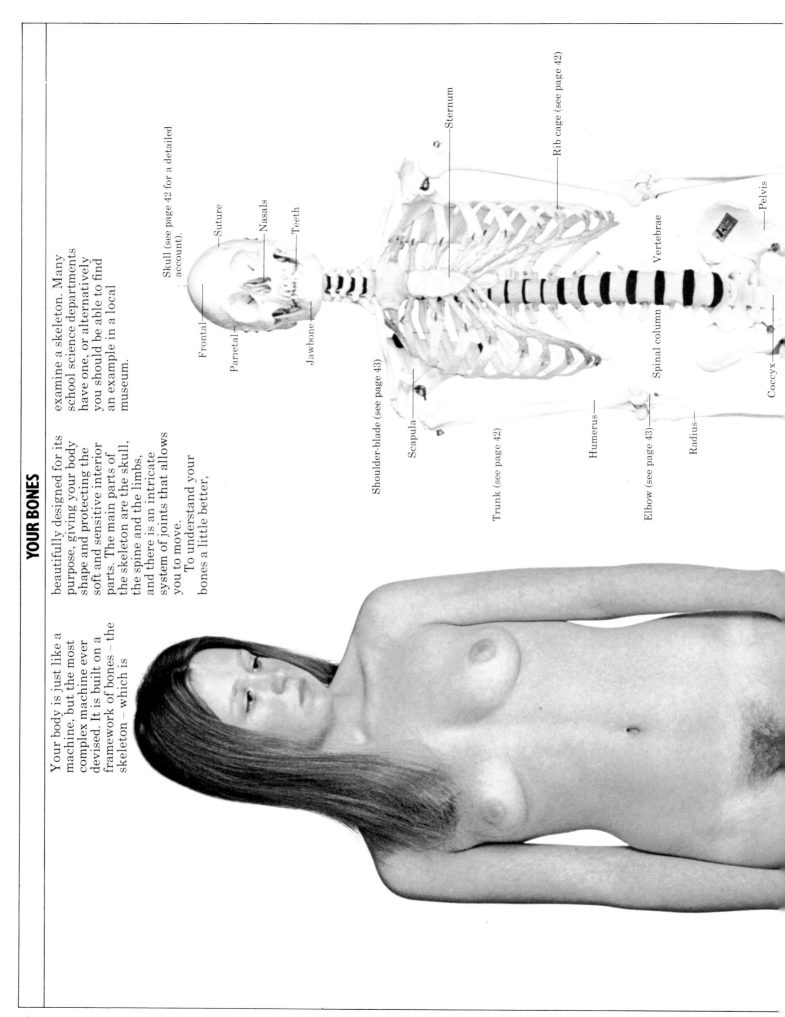

Skull (see page 42 for a detailed account).

Suture

Nasals

Teeth

Frontal

Parietal

Jawbone

Sternum

Rib cage (see page 42)

Shoulder-blade (see page 43)

Scapula

Trunk (see page 42)

Humerus

Elbow (see page 43)

Radius

Vertebrae

Spinal column

Coccyx

Pelvis

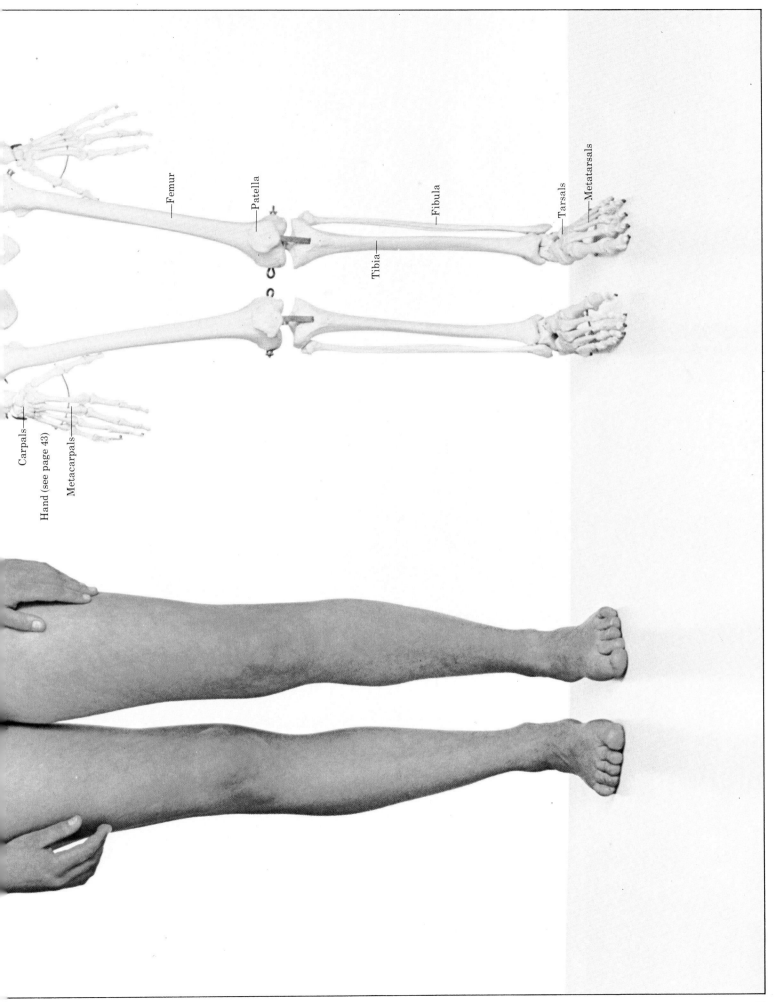

Carpals

Hand (see page 43)

Metacarpals

Femur

Patella

Tibia

Fibula

Tarsals

Metatarsals

Skull

The skull is made up of 22 separate bones, joined together to make a strong case for your brain, eyes, ears, nose and mouth. You will see two big holes for the eyes, and you may be surprised to find no bone at the tip of the nose. Feel your own nose to see why. Although it is joined to your forehead by bone at the top, its shape is formed by gristle, with skin and fatty tissue at the sides. Look at the teeth on the skull and count them. If it is the skull of an adult it will have 32 teeth; if it is that of a young teenager it will have only 28. If it is the skull of a young child, the teeth will look very different because they are the smaller, milk or first set of teeth. Compare the teeth at the front and back of the skull jaw. The front teeth are sharper for cutting into food, while the back teeth are blunt for grinding food. Look at the squiggly marks or sutures on the top of the skull. Babies have soft spots in the bones of their skulls, which allow their brains to grow. Then slowly the hard, bony parts of the skull grow together, filling in the soft spots and forming those strong squiggly joints.

Trunk

The trunk consists of the spinal column, or back-bone, the breast bone, the ribs and pelvis. If you look at the skeleton from the side, you will see a curve in the lower part of the spinal column. When you are

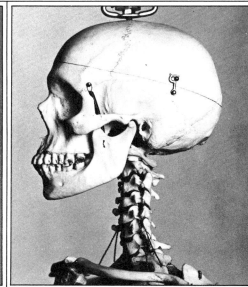

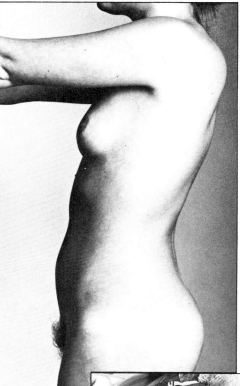

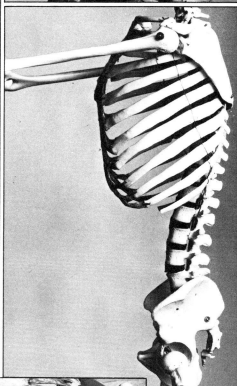

born you do not have that important curve, but it develops when babies begin to sit up and walk. Without curved spines it would be difficult to move about. Chairs are now often designed with back-rests in the same curved shape, because they are thought to be better for our backs. The spinal column itself has 33 knobbly bones called vertebrae, separated by discs of gristle or cartilage, which act rather like protective washers between metal machine parts. Feel them on your own back. These, acting as shock-absorbers, make it possible for us to move our back-bones. The vertebrae at the lower end of the spine are called the coccyx, and this is all that remains of the tail once possessed by man. In a museum, compare the coccyx of the human skeleton with the tail bones of other animal skeletons.

Rib cage

Your rib cage is a kind of fence of bones, protecting the important organs inside such as the heart, lungs and stomach. Count the ribs on the skeleton

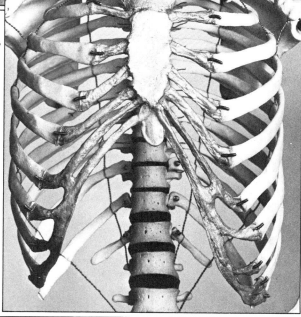

and see how many of them you can feel in your own body. You will find that 12 pairs of ribs are connected to your back-bone, of which 10 curve round to join the breast-bone.

Shoulder-blades

The shoulder blades or clavicles on the skeleton are flat because a large area is needed to attach all the muscles which are in that part of the body. A lot of muscle is required there for lifting, pushing, and many other activities. Reach back and touch one of your shoulder-blades. Now move your arm and free hand and find out which movements affect those muscles.

Elbow

Look at the skeleton's elbow. Here, three bones meet in a hinge-join. Bend your elbow so that you can feel what the bones do. There are three big bones in the arm, the humerus, radius and ulna. Poke your arm until you find them all. The elbow and lower arm bones twist round easily from the elbow, which is important for many arm movements.

Hand

The hand on the skeleton will give you some idea of just how complicated your own hands are. There are 29 bones in the wrist and hand. It is because you have so many bones that you can use your hands in so many different ways, for waving, hammering, poking with one finger, and doing delicate things like picking up a pin. Of all the animals with hands, only humans, apes and monkeys can rotate, or turn their thumbs to a position opposite each of the four fingers. That ability has been important in man's development; without it, for example, we could not hold a pen.

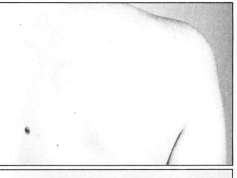
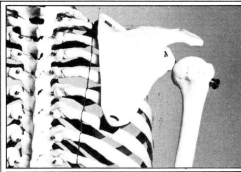
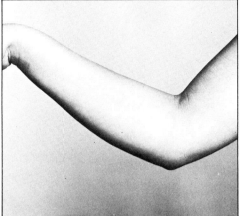
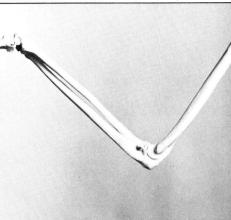
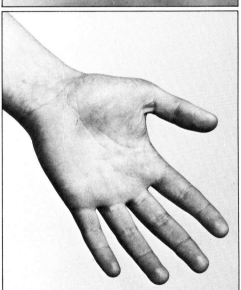
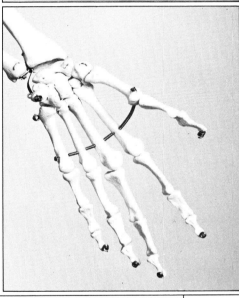

Ball-and-socket joints

Compare the elbow joint of the skeleton to the upper leg-bone, or femur, where it joins the hip. You will see that the types of joint are very different. Joints like the elbow and ankle joints are hinges, which allow movement in a general up-and-down direction. But the arms and legs are joined to the trunk by ball-and-socket joints that allow more movement. Try throwing a stone overarm. The ball of bone at the top of your arm-bone fits into a socket at the end of the shoulder blade. This makes it possible for you to move your arm freely in any direction. In the same way, the ball of bone

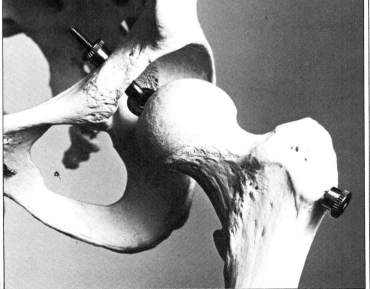

at the top of your thigh fits into a deep socket in the pelvis, a basin-shaped bone at the base of the spine.

Free movement is made possible by a whole series of joints. In your arm you have joints at the shoulder, elbow, wrist and fingers. The surface of the bones at joints is protected by cartilage to reduce friction. They are also bathed in a special fluid, just as moving parts of a machine are oiled. In fact, our skeleton functions so much like a machine that engineers and medical specialists have developed a new way to study the body which they call bio-engineering.

THE MUSCLES

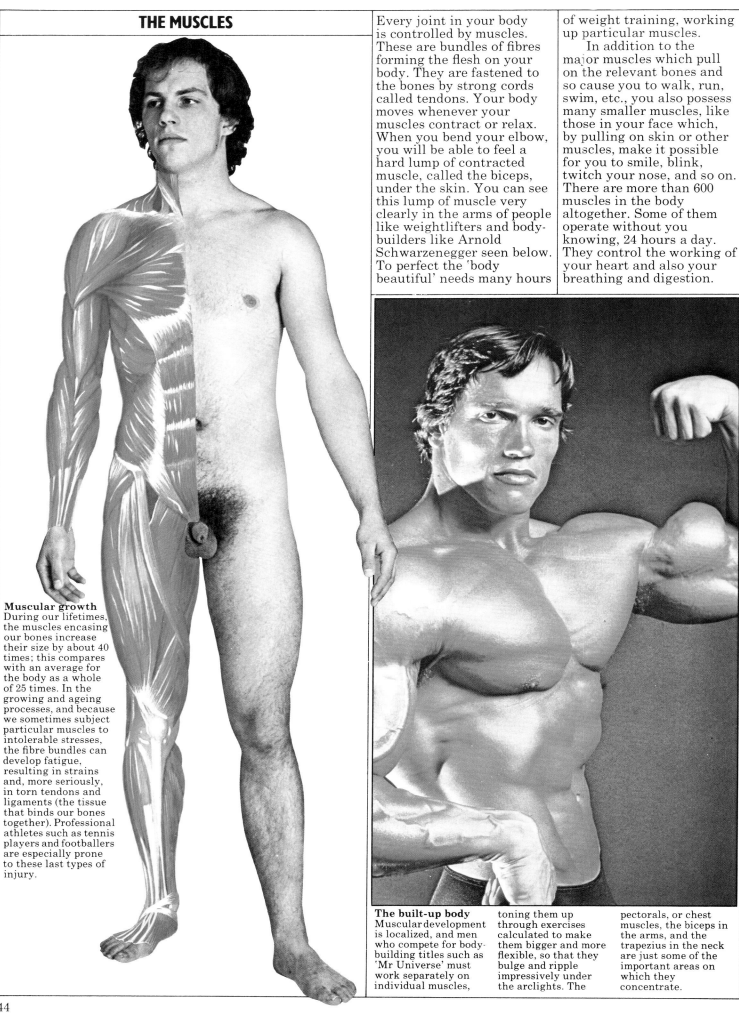

Every joint in your body is controlled by muscles. These are bundles of fibres forming the flesh on your body. They are fastened to the bones by strong cords called tendons. Your body moves whenever your muscles contract or relax. When you bend your elbow, you will be able to feel a hard lump of contracted muscle, called the biceps, under the skin. You can see this lump of muscle very clearly in the arms of people like weightlifters and body-builders like Arnold Schwarzenegger seen below. To perfect the 'body beautiful' needs many hours of weight training, working up particular muscles.

In addition to the major muscles which pull on the relevant bones and so cause you to walk, run, swim, etc., you also possess many smaller muscles, like those in your face which, by pulling on skin or other muscles, make it possible for you to smile, blink, twitch your nose, and so on. There are more than 600 muscles in the body altogether. Some of them operate without you knowing, 24 hours a day. They control the working of your heart and also your breathing and digestion.

Muscular growth
During our lifetimes, the muscles encasing our bones increase their size by about 40 times; this compares with an average for the body as a whole of 25 times. In the growing and ageing processes, and because we sometimes subject particular muscles to intolerable stresses, the fibre bundles can develop fatigue, resulting in strains and, more seriously, in torn tendons and ligaments (the tissue that binds our bones together). Professional athletes such as tennis players and footballers are especially prone to these last types of injury.

The built-up body
Muscular development is localized, and men who compete for body-building titles such as 'Mr Universe' must work separately on individual muscles, toning them up through exercises calculated to make them bigger and more flexible, so that they bulge and ripple impressively under the arclights. The pectorals, or chest muscles, the biceps in the arms, and the trapezius in the neck are just some of the important areas on which they concentrate.

HOW BLOOD CIRCULATES

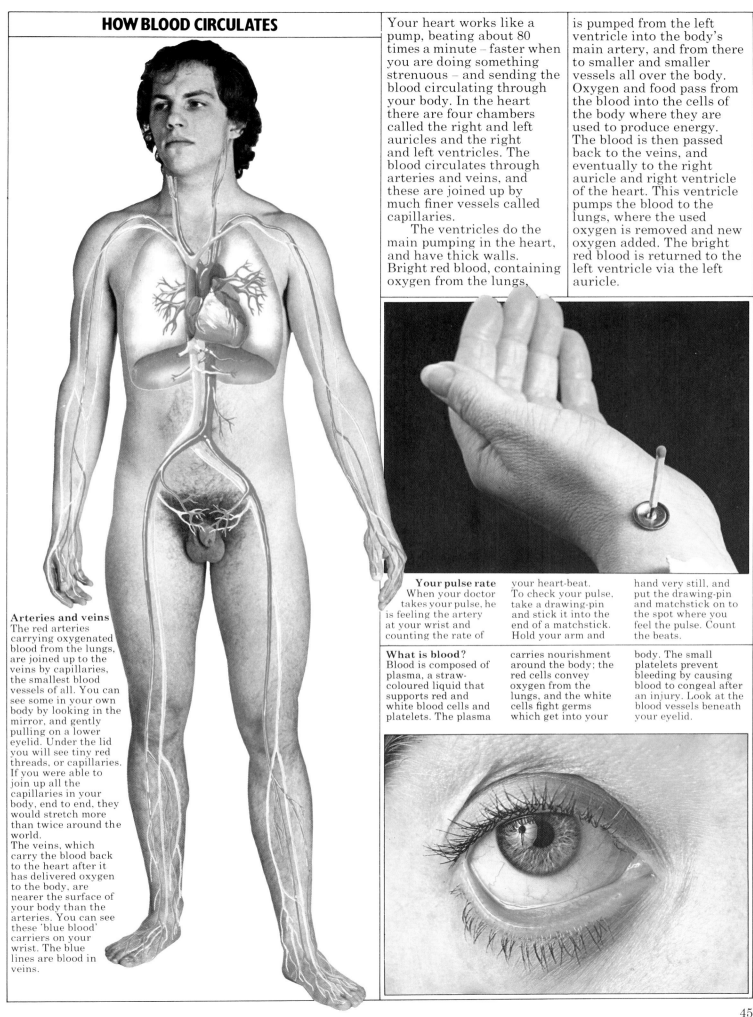

Your heart works like a pump, beating about 80 times a minute – faster when you are doing something strenuous – and sending the blood circulating through your body. In the heart there are four chambers called the right and left auricles and the right and left ventricles. The blood circulates through arteries and veins, and these are joined up by much finer vessels called capillaries.

The ventricles do the main pumping in the heart, and have thick walls. Bright red blood, containing oxygen from the lungs, is pumped from the left ventricle into the body's main artery, and from there to smaller and smaller vessels all over the body. Oxygen and food pass from the blood into the cells of the body where they are used to produce energy. The blood is then passed back to the veins, and eventually to the right auricle and right ventricle of the heart. This ventricle pumps the blood to the lungs, where the used oxygen is removed and new oxygen added. The bright red blood is returned to the left ventricle via the left auricle.

Arteries and veins
The red arteries carrying oxygenated blood from the lungs, are joined up to the veins by capillaries, the smallest blood vessels of all. You can see some in your own body by looking in the mirror, and gently pulling on a lower eyelid. Under the lid you will see tiny red threads, or capillaries. If you were able to join up all the capillaries in your body, end to end, they would stretch more than twice around the world.
The veins, which carry the blood back to the heart after it has delivered oxygen to the body, are nearer the surface of your body than the arteries. You can see these 'blue blood' carriers on your wrist. The blue lines are blood in veins.

Your pulse rate
When your doctor takes your pulse, he is feeling the artery at your wrist and counting the rate of your heart-beat. To check your pulse, take a drawing-pin and stick it into the end of a matchstick. Hold your arm and hand very still, and put the drawing-pin and matchstick on to the spot where you feel the pulse. Count the beats.

What is blood?
Blood is composed of plasma, a straw-coloured liquid that supports red and white blood cells and platelets. The plasma carries nourishment around the body; the red cells convey oxygen from the lungs, and the white cells fight germs which get into your body. The small platelets prevent bleeding by causing blood to congeal after an injury. Look at the blood vessels beneath your eyelid.

45

Your lungs (right) work like a pair of bellows. They are situated inside the rib cage, above an arched muscle called the diaphragm. Normally you breathe about 16 times a minute, but you often need more air, for example when you are running. Then you breathe faster and your lungs work harder. This is why, after a race, you see athletes' chests deeply rising and falling.

When you breathe in, the air passes into your windpipe, which then divides into two tubes called the bronchi. These pass into your lungs, where they divide and branch into numerous very fine tubes, each ending in an air-sac. The oxygen is able to pass through the thin walls of the air-sacs into the blood vessels in the lungs, and then on to the rest of the body, where it is used up by all cells. The used oxygen becomes carbon dioxide, which passes from blood vessels into the air-sacs and eventually the lungs. It is then breathed out.

Your lungs look rather like a sponge because they are full of tiny holes. The lungs fill up with air much as a sponge takes up water.

Lungs are also very important for speech. The air they bring in and out of the body is made to vibrate and produce sounds. To find out how you make sounds, stand with your hands on your chest and feel your ribs with your fingers (centre). Inside those ribs are your lungs. Now close your mouth and take a deep breath.

You will find that, as you breathe in, your chest swells out and air rushes in down your nose and throat into your lungs. Breathe in a lot of air and then say 'Ahhhhh', letting the air out slowly. You will only be able to make this sound when there is some air in your lungs. When you run out of air, you run out of 'Ahhhhh', which proves how important the lungs are for talking.

Take another deep breath, tip your head back and feel your throat with your fingertips (bottom).

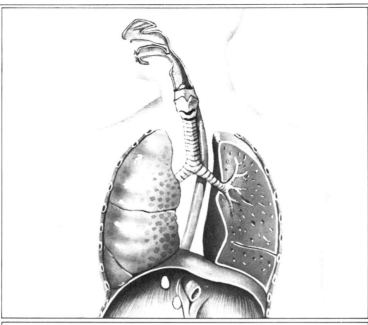

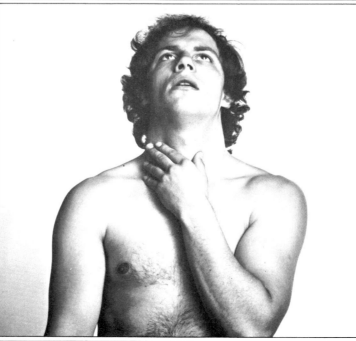

Breathe out again and say 'Ahhhh', placing your fingers so that you feel the larynx. This is located under the bulging part of the throat sometimes known as the 'Adam's apple'. At this place in your throat, the air goes through a narrow opening. You can experiment with a balloon to see how a larynx works.

Blow up the balloon, and regard the neck of the balloon as the larynx. First hold the neck of the balloon shut with both hands, then stretch it to make a narrow slit. As air escapes from the balloon through the slit, it makes a squealing sound; you will also find that when the slit is narrow the sound is high, and goes lower as the slit widens. Your larynx works rather like that slit in the balloon.

The larynx is a box-like instrument. Inside it, two membranes are stretched across, which are called the vocal cords. The narrow opening between them is called the glottis. When you speak or sing, air is forced through the glottis, making your vocal cords vibrate and produce sound. Just as happened with the neck of the balloon above, if the glottis is small, the voice will be high. If it is wide, the voice will be lower.

There is a wide variation in human sound. A low bass voice produces about 60 vibrations a second, while a high soprano may vibrate as many as 1,200 times a second. The special vocal effect known as vibrato is produced by exaggerating the natural vibrations of the human voice to make a controlled, wave-like sound. Singers often use it to hold one note for a long time, for a special emotional effect.

The human voice is rather like a musical instrument, although it has extra powers and is better than any man-made instrument in expressing feeling or emotion. Compared to the instruments of the orchestra, the voice is most like a wind instrument, with the hollow spaces inside the mouth, throat and nose being equivalent to the pipe (see pages 160–161).

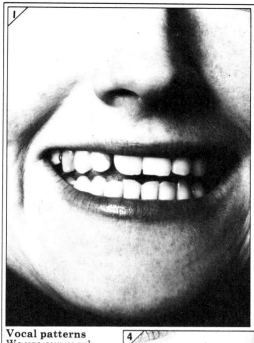

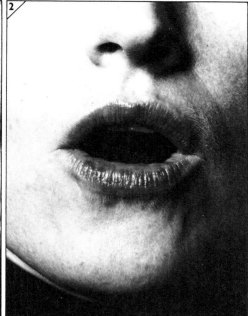

Vocal patterns

We use our vocal cords in conjunction with our mouth, throat, nose, lips and tongue to make different sounds, changing the size and shape of the spaces inside our mouth and throat by using special muscles. These spaces change rapidly all the time. Watch yourself in a mirror as you make the following vowel sounds:

1 EE. Your tongue is humped near the front of your mouth.

2 AW. Your tongue is humped much farther back, and your lips are still fairly close together, but they are in a different position.

3 AH. Your lips are now much farther apart and your tongue is more relaxed.

All vowel sounds are made with the lips apart. Consonants, however, are made with the lips closed, or almost so.

4 MMM. Your lips are closed, and the sound comes out through the nose, although the shape of your mouth space is helping to make the tone.

5 SSS and ZZZ. These consonants do not make use of the vocal cords. They are formed when air passes across small openings in the mouth. Most of the sound power of spoken words is carried by the vowels. The average word takes one-third of a second, with the vowel sounds using most of this time. Consonants need only about one-twentieth of a second each. But it is also interesting to know that in ordinary speech the sounds

themselves take up only about half the speaking time. Your own voice sounds strange to you and natural to other people because you hear your own voice from the 'inside'. The effect of the mouth and other spaces in your head make the tone of your speech sound different. One way to notice this is to hum loudly while pinching your nostrils lightly together, or while plugging both your ears with your fingers.

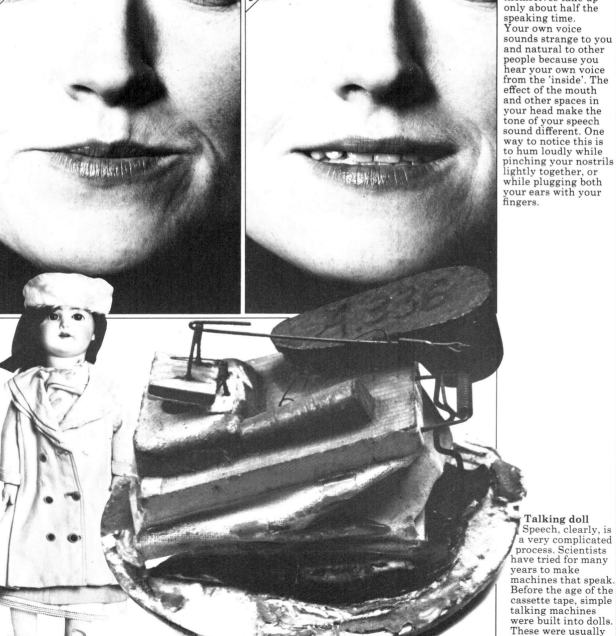

Talking doll

Speech, clearly, is a very complicated process. Scientists have tried for many years to make machines that speak. Before the age of the cassette tape, simple talking machines were built into dolls. These were usually worked by bellows.

The eye is such an important and delicate organ that it is particularly well protected. It is set in a large and very strong eye-socket in the skull (see page 42). This socket is lined by a lot of soft fat. The front of the eye is protected by eyelids, with lashes to keep out dust, eyebrows to keep out sweat and rain, and a supply of a liquid, that we call tears, to keep the eyeball washed clean.

Look carefully at your eyes in a mirror. You will see a coloured circle, the iris, with a small black circle in the centre called the pupil. The pupil looks black because it is the opening to the inside of the eye. Like that of a camera, this aperture has to be very dark to form a good picture on the retina at the back of the eye.

Eyebrow
The eye's outermost protective structure, the brow, traps moisture and dirt that would otherwise trickle down into the eye.

Eyelids
The lids are soft folds of skin that can close off the eye, either for a split-second through blinking or for longer periods such as when we are asleep.

Eyelashes
These extend from the eyelid and act as a screen to keep out dust and other particles.

Tears
We manufacture this salty fluid to keep the front of the eyeball clean. It is produced by the lachrymal glands, and is spread over the eyeball when we blink. The glands are vulnerable to emotional upset or physical irritation, and then produce the extra fluid generally called tears.

Pupil and iris
At the centre of the eye is the coloured iris with its central aperture, the pupil, through which light is admitted from the object being viewed.

Upside-down image

The picture or image of what you are looking at is formed upside down on the retina, just like the image on the film of a camera (see page 139). It is the brain which turns this picture the right way round. To prove that the retina forms an upside-down image, you need a small glass bowl filled with water, a piece of card and a lighted candle. Make a small hole in the card to represent the pupil of the eye. Stand the lighted candle a short distance away. Darken the room, and hold a piece of white paper behind the glass bowl on the opposite side to the candle to represent the retina. Looking through the card, adjust the paper until you see the candle in it. It will seem smaller and, even more important, it will be upside down.

Yellow spots

One particular part of the retina, called the yellow spot because it is that colour, is very sensitive to detail. Whenever you look at an object you are turning your eyeballs until the light from the object is focused by the lenses of your two eyes on to the yellow spot in each eye. If you look now at the tip of your finger, light from it falls on the yellow spot in each eye so that you see it in great detail. Now, while still looking at the finger, move your other hand about 25-30 cm (10-12 in) away from the finger. You can see it moving about but you cannot see any details unless you decide to focus light from that hand on to your yellow spots instead. Then the image of the nearer finger will become indistinct.

The blind spot

There is another, quite different, spot on each retina called the blind spot. Here the eye sees nothing at all because there are no sensitive nerve endings at this point, where the optic nerve leaves the eye. You can test your blind spots by making two marks on paper 5 cm (2 in) apart. Close the right eye and look at the right mark. Then move the paper nearer and nearer until the other mark disappears. Keep on moving the paper nearer and the mark will reappear. This happens when the rays of light have crossed over your blind spot.

●   ●

HEARING

You normally hear sound by catching the waves in the fleshy part of the ear that you can see, and reflecting them into the auditory canal and the inner part of the ear, as explained on page 152. But you can also hear sound through the bones of your head, including your teeth. This principle has been applied

in hearing aids for people who have healthy inner ears and auditory nerves, but are deaf because they have suffered some damage to the outer ear.

Do this experiment to prove that you can hear through your bones or your teeth. Strike a fork on the table and quickly put the handle against the bone just behind your ear, as demonstrated in the photograph on the left. You will be able to hear the sound because the vibrations are passed on by the bone. Repeat this, touching other bones in your head. Where the bones are covered by flesh, you will hear less. You will get the most powerful result when you clamp the vibrating fork handle firmly between your teeth.

EATING

Just as a stoker shovels coal into a boiler, which burns and generates heat and energy, you take food in at your mouth, which is used to produce the energy your body needs. Food is the body's fuel, and it is 'burned' in the cells of the body with oxygen provided by the blood. The waste product or 'smoke' is the carbon dioxide you breathe out.

Before your food can be used in this way, it has to be changed or digested. First of all, your sharp teeth cut the food up into pieces, the tongue then carries the food to your grinding teeth at the back of the mouth. They mash up the food before it is swallowed. The back teeth have bumps

which help to grind the food – and it is important to clean them carefully. The back teeth are very vulnerable to decay. Check this by asking some adults to open their mouths so that you can look at the number of fillings in their back teeth.

When food is ready to be swallowed, it passes down a soft, fleshy tube called the oesophagus, which goes down in front of your spinal column to your stomach. The pulp is again stirred up, this time by the stomach muscles. It is acted on by the gastric juices inside the stomach. They make the food taste sour, which you will know from the times you have been sick. To get rid of bad food, the muscles in your chest and near your

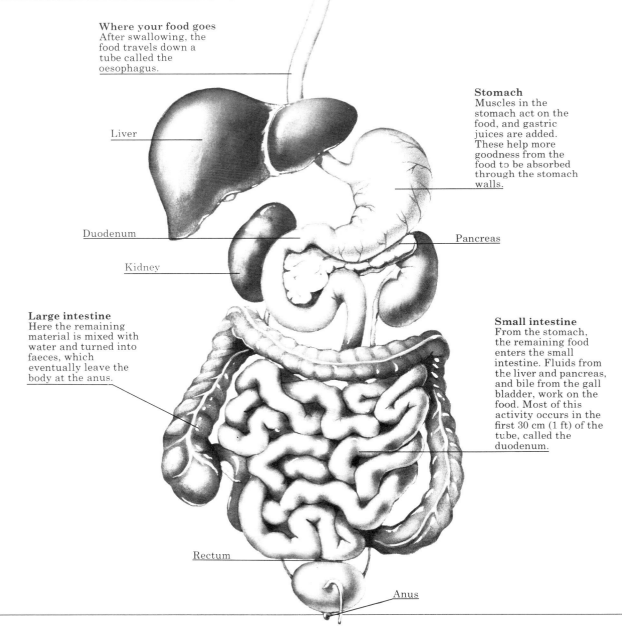

Where your food goes
After swallowing, the food travels down a tube called the oesophagus.

Liver

Duodenum

Kidney

Stomach
Muscles in the stomach act on the food, and gastric juices are added. These help more goodness from the food to be absorbed through the stomach walls.

Pancreas

Large intestine
Here the remaining material is mixed with water and turned into faeces, which eventually leave the body at the anus.

Small intestine
From the stomach, the remaining food enters the small intestine. Fluids from the liver and pancreas, and bile from the gall bladder, work on the food. Most of this activity occurs in the first 30 cm (1 ft) of the tube, called the duodenum.

Rectum

Anus

stomach squeeze together, and the 'gate' at the end of your stomach remains closed, so the food is forced to go up and you vomit.

After two to six hours in the stomach, any food which has not been broken down and absorbed through the stomach walls, passes into the small intestine, a folded tube which would be about 6 m (20 ft) long if it was straightened out. It is here that fluids from the liver and pancreas arrive to extract more goodness from the food, leaving the indigestible matter to pass on to the large intestine and rectum, until it eventually leaves the body through the anus.

Although we need food to provide energy for movement, that energy is also important when we are lying still. This is because there are always muscles, of the heart and diaphragm, for example, that have to move at all times. The amount of food a person needs depends on his age, size and job. A footballer will need more food than a radio announcer, while an old man will require a much smaller diet because he has become less active with age.

Over-eating can lead to obesity, the most harmful condition in the richer countries today, because it causes heart disease and other ailments. It does seem to be true that over-eating shortens life. Gerontologists point out that the greatest percentage of centenarians live in Georgia, USSR, where many people eat a sparse but healthy diet of fresh vegetables, herbs, honey, milk and cheese.

TASTE

Taste-buds on the tongue's surface connect directly with your brain and tell you what you are tasting. There are patches of different types of taste-buds, as the photograph below shows. You can prove this by putting sugar, salt and lemon on different parts of your own tongue. You probably know from experience that the bitter taste does not become apparent until you are ready to swallow. Your nose also tells your brain about flavours. If you hold your nose when you are eating, you will find that it affects the sensation of taste. Wine-tasters, for example, place great store by what their nose tells them about the quality of a particular vintage.

Wine is one of those substances we ingest which have a marked individual flavour. Oranges and cocoa (chocolate) are others, and these all tend to stimulate us by their aromas.

The route by which aromas travel to the brain is via the olfactory membrane. Here the odorous molecules stimulate tiny hairs to send messages to the olfactory bulb, and from there they are transmitted to the brain.

The classification of aromas is very complicated, and scientists are still looking for the best system. One way – equivalent to the taste buds on the tongue – is to regard all smells as a blend of four essential smells – acid, burnt, fragrant and rancid.

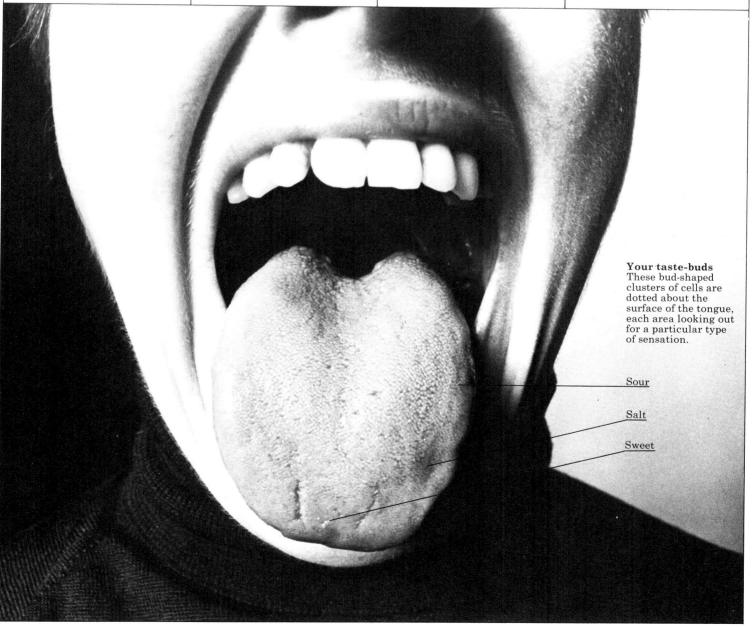

Your taste-buds
These bud-shaped clusters of cells are dotted about the surface of the tongue, each area looking out for a particular type of sensation.

Sour

Salt

Sweet

YOUR BODY AND HEAT

Because humans are mammals, you are warm-blooded and have an elaborate system for keeping your body temperature as constant as possible. The hypothalamus, at the base of the brain, acts as your 'thermostat', controlling your temperature by making your body adjust to conditions that increase the body's rate of heat loss and heat production.

If you stay in cold water for a long time, you will be able to watch how your body copes with this. You will shiver, you will notice goose pimples on your skin and your lips may turn a blue colour. This is part of your body's way of conserving heat. Your lips look blue for the following reason. The blood vessels near the surface of your skin become narrower to slow the rate of circulation. Now warm blood from deep inside your body does not reach the colder skin areas so quickly. Because your blood is flowing more slowly, there is plenty of time for the oxygen carried by the blood to be removed by cells. Since oxygen-poor blood is darker than blood rich in oxygen, skin that is thin and more transparent to blood vessels, like the lips, begins to look slightly blue. Goose pimples, which make hair 'stand on end', also help to conserve heat. In animals with fur,

EXERCISES

Imagine a car which is used only for occasional short trips. After a while it will fail to start properly and won't run very well. Your body is a bit like that. If you don't exercise it, the same thing will happen. Normally we have the advantage over machines in that we are able to repair ourselves, but if we neglect our bodies they become harder to adjust. Exercise will prevent this 'running down'; it will keep in check the surplus fuel – fat – and the body will function as it should.

You will not have to do anything complicated but all your efforts will be wasted unless you exercise regularly. Try one or more of the following: swimming 400 metres, running 3.2 km (2 miles), cycling hard for 10 minutes or skipping 100 times. If you exercise really hard you will notice that your heart beat (pulse) goes up, as does your breathing rate; you will sweat, and it may even feel painful. But it is doing you good and you will soon find it less tiring, your pulse rate will return to normal quicker and your breathing will be easier.

goose pimples actually make their hair stand up, trapping air and forming an insulating layer. When you become very cold you also begin to shiver. This makes your body produce more heat in the muscles.

When you become too hot, your body reacts so that as much heat as possible is lost to the atmosphere. Water needs heat to turn into a gas, and that makes your body cool off. Perspiration collects on the skin, and body heat is used to help it evaporate. That heat energy removed from your body makes you feel colder. The blood vessels near the skin become larger and your rate of circulation increases. You can see how your skin looks flushed when this happens. If the surrounding air is cool, the extra heat brought to the skin will pass out to the air by radiation and conduction. We also lose heat by the evaporation of fluid from the surface of the respiratory tract. On a winter morning we can often see this 'breath' (see also page 91). All these changes are brought about automatically by the body reacting to the 'thermostat' in the brain.

THUMP!
THUMP!
THUMP!

THUMP!
THUMP!
THUMP!

Step-ups

To monitor your progress, try these two simple tests. You have seen on page 45 how to take your pulse, and this method can be used to tell you how fit you are. Find a wooden box about 45 cm (16 in) high and put it where it can be stepped on. Take your pulse for 30 seconds to give a resting level. Now do 30 step-ups on to the box, beginning with your right foot only. Do this slowly but deliberately, and then change to the left foot. Immediately you have done 60 in all, check your pulse. Relax and repeat the pulse measurement every 30 seconds until it is back to normal. If you exercise regularly the time gap will shorten.

Fat test

The second test is to see how fat you are. You can do this by squeezing a fold of skin from the front of the stomach between your fingers and estimating its thickness. Every so often, measure it again. In time, if you keep up regular exercise, the thickness will be reduced. If you want to take a more precise measurement, use a pair of tweezers and measure the span with a ruler.

'Ever since the beginning of scientific thought in medicine, outstanding physicians of all civilized nations have been endeavouring to find the site where the sensitive soul fights its battles and the thinking mind shapes the world.' So claimed Paul Flechsig, a student of the human brain, in 1896.

It was among the highly civilized Greeks that this search began, when Hippocrates realized for the first time that the brain plays an essential part in our lives. While working as a physician, he had seen that brain injuries damaged a patient's ability to think and behave normally. He eventually challenged the established belief, first stated by Aristotle, that the seat of thought was in the heart.

During the Hellenistic period, when scientists in Alexandria were allowed to dissect the dead, progress was made in understanding the structure of the brain. Men distinguished between the cerebellum and cerebrum, and they observed the brain-like spinal marrow entering the brain from below. Eventually they recognized that the convolutions of the cerebrum were basic to man's judgment and intelligence. They then began to think of the brain, the spinal cord and the nerves as a single unit of fundamental importance to life.

It was not until the 19th century that scientists began to understand the role of different parts of the brain. They decided that the cerebellum recorded the general condition of the body as a whole, governing, for example, changes brought about by movement. They also found that if certain parts of the cerebrum were destroyed, faculties such as sight, hearing, speech and memory would be correspondingly put out of action.

It was a friend of the German thinker J W Goethe, one Samuel Thomas Sömmerring (1755–1830), who first drew attention to the large number of sensory nerves ending in the cerebrum. Many of these nerves can be seen in the drawing on this page of the brain seen from below. It was made in 1775 by the Italian anatomist Domenico Santorini.

In Santorini's picture, the spinal cord joins the hind-brain along the medulla or stem. The two sides of the cerebellum occupy the lower third of the image, and are joined by the strap-like pons (from the Latin for 'bridge'). At the white X-shape in the centre, the optic nerves are joined, and

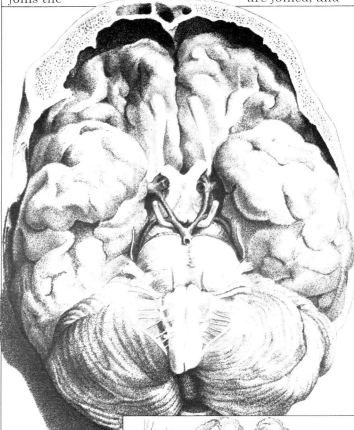

The brain from beneath
In 1775 the Italian anatomist Santorini drew this view looking up into the brain. In the lower area are the two sides of the cerebellum, and above these is the greater mass of the cerebrum.

The 'impulse tree'
In this diagram by Sir Charles Bell, the spinal cord descends from the brain, and nerves travel out from it to carry messages to and from various parts of the body.

above them the olfactory nerves are represented as worm-like shapes.

The spinal cord remained something of a mystery until Sir Charles Bell (1774–1842), a brain and nerve specialist, began to make great strides in his research, which involved experiments with animals. He discovered two sets of channels, the posterior and the anterior roots. Through the posterior root, messages from the sensory nerves travel to the spinal cord and on to the brain. Orders from the brain, or motor impulses, then pass through the anterior root to the muscles of the body, which respond to produce movement.

Bell then found that the brain could be bypassed for simple reflex actions, such as when we blink an eyelid.

On such occasions, a wave of sensory impulses passes along the posterior root into the spinal cord and directly stimulates motor nerve cells. The anterior root then immediately passes the impulse on to a muscle.

Bell concluded that the spinal cord could act like an 'accessory soul'. His drawing (left) demonstrates the network of impulses. Down the centre runs the spinal cord, with nerves branching off to various parts of the body. The uppermost ones, just below the brain-stem, lead to the neck, those at 3 and 4 lead to the chest, at 5 to the lumbar region, and at 6 to the sacrum. The cerebrum stands at the top of this tree-like form, and beneath it are the two sides of the cerebellum.

Another drawing by Bell (not shown) singles out one of the 31 places along the spinal cord where the posterior and anterior roots fasten on to it and relay messages to and from the brain. The roots grip the spinal cord like the spreading roots of a tree. There are two main branches and, as you can see in the picture of the 'impulse tree' (left) they then join up before travelling out to the various parts of the body. Nerve impulses move at 110 m (350 ft) per second.

Parts of the brain
The main areas of the brain are indicated here. In the column below, the brains of some other back-boned animals are shown.

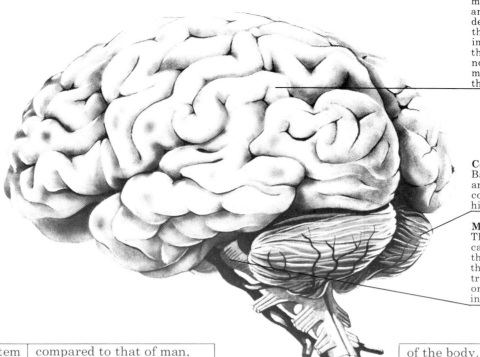

Cerebrum
This is the seat of man's ability to think and take reasoned decisions. In humans the cerebrum and its important outer layer, the cortex, are notably larger and more complex than in the 'lower' animals.

Cerebellum
Balance, movement and co-ordination are controlled in this hind-part of the brain.

Medulla
This part of the stem carries messages from the spinal system to the brain and transmits 'motor' orders back to nerves in the body.

The central nervous system of your body is made up of the brain, which is like a giant computer, and the spinal cord, which acts as the main message line leading out from the brain. Your brain is protected by the strong bone casing of the skull; it is also large, and weighs more than 1.3 kg (3 lb). Your brain enables you to think, remember, feel, and control the movements of your body. Each and every day the many million tiny cells of your brain solve problems and answer questions.

The brain is divided into three sections. The *medulla* is the busiest part: this is the message-centre of the brain, receiving and sending out all messages to and from the body. The *cerebellum* controls balance and co-ordination. It is about the size of a small apple, and is shaped like a partly open oyster shell. The *cerebrum* controls our ability to remember, think, see, speak, and make decisions about the body's actions. This part of the brain gives us the power of reason or common sense, which no other animal possesses. Look at the size of the brains of other animals (which you can find in a museum). The cerebrum of a frog, or even of a dog, is very small

compared to that of man, and the behaviour of these animals is controlled simply by instinct or reaction. The behaviour of man is, however, controlled by the ability to learn, to associate and to remember – activities that demand a large cerebrum.

The cerebrum is divided into the left and right cerebral hemispheres. These are so large that they have to be folded into convolutions that cover other sections of the brain. In each cerebral hemisphere there are special areas governing smell, touch, taste, muscle movement, thought, judgment, and hearing. Large parts of the cerebrum are also given to the use of the hands and the thumbs, uses which set man apart from other animals.

The spinal cord is an extension of the brain which continues down inside the spinal canal, in the centre of the spinal column. For the last third it tapers off into a thin thread. White nerves branch off in pairs from each side of the spinal cord between the vertebrae. These nerves link every part of your body to the brain, acting like a complicated network of telephone lines that pass signals from the brain to your skin, your fingers, your muscles, and all areas

Frog's brain
This has similar components to the human brain but the cerebrum is tiny. Most behaviour is instinctive.

Dog's brain
All parts are larger than in the frog but the cerebrum remains small.

Monkey's brain
Here the cerebrum and cortex are notably larger, though less complex than in the human version.

of the body.

Your brain reacts quickly to messages received. If it is an old, familiar message like 'Pick up your book', your computer-brain instantly goes through its many cells, finds the correct message, and passes it on to the motor nerves. The instruction goes through your message centre, the medulla, down the spinal cord, and out to the distant nerves in your hands and fingers. The nerves excite the muscles to action, and you pick up the book. This is called motor action.

Our brain is like a piece of new machinery which gradually runs down and loses its efficiency. The brain of a normal one-year-old baby contains its full supply of cells. Throughout our working and leisure hours, the nerve cells in the brain never rest. Even when we sleep they still use up about one-fifth of the body's oxygen supply, which is carried to them by the blood system. Every 24 hours some of these nerve cells wear out and cease to function. They are not replaced, and as we get older the accumulated loss of nerve cells affects our ability to reason and remember. This is part of the process of ageing and is quite natural.

Reflex actions

In addition to the controlled motor action described on the previous page, there is another kind of action which is unplanned. It is important in any emergency, as when a finger pricked by a pin sends a sudden call to the brain. Or it may be prompted by an unexpectedly loud noise in your ears, or a harsh light in your eyes. Reflex action immediately pulls your finger from the pin; raises your hands to protect your ears; or closes your eyelids to keep out the light. Do a little experiment yourself. Get a pin, close your eyes and prick a finger with the pin. You will be surprised how quickly you feel the pain and draw your hand away. Threaten a friend with a blow in the face, and watch the instant withdrawal.

Not all movement is controlled by the brain. Some occurs by the operation of another nervous system, the autonomic nerves, which control the many movements of the body essential for survival. These nerves, for example, keep you alive as you sleep, operating your breathing, keeping your heart pumping, controlling digestion, keeping your body temperature even, and providing moisture for your eyes, nose, mouth and throat. All this goes on without you being conscious of it.

When someone talks to you and asks you to do something, the words are heard by your ears and the message is sent to your brain. The brain then has to translate that message into instructions which are sent out along the nerves to muscles. The muscles obey and reports are sent back to the brain.

These messages speed along the nerve paths very fast, bounding from one nerve cell to the next. The time between recognition and response is called the *reaction time*. Sometimes it is not fast enough, as you can test in the following way.

Falling pencil test
Hold a pencil above a friend's open fist and ask him to catch the falling pencil by closing his hand. It is very unlikely that he will be able to do it. As his eyes see the pencil begin to fall, they have to send a signal to the brain. The brain then sends the message to the hand, telling it to grab the pencil. This takes very little time, but it is long enough for the pencil to pass through. But if you try the experiment yourself, you will succeed in grabbing the pencil because you are able

Versatility and the brain

The marvellous thing about the human brain is its ability to do many things at the same time. For example, you can read a book, listen to music, stroke your cat and hear it purr all at one moment. Different parts of your brain are making this possible, allowing you to enjoy things around you. Certain actions, however, which need concentration, are difficult to do together. Many people do not like to read or write while music is being played, for instance. To show how concentration can be upset, try writing your name while you make circular movements with your leg at the same time. You will probably manage little more than a messy scribble. You may find it possible to draw in the same direction as the circular leg movements, but when you begin to circle your leg in the other direction, the pencil movements will cross over completely. The leg movements are transferred to the writing, because both actions need so much concentration that it is virtually impossible to do both at the same time.

to send the messages to drop the pencil and grab at it simultaneously. The reaction time varies from one person to another, and it can be lengthened by tiredness or by the effect of alcohol or some medicines. The reaction time lost in dangerous situations, like car accidents, can make the difference between life and death.

Colours on the retina

Some colours remain longer on the retina than others, which can be confusing. Draw a house and colour it mostly in red to represent the brickwork. Put in a background of blue sky and a foreground of green for the grass. Hold this picture at the normal distance from your eyes in a dim light, and move it quickly from side to side. The house will appear to rock because warm colours like red and brown stay longer on the retina than cold colours like blue and green. When you move the picture the house and background obviously move together, but the house image remains on the retina, and therefore appears to move a little later.

Money trick

The reaction time can cause tricks with your eyes, as can be seen with the moving pictures on page 142. Try this money fraud trick too. Hold two large coins between your thumb and fore-finger, then rub them together as quickly as you can. When you watch them you will see a third coin, which appears to move backwards and forwards between the two real coins. This illusion is caused by your eyes reacting too slowly to follow the rapid movements of the coins. Each time, the image of the coins remains for a short time on the retina, even after they have moved away. You therefore see two coins moving, plus the after-image of a third coin.

YOUR VISUAL SENSE

Both eyes are vital for many things we do, especially judging distance. Close one eye and, holding two pencils not quite at arm's length, try to touch their tips together. To make the test purely one of vision, drop your arms out of position between each try. This simple test is very hard to do because two eyes, looking at something from slightly different angles, are important for judging depth or distance. When one eye is eliminated, objects are seen as flat. They can only look three-dimensional when there are two eyes to see partly around them.

Deceiving the eyes

Our eyes work together with our memory to prepare us for many tasks. Before we attempt to lift anything, for example, we unconsciously estimate its weight and key our muscles up to meet the task. If our estimate is wrong, our reactions can be hilarious. For proof of this, watch someone pick up something that looks heavy, like a log of balsa wood, which is, in fact, extremely light. Try this trick on a friend. Place two glasses, covered with paper handkerchiefs, at arm's length in front of him. At a signal, ask him to grasp a glass in each hand and lift both quickly and evenly into the air. To his amazement, one will fly up rapidly while the other will lag behind, because you will have made one glass very heavy by filling it with lead or wet sand.

How many fingers
Hold up one finger of each hand in front of your eyes about 20 cm (8 in) away from your face (lower drawing). Stare at something beyond your fingers, not at them, and you will soon see three or four ghostly fingers in front of your two fingers. Then focus on your two fingers and the other two will disappear. Because at first you are looking beyond your fingers, you see two fingers with each eye, making four in all.

The floating finger
Hold up one finger of each hand in front of your eyes as shown below, and stare hard between them. You should soon see a short finger appearing between them, which has a nail at each end. This is because the two extra fingers you see overlap to make one magic finger in the middle.

Make a hole in your hand
Make a tube by rolling up a sheet of stiff paper about 30 × 20 cm (12 × 8 in) in size. Stick the tube down with tape, hold it up to your right eye and hold your left hand up alongside the tube, as shown. Stare very hard down the tube with your right eye, keeping your left eye open. You can see your hand, and then you will see a hole in it that you can look through. The reason is that the two views mix together to produce a hand with a hole in it.

Nose sense
The 'taste' of food and medicine is really caused partly by its smell. True taste is a chemically initiated sensation originating in the taste buds on the tongue (see page 51). Only four things – sweet, sour, salt and bitter – can be distinguished. So the 'taste' of pineapple, roast beef or cabbage is also due to their aroma, which is why so many foods seem tasteless when you have a bad cold. You can easily prove how smell affects taste by eating an apple while holding a more odoriferous pear near your nostrils. The pear will pass on its flavour to the apple.

Ears and balance
Do not always believe your ears, because without help from your eyes or some previous knowledge about the source of a sound, you can become very confused. Ventriloquists owe their living to the directional deficiency of human hearing. When they 'throw' their voices, they merely throw your attention cleverly to the point from which the voice is supposed

to come, your sight and imagination do the rest. When you judge sound direction correctly, it is because the ear nearest the source receives the loudest impression. But when sound reaches both ears with similar intensity, your directional sense is poor. To test this, snap your fingers gently some distance above, in front of, and behind a blindfolded friend. He will not know which noise is which.

The balancing organ in your inner ear often plays tricks on you. Put a bottle upright on the ground and walk round it three or four times. If you then try to walk on in a straight line, you will find it very difficult. This is because a liquid in the ear moves around when you turn your head. The movement is picked up by small hairs inside the ear and nerves report the process to your brain. But if you stop the circular movements, the liquid carries on moving, your brain reacts as if you were still turning, and you find yourself walking in a curve.

What you see you feel

Sensations that we think we feel are often governed by what we see. Without the help of our eyes, we can easily be fooled. Here's a trick to prove it. While you are in a room where people are smoking, secretly get hold of a piece of ice, chipped at one end to the diameter of a pencil. Dry the end and touch it quickly on the back of the neck of someone in the room. He will feel sure that you have burned him with the lighted tip of a cigarette.

Nerve endings

Nerve endings are unequally distributed throughout the body, and therefore our sensitivity to touch varies from one part of the body to another. To test the concentration of nerve endings, push two pins about 2.5 cm (1 in) apart through a strip of heavy cardboard. Blindfold a friend and touch his arm with the points. He will only feel one point. Repeat the experiment on other parts of the body and you will find that his sense of touch is differently developed on various parts of the body. On the back, sensitive nerve endings are not as abundant, for example, as on the face. But on the fingertips your friend will feel both pin points immediately because there are far more nerve endings.

Doubling up

Despite the profusion of nerve endings on your fingers, it is possible to confuse your brain with messages from this area. Prove that you cannot always believe what you feel by doing this experiment. Try rolling a large marble between your index and middle fingers, after crossing them. Keep your eyes closed while you do so. Roll the marble so that it touches first one finger and then the other. Although your brain tells you that you only have one marble at your fingertips, your sense of touch tries to convince you that there are two.

Aristotle (384–322 BC) mentioned this illusion, and it still puzzles people today. If you cross the same fingers and rub them sideways over the tip of your nose, the same thing will happen. To your surprise, you will feel two noses. Your brain is again confused, by sense stimuli coming to the brain by unfamiliar paths. When you cross the fingers over, the position of their sides is exchanged, and the sides normally facing away from one another are now adjacent, and both touch the nose or marble together. Each one reports separately as normal, which confuses the brain.

Cold feet

Your senses work by comparison, and this experiment is one way to fool them. Take three bowls and fill one with hot water, one with cold and the third with an equal mixture of both. Sit with one foot in the cold water and the other in the hot. Then remove them and put both feet in the half-and-half bowl. You will still find that one foot will feel cold and the other hot because your senses are comparing sensations. The half-and-half bowl is hotter than the cold bowl, but colder than the hot bowl, and this is what makes your senses report two different findings.

On these pages is a set of optical illusions. They illustrate some of the themes discussed on pages 56–59, and in particular the idea that we often see what we think is in front of us rather than what is really there. This applies mainly to shapes and colours. Movement is also an important factor. When the object viewed begins to move, or we shift our viewpoint, then other strange images can appear. Try out your brain on these eight puzzlers.

1 How many cubes?
When you first look at this shape you will probably see nine cubes, the yellow diamonds forming the tops of the cubes. Stare hard for a while, and they will suddenly change. Now only four cubes are visible, the yellow diamonds forming their bases.

2 Cup and ball
Hold the book sideways about 23 cm (9 in) from your face. Look intently at the white circle in the cup. Bring the book slowly nearer to your eyes, and the red ball will slip into the place occupied by the white one.

3 Cheese slice
Most people would react to this image by saying that it showed a cheese with a section cut out of it. But look again, and tell yourself that the slice is not cut out but stuck on, and in reality protrudes from the cheese. This is not an unduly difficult proposition for the brain to accept, and soon you will be able to see the object in either of these two different ways.

4 Line lengths
In the drawing, the lines AB, CD, and EF are all the same length. They appear to be unequal because the side lines of the yellow diamonds distract the brain into thinking that AB and EF are shorter than CD. If you can't believe your eyes, test the line lengths with a ruler.

5 Circle and dot
Turn the book to make the image a horizontal one, and hold it about 30 cm (12 in) from your face. Look steadily with both

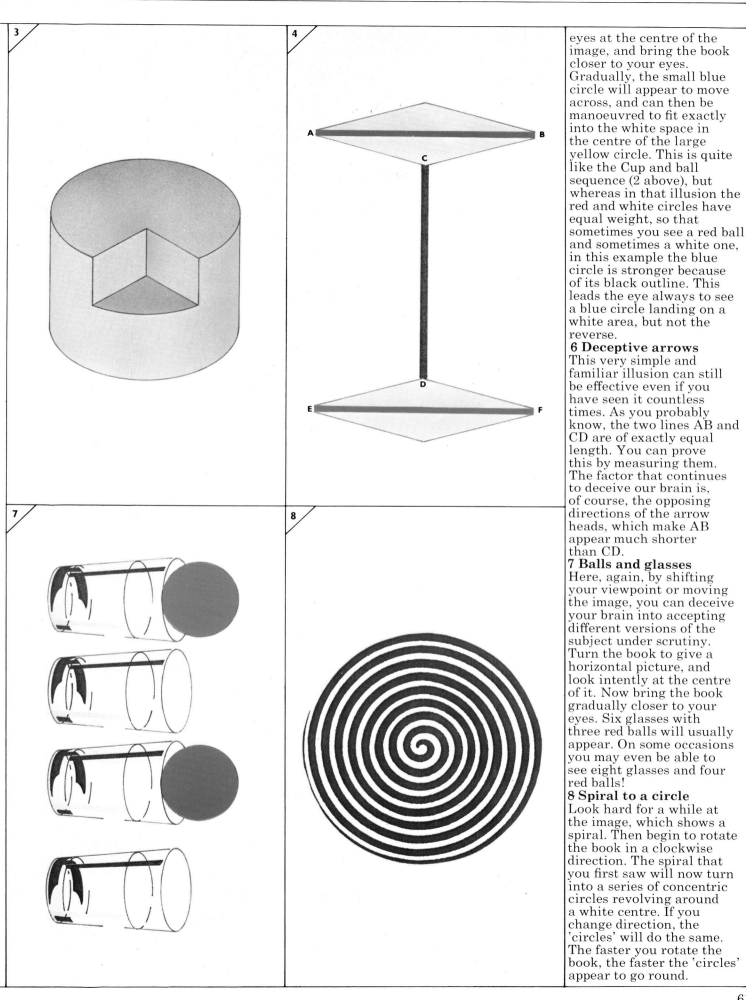

eyes at the centre of the image, and bring the book closer to your eyes. Gradually, the small blue circle will appear to move across, and can then be manoeuvred to fit exactly into the white space in the centre of the large yellow circle. This is quite like the Cup and ball sequence (2 above), but whereas in that illusion the red and white circles have equal weight, so that sometimes you see a red ball and sometimes a white one, in this example the blue circle is stronger because of its black outline. This leads the eye always to see a blue circle landing on a white area, but not the reverse.

6 Deceptive arrows
This very simple and familiar illusion can still be effective even if you have seen it countless times. As you probably know, the two lines AB and CD are of exactly equal length. You can prove this by measuring them. The factor that continues to deceive our brain is, of course, the opposing directions of the arrow heads, which make AB appear much shorter than CD.

7 Balls and glasses
Here, again, by shifting your viewpoint or moving the image, you can deceive your brain into accepting different versions of the subject under scrutiny. Turn the book to give a horizontal picture, and look intently at the centre of it. Now bring the book gradually closer to your eyes. Six glasses with three red balls will usually appear. On some occasions you may even be able to see eight glasses and four red balls!

8 Spiral to a circle
Look hard for a while at the image, which shows a spiral. Then begin to rotate the book in a clockwise direction. The spiral that you first saw will now turn into a series of concentric circles revolving around a white centre. If you change direction, the 'circles' will do the same. The faster you rotate the book, the faster the 'circles' appear to go round.

4

THE SCIENCE OF HEAT AND COLD

Long before scientists began to study the subject, heat was of the greatest importance to man. We do not know for certain when early man first learned to make use of fire, but once the discovery was made, it changed life dramatically. Man used fire in many ways: to keep himself and his family warm, to cook his food and to frighten away wild animals.

Once men had discovered how to create and make use of heat, their way of life began to change. People who had once lived as wandering hunters now found that they could settle down and become farmers and craftsmen.

Next they discovered that fire could also be used to extract various metals from ores which they dug from the ground. They learned to shape these metals into weapons, tools and ornaments. Later still they made another important discovery: when certain metals are mixed together, they form an alloy. Copper and tin produce bronze, for example, which remained an important metal for many hundreds of years.

Although scientists now know that flames are produced by burning gases, fire was for a long time a complete mystery. Our early ancestors thought of it as a gift of nature, and they worshipped natural sources of heat or fire, like volcanoes, the Sun and lightning, as gods. In ancient Egypt the Sun God, Ra, was portrayed both as a human being and a hawk because people believed that the hawk could fly directly into the Sun.

Fire was used in many religious ceremonies and it was thought to have the power of doing both good and evil. Heat was also associated with life. The death of a warm-blooded animal was thought of as the point at which the corpse grew cold and the 'fires of life' were extinguished.

Philosophers in ancient Greece believed that there were four basic substances, or elements, in the world: fire, earth, air and water. (In the illustration, above right, you can see a 17th-

Fire and the gods
The picture above is one of a series of four paintings by the Italian artist, Albani (1578–1660), depicting the elements of earth, fire, air and water. It is called *The Element of Fire*.

Early thermometers
The tubes contained a liquid, such as alcohol or coloured water. The little 'bobbles' on the outside of the tube served as a scale. The illustration comes from a book of scientific experiments published in Italy at the end of the 17th century.

century Italian painting showing an artist's interpretation of the element of fire.) Aristotle (384–322 BC) held that everything was composed of these four elements. He thought that air was contained in a sphere which surrounded the Earth, and this explained why air is always around us. He observed that a flame always travels upwards, whichever way a burning object is held. He therefore believed that fire must be contained in a further sphere above the one which held the air; a flame burns upwards because it is always trying to return to its place of origin.

The first attempt to measure the temperature of an object scientifically was made early in the 17th century by the Italian astronomer, Galileo (1564–1642). He did this by heating air in a tube which was closed at one end and open at the other. He then turned the tube upside down and put the open end in a bowl of water. As the air in the tube cooled, its pressure and volume decreased. This meant that the air pressure on the surface of the water was greater than the pressure in the tube. So the water rose up the tube, and the column of air inside got shorter. When the air in the tube was heated once more, it expanded to its previous volume. In this way it was possible to gauge the temperature of the air by measuring the length of the air column.

There was one problem with Galileo's thermometer, however. The length of the air column was not only affected by heat, but also by changes in the atmospheric air pressure. On sunny days, when the air pressure was high, the air column was short. On stormy days, when the pressure was low, the column was longer.

In order to overcome this difficulty, scientists started to use liquids instead of air in their thermometers. In the picture on the left you can see some of these early thermometers.) Mercury was particularly suitable because, like air, it expands

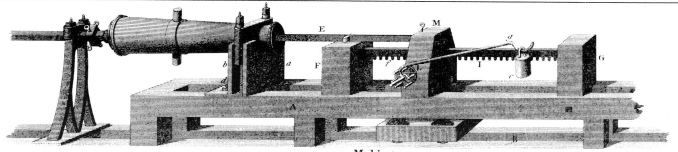

when heated and contracts when cooled. In modern thermometers the mercury is contained in a glass bulb which is connected to a glass tube. Because the apparatus is not open to the atmosphere, it cannot be affected by changes in the air pressure. The tube is very narrow so that even small changes in the volume of the mercury can be detected.

The final step was to add a scale. This was done at the beginning of the 18th century by a German scientist called Gabriel Fahrenheit (1686–1736). He measured the length of a mercury column at the coldest temperature he could produce in his laboratory and called this point 0 degrees. He called the length of the mercury column in iced water 32 degrees, and its length in boiling water 212 degrees. He divided the distance between the freezing and boiling points into 180 equal sections. The average temperature of the human body fell conveniently in the middle of the scale, at 98.6 degrees.

Most scientists now use thermometers with a Centigrade scale. This was invented by the Swedish astronomer, Anders Celsius (1701–44). He was the first person to use a scale which showed the freezing point of water as 0 degrees and the boiling point as 100 degrees.

Later on in the 18th century Joseph Black (1728–99), a Scottish chemist, was the first person to use a Centigrade thermometer to study the nature of heat. Black wanted to find out what happens to temperature when hot and cold objects are brought together, and when liquids of different temperatures are mixed.

He discovered that heat and temperature are not the

Making cannon barrels
While supervising this mechanical process Count Rumford, seeing the heat generated, developed the idea that this heat was a form of energy.

Heat and energy
Joule's apparatus for determining the mechanical equivalent of heat. As the paddle wheels turned, the temperature was raised and the amount measured by the thermometer fixed in the lid.

same thing. For example, a candle has a higher temperature than a radiator, but it cannot heat a room. So he created another measure of heat, called a calorie. A calorie was defined as the amount of heat needed to raise the temperature of one gram of water by one degree Centigrade.

Black reached his understanding of the difference between temperature and heat by heating equal quantities of different substances. He found, for example, that copper needs less heat to raise its temperature by one degree than glass does. The amount of heat needed to raise the temperature of 1 g of a material by 1°C is called the specific heat of that material.

The next step towards our understanding of the nature of heat was taken by Count Rumford (1753–1814), who discovered that heat and mechanical energy are related. As Minister of War for the German State of Bavaria, Rumford had been put in charge of making cannons. Each cannon was first cast as a solid cylinder of brass; this was then bored

to form a hollow tube (see the illustration at the top of the page). Rumford found that a brass gun got very hot while it was being bored and he realized that the heat must be created by friction. He therefore suggested that heat is a form of motion, or internal energy. (Count Rumford applied his knowledge of heat in the kitchen as well as the armoury, and made a considerable contribution to the Science of Cooking, described in Chapter 8 on pages 122–129.)

It was left to an English physicist, James Prescott Joule (1818–89), to confirm this theory. He designed a well insulated, drum-shaped container and fitted a paddle-wheel to the inside. Weights were fixed to the outside of the container. When the weights were released, they fell, thus causing the paddle wheel to turn. When Joule had constructed his container, he put a weighed amount of water inside. As the weights fell, they made the paddle wheel spin and stir up the water. Joule used the weights as a measure of the mechanical energy needed to heat water. After many

experiments, he was able to state that a measured amount of heat was produced by a measured amount of mechanical energy. In the illustration on the left the paddle-wheels are shown as flat boards inside the cross-section view of the container. To make them turn, the operator stood beside the apparatus and rotated the handle shown at the top of the picture.

This discovery coincided with the results of other scientific work of the time. Light, sound and magnetism, to name only a few examples, were now being thought of as forms of energy, and scientists were starting to find ways of changing one kind of energy into another. The Law of Conservation of Energy stated that energy cannot be created or destroyed, but can be changed from one form into another. In other words, for every measured amount of electricity, light or sound, there is a corresponding amount of heat.

Joule's work led to his Kinetic Theory of Heat. The theory states that, although whole objects do not necessarily move when heated, there is invisible motion nevertheless. This is because molecules – the tiny particles of which everything on Earth is made up – are perpetually in motion in all objects. When a material is heated, its molecules move faster. They collide with one another and thus cause the temperature to rise. The faster the molecules move, the hotter the material gets. On the following pages you will see some examples of this principle at work. You will be able to carry out your own experiments to help you understand the nature of heat and cold.

Watch the molecules move

To show that molecules move at different rates, fill one bowl with very hot water and another with cold. When the water is still, carefully put a drop of food colouring into the middle of each bowl. You will see that the colouring hardly moves in the cold water, while in the hot water it moves around very fast. You can watch the movement of molecules more precisely with a microscope. Sprinkle some fine powder on to water. Look at a drop of this water under the microscope: the powder particles are never still. Water molecules constantly bump into one another, pushing the powder particles around. In heated water the powder moves faster still; compare hot and cold water with powder in it.

The transfer of energy

The experiment above has shown us that there is a greater movement of molecules in a hot material than in a cold one. The explanation for this is as follows. When molecules move more quickly, they give off more heat. The movement makes them push harder against each other, thus transferring the heat, or kinetic energy, as it is called.

You can also see that collisions between moving bodies cause kinetic energy to be transferred if you do this simple experiment. Take two equal-sized billiard balls (or you could use marbles); place one ball on a flat surface so that it is quite still. Roll the other ball towards it so that the two balls collide. If you score a direct hit, the moving ball will stop and the other one will move away at almost exactly the same speed. This is because the kinetic energy of the moving ball has been transferred to the ball which was stationary.

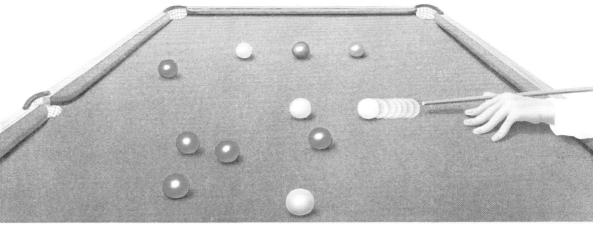

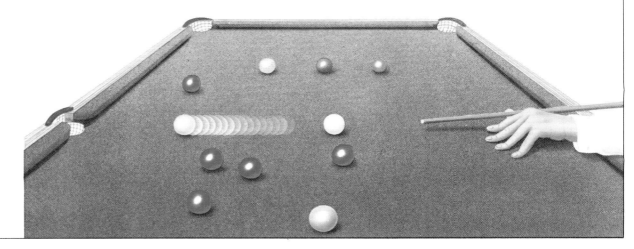

SOLIDS, LIQUIDS AND GASES

As molecules push hard against each other, the distance between each molecule increases. This can cause the material to change from one form to another, as happens with water, for example (see the experiment below). At the molecular level, the explanation for this is as follows. When a solid is heated, the molecules nearest the heat source vibrate faster, causing the neighbouring molecules to vibrate faster as well, so that heat spreads through the solid. This transfer of heat is known as conduction.

When the movement of the molecules is violent enough, they move too fast to stay in fixed positions and the solid changes into a liquid. As the temperature of the liquid rises, more and more surface molecules move fast enough to escape the forces of attraction to other molecules. At that stage they take on an increasing amount of heat energy. The surface molecules are much more loosely packed than before, and eventually they leave the surface as a gas.

Ice to water to steam

You can see the effect of the violent movement of molecules by heating a few ice cubes in a pan. The ice will change from a solid to a liquid, and then to a gas which disappears into the atmosphere. When water is in the form of ice, the molecules are packed tightly together (as in all solids); they have little heat energy and so move about slowly. When water is in liquid form, the molecules can move about more freely. (As we have seen, they move faster in hot water.) When water is heated to boiling point, steam is produced. As in all gases, the molecules are loosely packed.

CONDUCTION

Conduction, or heat transfer, occurs because molecules are constantly in motion. If you put a cold spoon into hot water the handle can become too hot to hold. The spoon is getting hotter because the water molecules are moving faster than the molecules in the spoon; the water molecules push against those in the spoon and make them move faster too. At the same time, the water molecules are slowed down and so the water cools. When the molecules in both the water and the spoon are moving at the same speed, the liquid and the solid are at the same temperature.

To test this, take one bowl of ice-cold water and one bowl of hot. Put a hand in each and count to 10. One hand will feel cold because heat has passed from it to the iced water. The other hand will get hot as heat passes to it from the hot water. If you test the temperature of both bowls before and after putting your hands in, you will see that the cold water has got warmer and the hot water has become cooler. Transfer of heat has taken place because you introduced another element – your hands – which influenced the temperatures of the two liquids.

You can also see the effect of heat moving from a hotter to a cooler material if you put some ice cubes into a glass of lemon squash, for example. Heat will pass from the drink to the ice, the ice will melt as it uses up the heat, and this has the effect of lowering the temperature of your drink.

Conductors of heat

You can test which materials are good heat conductors. Put some spoons made of silver, plastic, bone, steel, wood or whatever you have into a glass. Add a glass rod. With a dab of butter, fix a dried pea to each handle at the same height. Pour some very hot water into the glass and watch the order in which the butter melts and the peas fall off. Silver is first, then steel, glass, bone, wood and plastic. Plastic is a very poor conductor of heat and saucepans often have plastic handles.

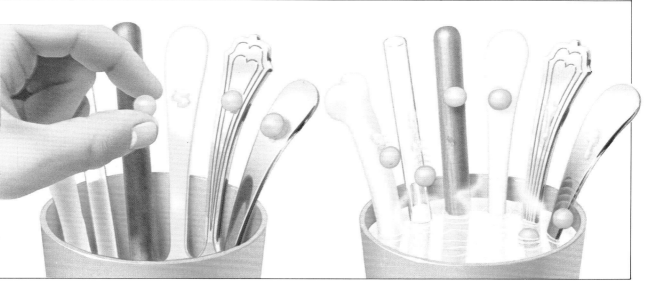

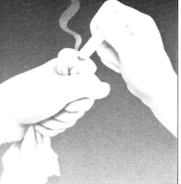

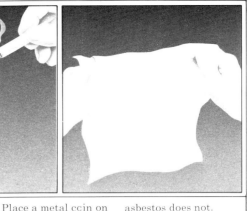

Metal conducts heat

You can do a clever trick if you stretch a cotton handkerchief over a metal coin and then press a burning cigarette onto the handkerchief. Contrary to expectations, the handkerchief does not burn and only a small amount of ash is left. Metal is a much better conductor of heat than cotton is. The coin takes away the heat of the cigarette so that the cotton cannot reach a high enough temperature to burn. Next try putting some asbestos over a hotplate on the stove. Place a metal coin on top and touch the coin and the asbestos at regular intervals. The coin soon becomes too hot to touch, but the asbestos does not. Asbestos is a poor conductor of heat and for that reason is often used as an insulating material.

The fire-guard

Both fire-guards and miners' safety lamps (see engraving, left) work by using metal lattices. These absorb heat from a naked flame so that the flame cannot pass through and cause damage in the home or ignite gases in a mine. You can see how a lattice works by holding a metal kitchen sieve over a candle flame. The metal in the sieve absorbs so much heat that the flame cannot pass through the net.

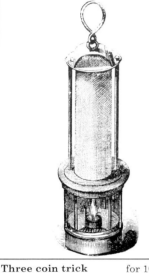

Three coin trick

We have already seen the ability of metal to conduct heat (see above). Use this as the basis of another good coin trick to surprise your friends. Put three coins in a plastic dish. Ask one of your friends to choose a coin while you are out of the room. Tell him to take his coin out of the dish and hold it in his closed hand for 10 seconds, then return the coin to the dish and call you back into the room. To everyone's amazement, you will be able to tell which coin was chosen. You can do this by holding all three coins in turn to your upper lip. The upper lip is very sensitive and you will feel the smallest difference in temperature between the coins. One will be warmer than the others because metal is a good conductor of heat and will have warmed up quickly in the hand. The coin which feels warmest is the one chosen by your friend. (Plastic is a poor conductor of heat and so little heat will have been lost in the interval between the coin leaving your friend's hand and being picked up for the lip test.)

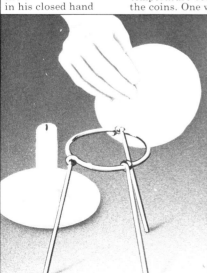

The paper pot

You can boil water in a paper pot or cup! Use a circle of thick paper with wire bent round it and put it on a stand over a candle. Or push a skewer or knitting needle through the rim of a paper cup and rest the skewer on the stand. Fill the container with water and light the candle. The candle boils the water without scorching the paper. The water takes the heat away from the paper and boils at 100 C (212 F) without getting any hotter. So the paper never reaches a high enough temperature to catch fire.

Heat also causes substances to expand. Air is a good example. When air becomes warmer, it takes up more space. This can be put to good use in many ways.

For example, a hot-air balloon floats up in the air when the burner in the basket heats the air in the balloon. As the air expands, some of it escapes so that the remaining air weighs less. The first manned balloon flight was made in 1783. The photograph above is part of a record of a recent trans-African journey by hot-air balloon.

You can also make use of expansion if you have a dented ping-pong ball. Put the ball in warm water; this will heat the air inside, making it expand and push out the dent (see pictures at right).

You can see expansion at work again if you have a beach ball which is not fully inflated. When the ball is left out in the Sun, it will often expand to its full size. As the Sun heats the air inside the ball, the air molecules move faster. They bounce against each other and against the sides of the ball and so push it out to its full size. As the day gets cooler, the ball shrinks in size again.

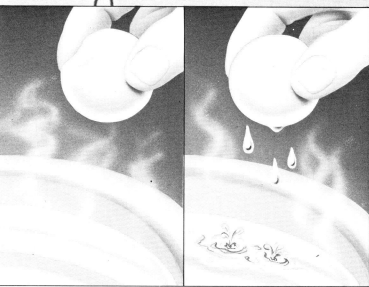

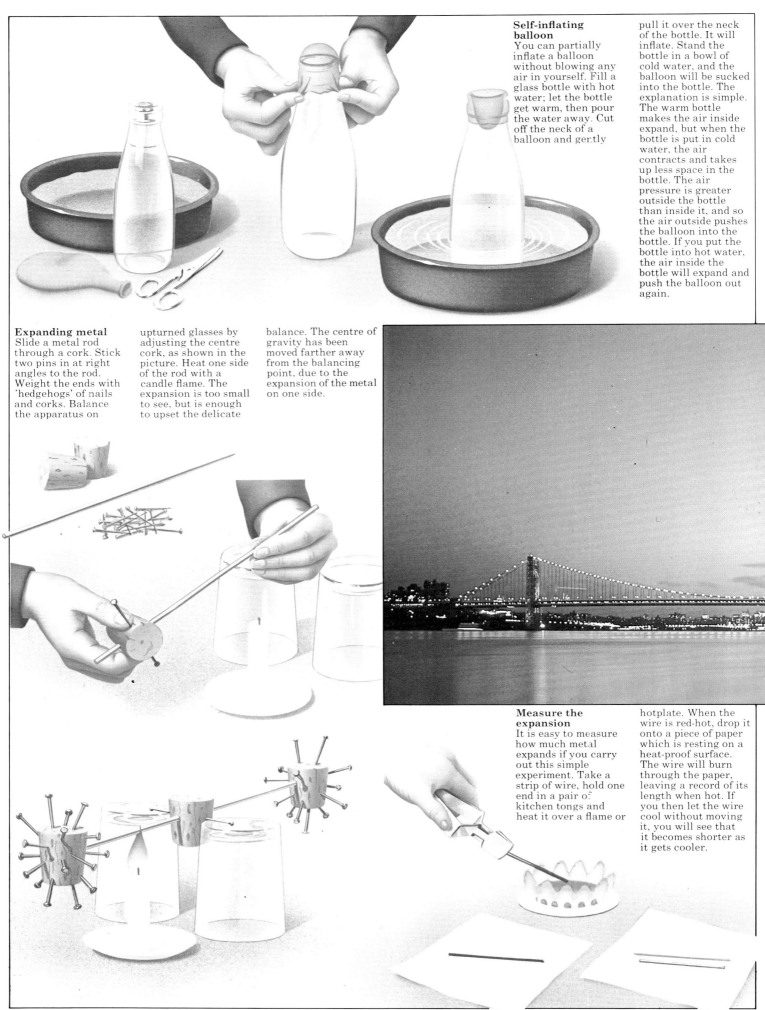

Self-inflating balloon

You can partially inflate a balloon without blowing any air in yourself. Fill a glass bottle with hot water; let the bottle get warm, then pour the water away. Cut off the neck of a balloon and gently pull it over the neck of the bottle. It will inflate. Stand the bottle in a bowl of cold water, and the balloon will be sucked into the bottle. The explanation is simple. The warm bottle makes the air inside expand, but when the bottle is put in cold water, the air contracts and takes up less space in the bottle. The air pressure is greater outside the bottle than inside it, and so the air outside pushes the balloon into the bottle. If you put the bottle into hot water, the air inside the bottle will expand and push the balloon out again.

Expanding metal

Slide a metal rod through a cork. Stick two pins in at right angles to the rod. Weight the ends with 'hedgehogs' of nails and corks. Balance the apparatus on upturned glasses by adjusting the centre cork, as shown in the picture. Heat one side of the rod with a candle flame. The expansion is too small to see, but is enough to upset the delicate balance. The centre of gravity has been moved farther away from the balancing point, due to the expansion of the metal on one side.

Measure the expansion

It is easy to measure how much metal expands if you carry out this simple experiment. Take a strip of wire, hold one end in a pair of kitchen tongs and heat it over a flame or hotplate. When the wire is red-hot, drop it onto a piece of paper which is resting on a heat-proof surface. The wire will burn through the paper, leaving a record of its length when hot. If you then let the wire cool without moving it, you will see that it becomes shorter as it gets cooler.

Moving coin mystery

Use an empty glass bottle which has been stored in a cool place to convince your friends the bottle has a ghost in it! Moisten the rim of the bottle with water and put a coin on top. Put your hands round the sides of the bottle and the coin will start to move. There is a scientific explanation for this. The cold air in the bottle expands as it is heated by your warm hands. The expanding air is at first prevented from escaping because of the coin. But the pressure eventually becomes so great that the coin is lifted up, allowing the expanding air to escape.

The bottle fountain

Half fill a screw-top bottle with cold water and colour the water with some ink, paint or food colouring. Make a hole in the top and screw it on very tightly. Push a straw through the hole and press modelling clay round the hole to seal it. Put a plug of clay in the end of the straw too. Poke a hole through the plug with a needle. Put the bottle in a bowl of hot water. After a few minutes a fountain will spray out of the end of the straw. As the hot water warms the bottle, the air inside expands, pushing the water up the straw and out in a spray.

Expansion at work

You can make a hot-air balloon – but only if an adult is there. Roll a thick paper napkin into a tube; twist one end, stand it on a saucer as shown, and light the top. The paper will rise while still burning. As the air inside expands, some escapes, making the 'balloon' lighter. Buildings and bridges (like the George Washington Bridge above) expand and contract too. Paving stones and railway tracks are laid with enough room to expand, and telegraph wires are strung loosely so as not to snap in cold weather. You can make a stone explode in winter by pouring boiling water over a frozen flint. The outer layers heat up and expand faster than the centre, causing tension which makes the stone crack.

HEAT ENERGY

There are many sources of heat. It can be produced by friction (rubbing two things together); this speeds up the movement of molecules, so heat is given off. Fires can be made like this using two sticks, and we all rub our hands together when we are cold. A nail heats up when struck by a hammer, and a power drill quickly gets very hot. Meteors, or shooting stars, are also caused by the heat of friction. A meteor travels very fast as it enters the air blanket round the Earth. Friction between the meteor and the air molecules creates so much heat that the meteor burns brightly. In the picture below is Halley's Comet, which leaves a bright trail visible from Earth when its orbit brings it close enough.

When an electrical current passes through metal, some of the electrical energy is changed to heat. The metals in light bulbs, cookers and toasters do not allow electricity to pass easily; this resistance helps make the heat and light we need in our homes.

When substances combine chemically, they often produce heat. When fuel burns, a chemical change occurs in the flame and heat is given off. When gas, oil and wood burn, their carbon joins with oxygen in the air to form carbon dioxide molecules. Their hydrogen joins with oxygen in the air to make molecules of water vapour. Scientists have measured the amount of heat given off when these chemical changes occur. They have found that whenever two atoms of hydrogen and one atom of oxygen join to make a molecule of water, the same amount of heat is given off.

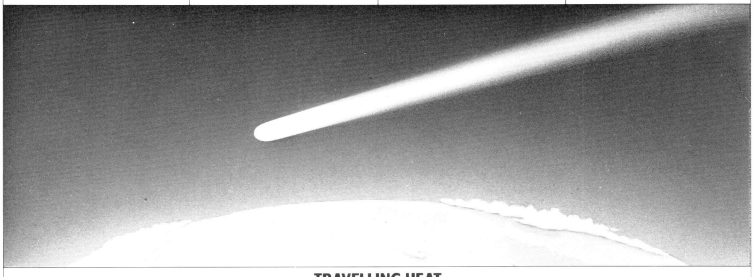

TRAVELLING HEAT

Heat travels through liquids and gases in several different ways. The flow of heat in liquids and gases is called convection. Convection currents help gliders and birds to stay up in the air; they also help ventilate our homes. The principle is as follows. As liquids and gases become hot, they expand and get lighter and will rise if the material around them is cool. As liquids and gases become cool, they get heavier and will sink if the material around them is warm.

Heat travels from the Sun to the Earth by radiation. During the Sun's journey of millions of miles through space, there are no molecules or convection currents to help. Radiant heat waves are very similar to light waves, but they cannot be seen as they travel at about 300,000 km (187,500 miles) a second. These radiant heat waves are not themselves hot; they can only heat materials when the heat waves are stopped and absorbed. Dark materials absorb more radiant heat than light-coloured materials. This is why darker colours are worn in the winter.

HEAT AND ANIMALS

Nowadays we are able to live far easier, more comfortable and more exciting lives than our ancestors did because we have learned how to harness and make use of heat and energy.

Heat helps us in many different ways. It makes it possible for us to travel by air, for example, by providing the energy needed to move a jet engine. It also encourages space research because space rockets use oxygen to burn fuel and thus produce heat energy. Heat from burning fuels produces the steam needed to drive the steam turbines which help to make electricity. Heat and electricity keep our homes warm and well-lit throughout the day, and some people even live in solar-heated houses.

We are only able to live on the Earth because the temperature is ideal for us. But space exploration has indicated that life probably does not exist on Mercury or Venus. This is because these planets are too hot. High temperatures destroy the delicate chemical compounds of which living things are made.

In different parts of the Earth, variations in temperature have led to the evolution of the animals and plants most suited to a particular area. For example, plants in cold regions must be able to adjust to periods when water is scarce because it is frozen. In cold areas some animals adapt by sheltering in rock crevices or on the mud floors of ponds. Others migrate to warmer areas or go through a dormant period. During this period, the animal's metabolism slows down so that it needs very little energy in order to stay alive. Trees can reduce their activity by shedding their leaves.

In hot areas, plants have had to develop ways of preventing themselves drying out; they may do this by storing water and preventing evaporation. Some animals have a dormant period during the dry season of a tropical climate. Birds and mammals are protected from environmental temperature changes by their fur, fat or feathers. The mudskipper (left) has fleshy pectoral fins which it uses to crawl overland from pond to pond during droughts.

HEAT AND COLD

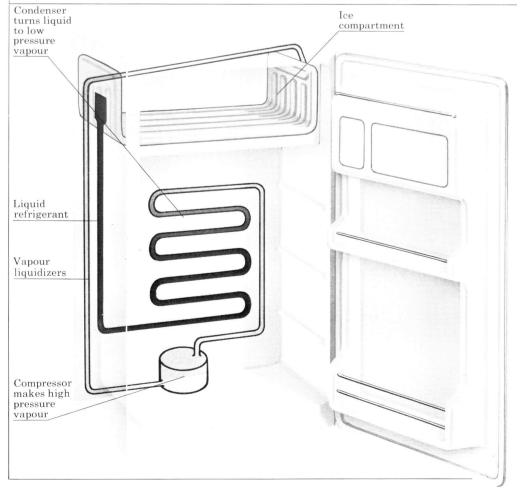

Condenser turns liquid to low pressure vapour

Ice compartment

Liquid refrigerant

Vapour liquidizers

Compressor makes high pressure vapour

How does a refrigerator work? An electric cooker uses electrical energy to make heat; a refrigerator uses it to take heat away. We have seen that heat is used up as a liquid changes into a gas (see page 65). In order to evaporate, a liquid takes heat from its surroundings. A refrigerator works on the same principle. A liquid which evaporates easily (called a refrigerant) flows through small pipes inside the refrigerator. In order to evaporate, the refrigerant takes heat out of the food. The vapour from the evaporating refrigerant flows through the pipes to a compressor, run by an electric motor. The compressor squeezes the vapour, turns it back into a liquid and warms it up again. It then flows through pipes on the outside of the refrigerator. Air on the outside takes heat out of the liquid, thus cooling it. The cooled liquid then goes back through the pipes inside and the whole process is repeated.

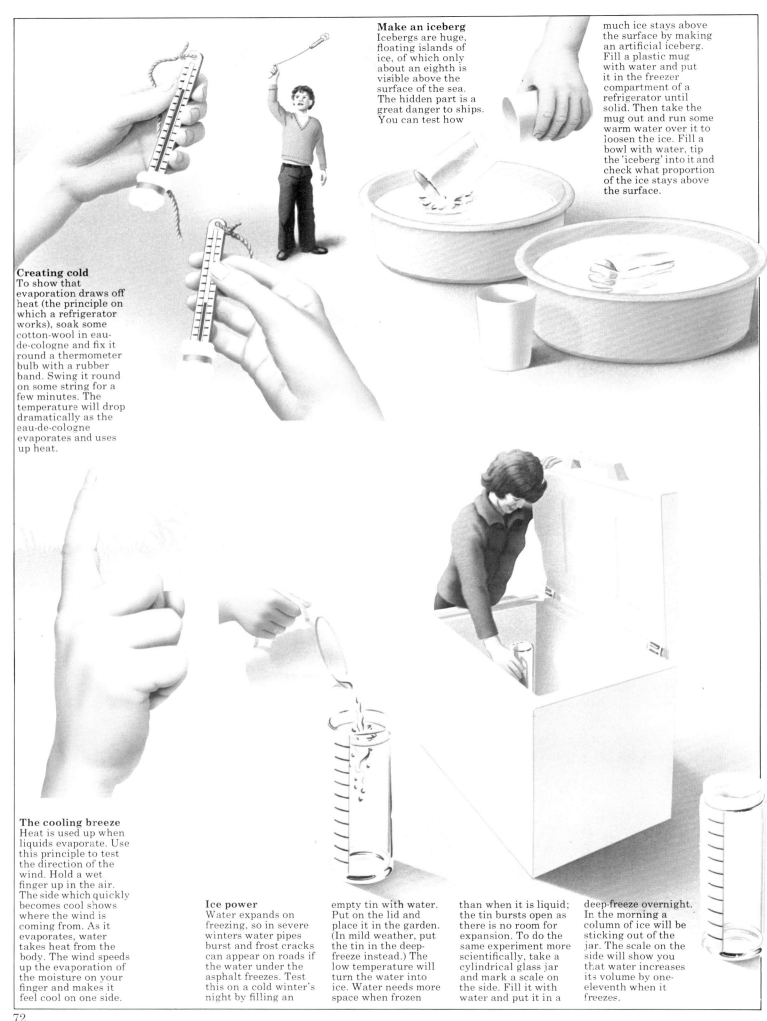

Make an iceberg
Icebergs are huge, floating islands of ice, of which only about an eighth is visible above the surface of the sea. The hidden part is a great danger to ships. You can test how much ice stays above the surface by making an artificial iceberg. Fill a plastic mug with water and put it in the freezer compartment of a refrigerator until solid. Then take the mug out and run some warm water over it to loosen the ice. Fill a bowl with water, tip the 'iceberg' into it and check what proportion of the ice stays above the surface.

Creating cold
To show that evaporation draws off heat (the principle on which a refrigerator works), soak some cotton-wool in eau-de-cologne and fix it round a thermometer bulb with a rubber band. Swing it round on some string for a few minutes. The temperature will drop dramatically as the eau-de-cologne evaporates and uses up heat.

The cooling breeze
Heat is used up when liquids evaporate. Use this principle to test the direction of the wind. Hold a wet finger up in the air. The side which quickly becomes cool shows where the wind is coming from. As it evaporates, water takes heat from the body. The wind speeds up the evaporation of the moisture on your finger and makes it feel cool on one side.

Ice power
Water expands on freezing, so in severe winters water pipes burst and frost cracks can appear on roads if the water under the asphalt freezes. Test this on a cold winter's night by filling an empty tin with water. Put on the lid and place it in the garden. (In mild weather, put the tin in the deep-freeze instead.) The low temperature will turn the water into ice. Water needs more space when frozen than when it is liquid; the tin bursts open as there is no room for expansion. To do the same experiment more scientifically, take a cylindrical glass jar and mark a scale on the side. Fill it with water and put it in a deep-freeze overnight. In the morning a column of ice will be sticking out of the jar. The scale on the side will show you that water increases its volume by one-eleventh when it freezes.

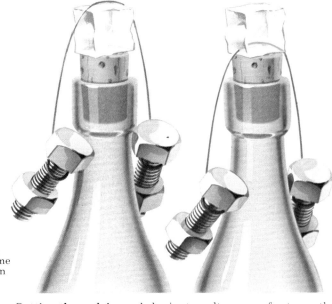

Melting ice
Put a cube of ice in a glass and fill it to the brim with water. Ice floats with about an eighth of its volume above the surface, but the water does not overflow when the ice melts. Water increases its volume by one-eleventh on freezing. The ice is lighter than the water and so it floats, projecting slightly above the surface. On melting, it loses enough volume to fill the space taken up by the cube in the water.

Cutting through ice
You can skate on ice because pressure makes the ice melt under the blades of your skates, thus reducing the friction. To see how pressure helps ice to melt, stand an ice cube on a corked bottle. Fix objects of equal weight to each end of a piece of wire, hang it over the ice and put the apparatus outside in frosty weather, sheltering it from the wind.
Because ice melts under pressure, the wire will gradually cut through the ice without splitting it.

Subarctic cold
To test the effect of subarctic cold (38° C/100° F below zero) fold about 114 g (4 oz) of dry ice in a heavy cloth and break it into small pieces with a hammer. (It is dangerous to handle dry ice with bare hands; always use kitchen tongs or a spoon.) Put about 57 g (2 oz) of acetone in a beaker and add the dry ice very gradually until you have a mush. Dip the end of a sausage into this mixture for a minute or two. It will become as hard as a rock and break into tiny pieces if hit with a hammer. Even rubber shatters in the same way if subjected to subarctic cold.

Salt makes ice melt
Here is an interesting trick using salt, ice and a matchstick. Put a matchstick on an ice cube and scatter salt over it. You will find that the ice and the matchstick quickly freeze together and you will be able to lift the cube out of a bowl of water with the matchstick. By scattering salt on the ice you have made it melt, thus using up heat. This heat is taken from the moisture under the match, where no salt fell, and so it freezes.
This principle is useful in cold winter weather: salt is scattered on icy roads to melt the ice and so reduce the chances of motorists skidding and perhaps suffering a dangerous accident.

Ice prevents water heating
To keep an iced drink at freezing point, you do not have to keep adding ice cubes as long as even a fraction of one cube remains. To test this, put some ice cubes and water into a small, heat-proof glass container. Stir with a thermometer until the temperature goes down to freezing point. Now put the container on a hotplate or low flame and stir. The temperature of the water will not rise if there is any ice left. It takes a lot of heat to melt ice, so all the heat applied to the container is being used to melt the ice first. Only when all the ice has melted can the heat source beneath the container concentrate on the task of raising the temperature of the water.

The Sun is your slave

In this trick (which only works if it is a sunny day) you can use radiated heat from the Sun to make something burn by remote control! Take a small metal nut, or something similar which will act as a weight, and tie it to one end of a piece of thread. Fix the other end of the thread to a bottle cork. Drop the weighted thread into a clear glass bottle and seal it with the cork. Ask your friends to try and cut the thread without touching the cork or the bottle. When they have all given up, take the bottle and put it in the Sun. With a magnifying glass, concentrate the Sun's rays onto the thread. It will eventually get hot enough to burn, and the weight will drop to the bottom of the bottle.

The magic moving tumbler

Take a plastic-covered tray or an old picture behind glass and tilt it very gently. Wet the rim of a glass tumbler and place it upside down on the glass or plastic surface. (The slope must be gentle enough for the tumbler to stay in position.) Then light a candle and gently heat one side of the tumbler. It will soon start to move by itself.
The secret of this trick is as follows. Heat from the candle makes the temperature of the air inside the tumbler rise. Hot air expands, so the tumbler is lifted up from the surface. The water on the rim acts as a seal so that the air inside cannot escape. Because the tumbler is supported by a thin cushion of water, its own weight sends it 'floating' down the slope.
A hovercraft rides on a cushion of air in rather the same way. But the principle of the moving tumbler was first used for a new kind of railway shown at the Paris Exhibition as long ago as 1878 (right). The train had runners instead of wheels; they floated on water-filled rails to give a smooth ride, very much like the gliding movement of the tumbler in the experiment above. No manufacturer has yet taken up this idea of a sliding railway.

The fire-proof thread

Before trying this trick on your friends, soak some thread in a salt solution and let it dry. Do this several times. With your audience present, show them the thread (it will look no different after its soaking) and tie a light ring to one end. Light the thread near this end and let your audience watch the flames move along it. Everyone will be amazed to see that, despite the flames, the thread is still intact. A thin, flimsy column of ash will seem to hold the ring in place. You will be the only person who knows that, although the fibres of the thread have been destroyed by the flames, a thin tube of salt has survived; this is strong enough to hold the ring, as long as there are no draughts.

Two bottle tricks

Here are two more amusing tricks. You will need a small glass bottle with a stopper. Fill it with water to about 2.5 cm (1 in) from the top and put it (without the stopper) in a pan of salt water. Heat the pan until the water in the bottle is boiling. Allow the water vapour time to drive out any air in the bottle and then put the stopper on very firmly. Take the bottle out of the pan; as the bottle cools, the water vapour will condense, leaving a vacuum inside.

Now for the first trick. Tip the bottle up and right it again. As the water pounds about in the vacuum it will make a sound like the banging of a hammer!

For the second trick, put the bottle back into the pan of water and boil it again. Let the bubbling die down and then call your friends. Tell them you can make the water bubble and boil again by magic. To do this, blow through a straw (or put an ice cube) on to the surface of the bottle and the water will boil. This is because, by blowing on the bottle, you have cooled it, so that the water vapour condenses. As the pressure decreases, the heat left in the water is enough to start it boiling again. (The lower the pressure, the lower the boiling point of water.)

Science has proved successful in solving most of the major mysteries of nature. Of those that remain, perhaps the Universe and the atom still have the most secrets to unfold – the largest and the smallest of scientific mysteries today.

The study of the Universe is called astronomy, a name that means 'star knowledge' and comes from the ancient Greek. As a science, astronomy has an

immensely long history, and hundreds of years before the Greeks founded their civilization men living in Sumeria took a great deal of interest in the night sky.

At first they did not realize that the stars that impressed them at night were also present during the daytime, and that their light was not visible only because the Sun outshone them. The early observers found out the truth during that one event which does allow us to see daytime stars – the total eclipse of the Sun, when the Moon passes in front of the Sun and hides it from view. When this happens, the sky darkens and stars can be seen. Total eclipse only happens about twice every century, and it must have been a dramatic event when it was seen for the first time by early man.

In looking at the stars, people soon began to notice that they formed groups, or constellations as we know them today. They made pictures of these star groups and eventually developed the 12 Zodiac signs, which we still use for less serious purposes such as fortune-telling. As

5

THE SCIENCE OF THE SKY

well as being in awe of the stars, early man gave the Sun and the Moon an elevated role in their lives,

Earth at the centre
This 16th-century picture conveys the common view that the Earth lay at the centre of the Universe. Around it were the four elements, the planets in their orbits and the fixed stars, represented by the Zodiac.

worshipping both as gods.

Although we all know that the Earth is round, and have seen proof of this from astronauts' photographs of our world as seen from space, the first astronomers believed that the Earth was completely flat. Although it is not clear why they began to change their ideas, the

first to decide that the Earth must be a sphere were pupils of the famous Greek philosopher Pythagoras (6th century BC). You can prove their statement by standing on a beach and looking through binoculars at a ship approaching on the horizon. The fact that the tips of the masts are seen first, and then the funnels, before the whole ship comes into view, is visible proof

that the Earth is round. If it were flat, the whole ship would be seen from the start. It was very probably this kind of observation that made the Greek scholars change their thinking.

The majority of people nevertheless believed in a flat Earth until well into

the 15th century, and adventurous sailors went off in their ships to search for the edge of the world. Columbus (1451–1506) helped to refute the flat-Earth theory when in 1492 he sailed west (not east, around Africa) and discovered America, although he thought he had landed in 'the Indies'.

At about this time Copernicus (1473–1543) formulated his revolutionary theory that the Sun, and not the Earth, was the centre of the Universe. The idea did not gain much ground until his book proving the theory was published after his death. Copernicus was too frightened of the trouble it would cause among Church leaders to publish during his lifetime.

Tycho's observatory
The domes and instruments *(left)* on the 'roof' of Tycho Brahe's underground observatory.

Galileo's Moon
Sketches of the Moon's surface *(above and right)* made by Galileo from telescopic observations.
Halley's comet
The comet's passing is recorded in the Bayeux Tapestry *(c1092)*.

A Dane, Tycho Brahe (1546–1601), was the next to introduce new ideas. He set up an observatory near Copenhagen, and used it to make accurate observations of the Moon, stars, Sun and planets, and he designed quadrants and sextants to improve his work.

Tycho's assistant,

Johannes Kepler, (1571–1630) used these measurements to work out his own laws of planetary motion. He eventually found that planets move around the Sun in an oval path, and that the nearer a planet is to the Sun during its orbit the faster it moves, so that its average speed varies according to its distance from the Sun. This upset all previous theories, first proposed by Pythagoras and Aristotle, that planets move in circles at constant speeds.

A contemporary of Kepler, living in Italy, was the first to develop the telescope from a Dutch invention and use it to see mountains on the Moon, spots on the Sun and details of beautiful planets. But this man, Galileo (1564–1642), was hated by traditionalists for his new evidence. He was even placed under arrest and forced to withdraw many of

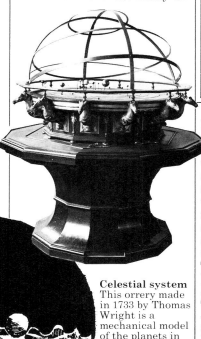

Celestial system
This orrery made in 1733 by Thomas Wright is a mechanical model of the planets in orbit round the Sun.

his newly discovered facts about the Universe.

Isaac Newton (1642–1727) was determined to carry on with the work begun by Galileo. He developed laws of motion which are still accurate today. He worked out the different paths of a

projectile if launched at varying speeds from a great height above the Earth. At the right speed and height it would have orbited the Earth in just the same way as satellites do today. In 1687 he published a book on his work, encouraged by a friend, Edmund Halley.

Halley (1656–1742) has

become a household name, too, because of the way he applied Newton's laws to work out the paths of comets. He predicted that a comet, which he and others watched in 1682, would reappear in 1758. When it did, Newton's laws were accepted more readily by the scientific community. That comet, now called Halley's Comet, is the same one shown on the Bayeux Tapestry during a previous visit. As Halley predicted, it appears regularly. The next time we shall be able to see it will be in 1986.

During the 19th century, more efficient telescopes were developed. Refractor telescopes improved when flint glass could be used for high-quality lenses, and by the end of the century enormous telescopes of this kind were being built in America. Since it was impossible to build telescopes with a lens size greater than 101 cm (40 in), scientists developed reflecting telescopes, using mirrors instead of lenses.

Today there are telescopes with mirrors 505 cm (200 in) in diameter.

The study of astronomy progressed even further when giant radio telescopes which developed out of the use of radar during World War II, were used to detect radio waves coming from stars that are so far away

that we cannot see them. Now the radio telescopes themselves are used to send out signals. These bounce off the Sun, Moon, planets or artificial satellites, and are picked up again on their return. They are also used to track and contact the man-made space travellers which orbit the Earth.

Surface of the Moon
Another early observer of the Moon was Johannes Hevelius (1611–87). He charted the surface of the Moon (this drawing was made in 1645), catalogued many stars, and studied the phases of Saturn.

Radio telescope
The famous radio telescope at Jodrell Bank, shown in 1958 in the last stages of building. In the foreground is a model of the finished telescope. Radio waves from space are focused at the centre of the giant dish.

THE EARTH OUR HOME

Although it has been accepted since Columbus's day that the Earth is round, it is actually slightly flattened at both poles, like a firm rubber ball pressed lightly between two hands. This shape is called geoid, and is the reason why the Earth's diameter from pole to pole is 12,714 km (7,900 miles), while at the equator it is 42 km (26 miles) more.

So, if the Earth is a sphere, why don't people living on the other side of the globe fall off? Why does a ball always come down when it is thrown up into the air? The reason is the Earth's mysterious pull towards its centre, a force we call gravity. Without it, a ball would not come down when it is thrown into the air. And the air itself would just float away into space, leaving us no air to breathe, and we would suffocate.

Every time you weigh yourself you are really measuring the force of gravity. Whatever your weight, you are getting pulled towards the centre of the Earth with an equal force. The farther away you go from the Earth's surface, the less you weigh, until, in space, you become weightless.

This law of gravity operates both on Earth and throughout the Universe. Put simply, it states that a heavy body attracts a lighter body and the attraction increases with the difference between the two masses. Obviously the Earth has a much greater mass than a human being and even the highest skyscraper. So both are held on the surface of the Earth by gravity. And they are always pulled towards the middle of the Earth, where the centre of gravity lies.

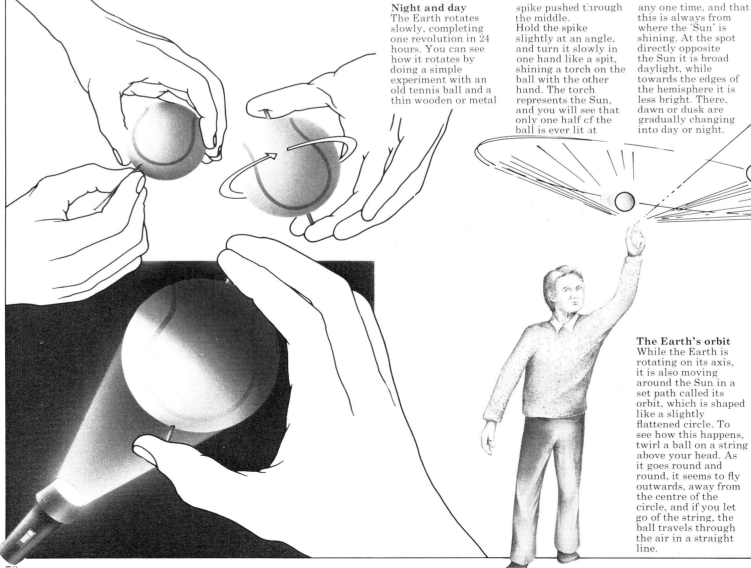

Night and day
The Earth rotates slowly, completing one revolution in 24 hours. You can see how it rotates by doing a simple experiment with an old tennis ball and a thin wooden or metal spike pushed through the middle.
Hold the spike slightly at an angle, and turn it slowly in one hand like a spit, shining a torch on the ball with the other hand. The torch represents the Sun, and you will see that only one half of the ball is ever lit at any one time, and that this is always from where the 'Sun' is shining. At the spot directly opposite the Sun it is broad daylight, while towards the edges of the hemisphere it is less bright. There, dawn or dusk are gradually changing into day or night.

The Earth's orbit
While the Earth is rotating on its axis, it is also moving around the Sun in a set path called its orbit, which is shaped like a slightly flattened circle. To see how this happens, twirl a ball on a string above your head. As it goes round and round, it seems to fly outwards, away from the centre of the circle, and if you let go of the string, the ball travels through the air in a straight line.

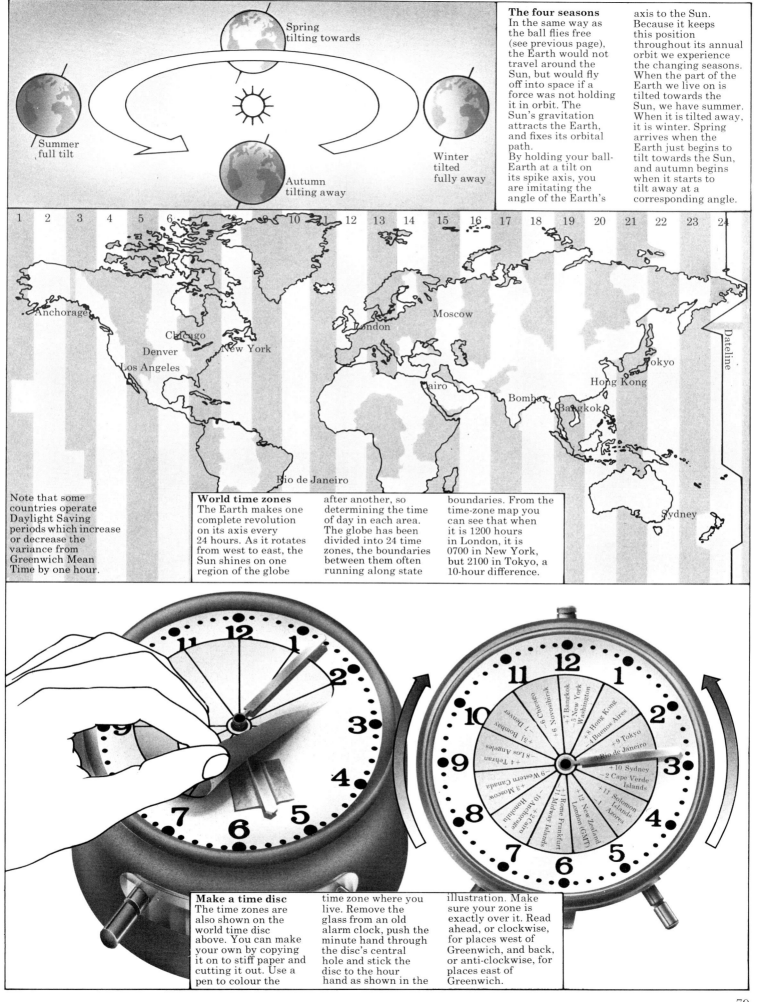

The four seasons

In the same way as the ball flies free (see previous page), the Earth would not travel around the Sun, but would fly off into space if a force was not holding it in orbit. The Sun's gravitation attracts the Earth, and fixes its orbital path.

By holding your ball-Earth at a tilt on its spike axis, you are imitating the angle of the Earth's axis to the Sun. Because it keeps this position throughout its annual orbit we experience the changing seasons. When the part of the Earth we live on is tilted towards the Sun, we have summer. When it is tilted away, it is winter. Spring arrives when the Earth just begins to tilt towards the Sun, and autumn begins when it starts to tilt away at a corresponding angle.

Spring
tilting towards

Summer
full tilt

Autumn
tilting away

Winter
tilted
fully away

Note that some countries operate Daylight Saving periods which increase or decrease the variance from Greenwich Mean Time by one hour.

World time zones

The Earth makes one complete revolution on its axis every 24 hours. As it rotates from west to east, the Sun shines on one region of the globe after another, so determining the time of day in each area. The globe has been divided into 24 time zones, the boundaries between them often running along state boundaries. From the time-zone map you can see that when it is 1200 hours in London, it is 0700 in New York, but 2100 in Tokyo, a 10-hour difference.

Make a time disc

The time zones are also shown on the world time disc above. You can make your own by copying it on to stiff paper and cutting it out. Use a pen to colour the time zone where you live. Remove the glass from an old alarm clock, push the minute hand through the disc's central hole and stick the disc to the hour hand as shown in the illustration. Make sure your zone is exactly over it. Read ahead, or clockwise, for places west of Greenwich, and back, or anti-clockwise, for places east of Greenwich.

79

THE TELESCOPE

There are two main types of telescope, refracting and reflecting telescopes. Refracting telescopes are the most common and were first put to effective use by Galileo in about 1610.

A simple refracting telescope (see diagram below) consists of a tube with a special convex lens at one end, and a magnifying lens at the other. The convex lens is called the objective lens, and the other lens is the eyepiece. The objective lens collects light lenses. This is because a single lens acts like a prism, causing irritating rims of colour in the picture, which can only be removed by employing compound lenses.

In 1663 James Gregory suggested using mirrors instead of lenses, and Sir Isaac Newton went on to make the first satisfactory reflecting telescope five years later.

The principle of this type of telescope is shown in the diagram. The concave mirror collects light from

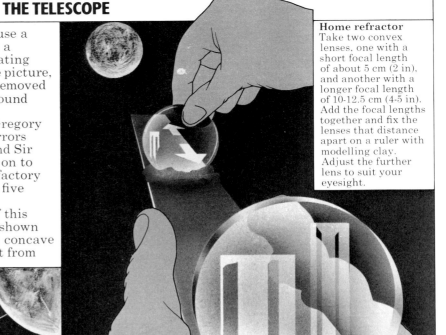

Home refractor
Take two convex lenses, one with a short focal length of about 5 cm (2 in), and another with a longer focal length of 10-12.5 cm (4-5 in). Add the focal lengths together and fix the lenses that distance apart on a ruler with modelling clay. Adjust the further lens to suit your eyesight.

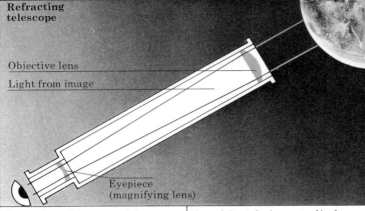

Refracting telescope

Objective lens

Light from image

Eyepiece (magnifying lens)

from the object, and forms a small image of the object inside the tube, which is then magnified by the eyepiece. The distance between the two lenses is adjusted to sharpen the image.

In modern telescopes the single lenses are replaced by a combination of two or more individual the object being studied, and reflects it on to the flat (plane) mirror. The flat mirror then reflects the light and the image through the side of the tube to the eyepiece, which magnifies it. Reflecting telescopes have fewer distortion problems, and most large observatory telescopes now use this principle.

Home reflector
Stand a shaving mirror outside to face the Moon. Hold a flat mirror so that you can see an image of the shaving mirror in it, with the Moon in the centre. Then look at that reflection with a magnifying glass and you will see a magnified image of the Moon.

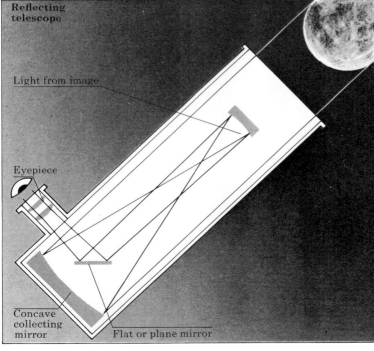

Reflecting telescope

Light from image

Eyepiece

Concave collecting mirror

Flat or plane mirror

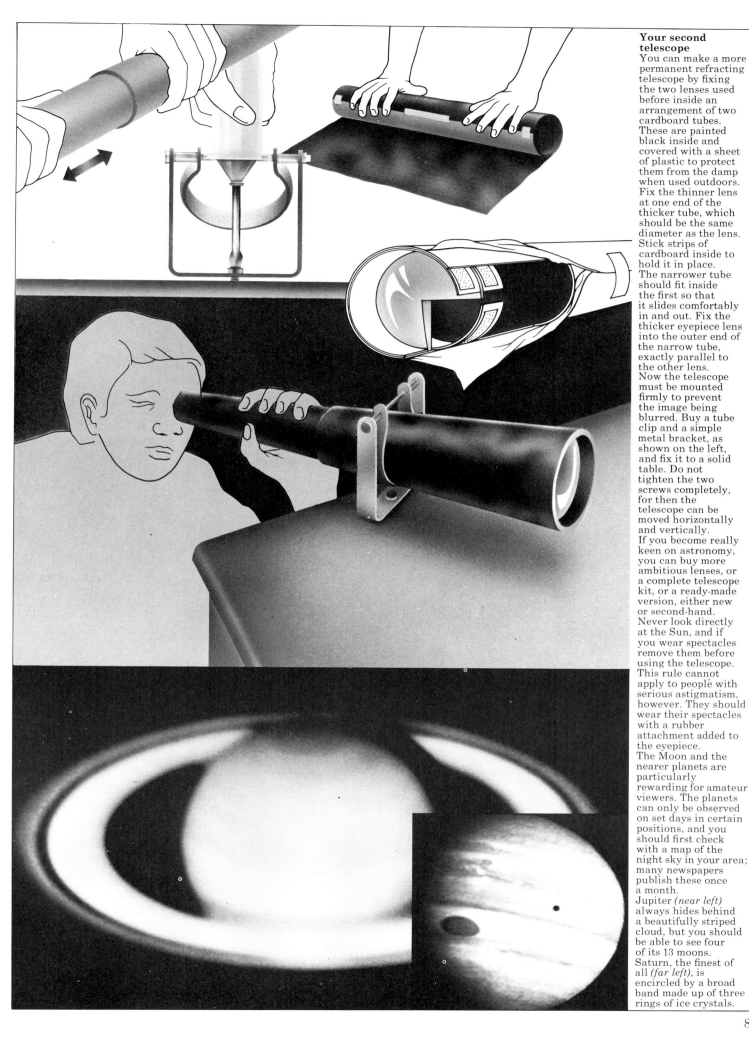

Your second telescope

You can make a more permanent refracting telescope by fixing the two lenses used before inside an arrangement of two cardboard tubes. These are painted black inside and covered with a sheet of plastic to protect them from the damp when used outdoors. Fix the thinner lens at one end of the thicker tube, which should be the same diameter as the lens. Stick strips of cardboard inside to hold it in place. The narrower tube should fit inside the first so that it slides comfortably in and out. Fix the thicker eyepiece lens into the outer end of the narrow tube, exactly parallel to the other lens.

Now the telescope must be mounted firmly to prevent the image being blurred. Buy a tube clip and a simple metal bracket, as shown on the left, and fix it to a solid table. Do not tighten the two screws completely, for then the telescope can be moved horizontally and vertically.

If you become really keen on astronomy, you can buy more ambitious lenses, or a complete telescope kit, or a ready-made version, either new or second-hand. Never look directly at the Sun, and if you wear spectacles remove them before using the telescope. This rule cannot apply to people with serious astigmatism, however. They should wear their spectacles with a rubber attachment added to the eyepiece.

The Moon and the nearer planets are particularly rewarding for amateur viewers. The planets can only be observed on set days in certain positions, and you should first check with a map of the night sky in your area; many newspapers publish these once a month.

Jupiter *(near left)* always hides behind a beautifully striped cloud, but you should be able to see four of its 13 moons. Saturn, the finest of all *(far left)*, is encircled by a broad band made up of three rings of ice crystals.

THE MOON

The Moon, our nearest neighbour, is approximately 385,000 km (239,000 miles) away. Just as the Earth turns round the Sun, the Moon moves in a nearly circular path around the Earth, held there by gravity. It makes one complete circle around the Earth in 27¼ days.

There is one side of the Moon that we never see.

The same side is always facing Earth because the Moon turns once on its axis in exactly the same length of time that it goes once round the Earth. To see how this works, walk round a chair, always facing it. In doing so, you also turn round once in relation to the room.

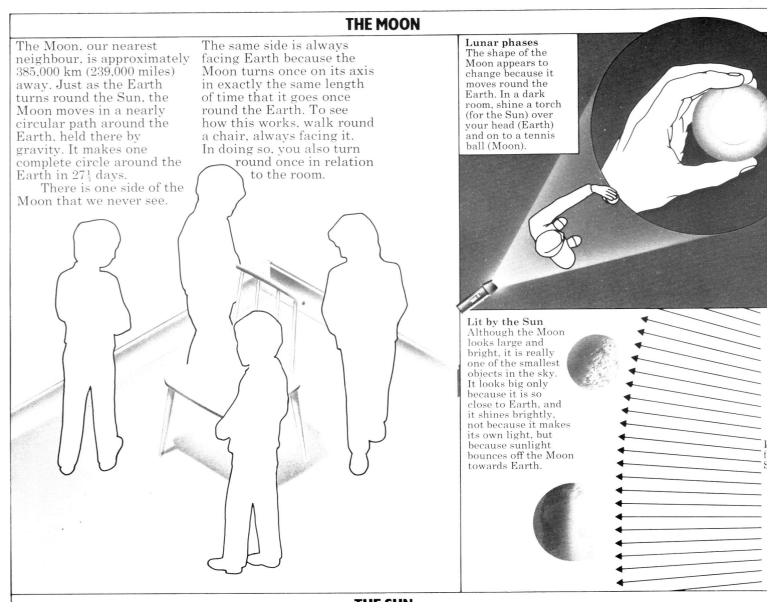

Lunar phases
The shape of the Moon appears to change because it moves round the Earth. In a dark room, shine a torch (for the Sun) over your head (Earth) and on to a tennis ball (Moon).

Lit by the Sun
Although the Moon looks large and bright, it is really one of the smallest objects in the sky. It looks big only because it is so close to Earth, and it shines brightly, not because it makes its own light, but because sunlight bounces off the Moon towards Earth.

THE SUN

A star is made of gas so hot that it shines with its own bright light, and not with reflected light as the Moon does. We can see thousands of stars with the naked eye, and millions more through a telescope. Our nearest star is the Sun, and Earth revolves around it along with eight other planets. In order of distance from the Sun these are Mercury (the Sun's nearest neighbour), Venus, Earth, Mars, Jupiter, Saturn, Uranus, Neptune and Pluto.

The planets, whose name is derived from the Greek word for 'wanderer', travel in roughly circular orbits. They have no light or heat of their own, but acquire it from the Sun. On Earth we see the other planets as luminous stars only because they reflect the light radiated from the Sun. Even Earth, when seen from space (see page 78) looks like a luminous star.

Another interesting feature of the Solar System are the Asteroids, a continuous belt of planetary material, most of which orbits the Sun between Mars and Jupiter.

Although the planets travel in regular orbits that bring them back to their starting points, the patterns of their paths vary quite a lot. Mercury, for example, wanders at distances ranging from 47 million km (29 million miles) at its nearest point to the Sun (its perihelion), to 69 million km (43 million miles) at the farthest point (known as the aphelion). Pluto is the most eccentric, and at one point it passes inside the orbit of Neptune – though at an angle of inclination that ensures they will never collide.

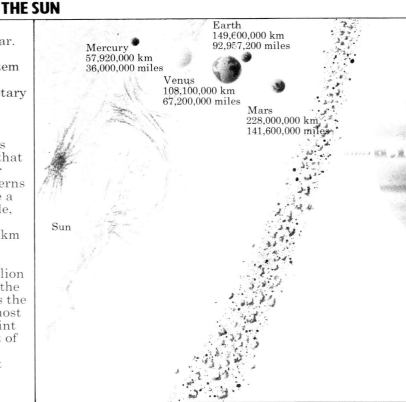

Mercury
57,920,000 km
36,000,000 miles

Venus
108,100,000 km
67,200,000 miles

Earth
149,600,000 km
92,957,200 miles

Mars
228,000,000 km
141,600,000 miles

Sun

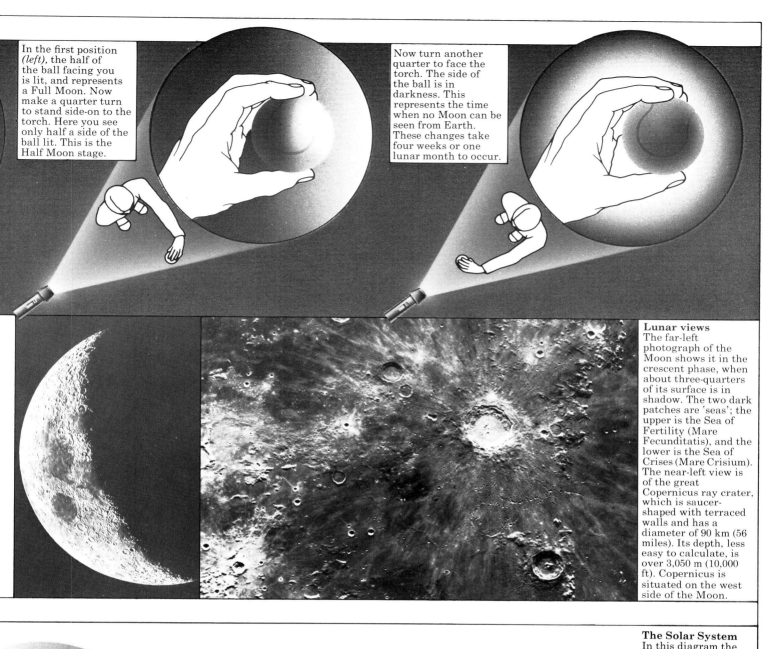

In the first position (*left*), the half of the ball facing you is lit, and represents a Full Moon. Now make a quarter turn to stand side-on to the torch. Here you see only half a side of the ball lit. This is the Half Moon stage.

Now turn another quarter to face the torch. The side of the ball is in darkness. This represents the time when no Moon can be seen from Earth. These changes take four weeks or one lunar month to occur.

Lunar views
The far-left photograph of the Moon shows it in the crescent phase, when about three-quarters of its surface is in shadow. The two dark patches are 'seas'; the upper is the Sea of Fertility (Mare Fecunditatis), and the lower is the Sea of Crises (Mare Crisium). The near-left view is of the great Copernicus ray crater, which is saucer-shaped with terraced walls and has a diameter of 90 km (56 miles). Its depth, less easy to calculate, is over 3,050 m (10,000 ft). Copernicus is situated on the west side of the Moon.

The Solar System
In this diagram the planets are shown in scale with each other and with their mean distances from the Sun.

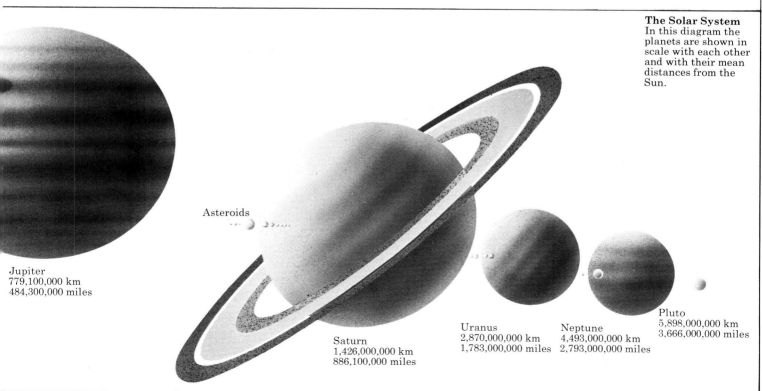

Jupiter
779,100,000 km
484,300,000 miles

Asteroids

Saturn
1,426,000,000 km
886,100,000 miles

Uranus
2,870,000,000 km
1,783,000,000 miles

Neptune
4,493,000,000 km
2,793,000,000 miles

Pluto
5,898,000,000 km
3,666,000,000 miles

Make a Sun clock

The simplest of sundial-clocks can be made with a flowerpot and a stick about twice as long as the height of the pot. Fix the stick in the hole at the bottom of the flowerpot and place in a sunny spot. The shadow formed by the stick moves around the rim of the pot as the Sun moves. Mark the position of the shadow as each hour passes. Then, once you have a complete set of marks, you will be able to tell the time whenever the Sun is shining.

The compass-watch

Using the position of the Sun, your wrist watch and a spent matchstick, it is always possible to make a simple compass to locate North, South, East and West. Holding the watch horizontally, with the hour hand pointing directly at the Sun, halve the distance between the hour hand and the 12 with a match, and the end of that match is then pointing directly South. For times before midday, halve the distance from the hour hand forward to 12, and after midday count forward from 12 to the hour hand.

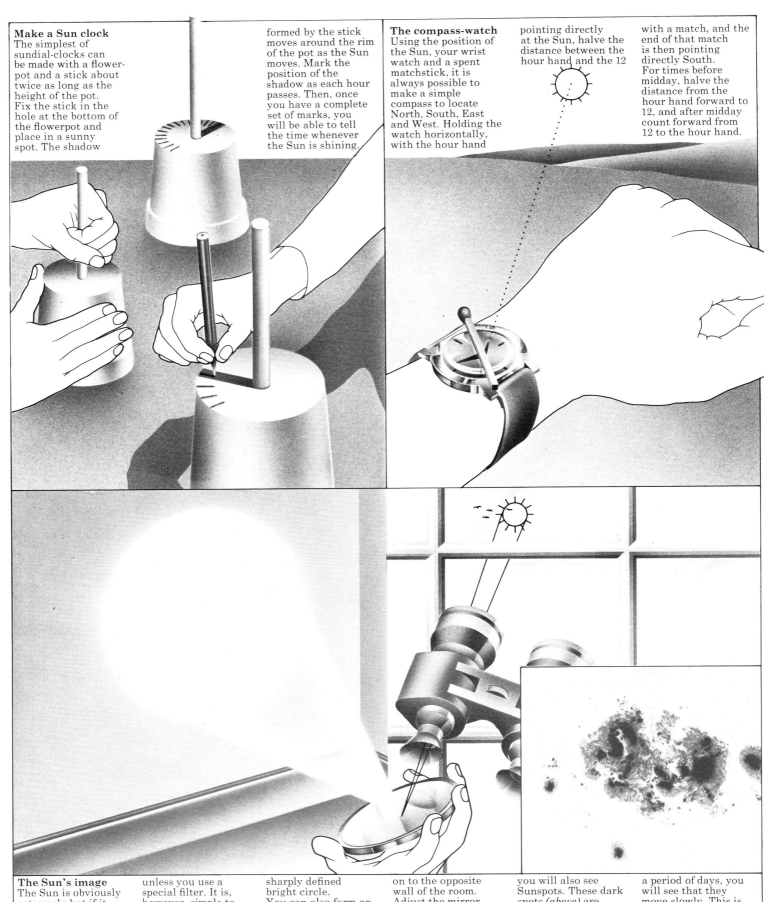

The Sun's image

The Sun is obviously extremely hot if it can light and heat Earth so well from a distance of about 150 million km (93 million miles). In fact it is so brilliant that it is unsafe to look at the Sun directly through a telescope, unless you use a special filter. It is, however, simple to look at it indirectly. Point a telescope towards the Sun and move a piece of white card to and fro at a distance from the eyepiece until the outline of the Sun appears on it as a sharply defined bright circle.

You can also form an image of the Sun by standing a mirror in the eyepiece of your telescope, or in front of one eyepiece of a pair of binoculars. Move the mirror slightly until it throws an image of the Sun on to the opposite wall of the room. Adjust the mirror until the image is sharp, and then darken the room to see it more clearly. If the magnification is good, not only will you see birds and clouds passing over the face of the Sun, you will also see Sunspots. These dark spots (*above*) are mysterious phenomena on the Sun's surface, which stay for a few days or weeks and then disappear. If you watch the Sunspots on your image of the Sun over a period of days, you will see that they move slowly. This is proof that the Sun also revolves on its axis. It takes 27 days to complete one revolution, but this has no effect on Earth because the Sun is equally brilliant on all sides.

THE STARS

Great Bear

Great Bear
Ursa Major, a familiar group seen in Northern latitudes. It is easy to find, and the seven brightest stars form the famous Plough.

Orion
Visible from everywhere on Earth. Its bright stars include Betelgeux and the central Belt of Mintaka, Alnilam and Alnitak.

Orion

Cygnus
The Swan, visible from Europe and northern USA. Deneb forms the end of one arm of this group's famous Northern Cross.

Pegasus
A large constellation in the Northern Hemisphere, its four principal stars are bright and make up the Great Square of Pegasus.

Cygnus

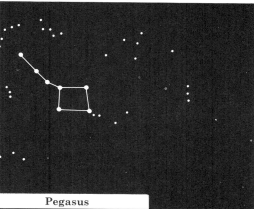

Pegasus

Southern Cross
Crux, the best-known constellation in the Southern Hemisphere, whose four brightest stars form a cross. Never seen from Europe.

Crane
Grus, another Southern constellation never visible from Europe – although Europeans can see part of nearby Eridanus.

Southern Cross

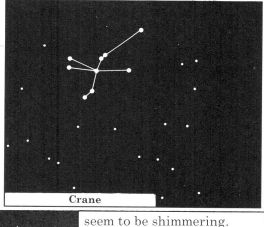

Crane

On a clear night the sky seems crammed with stars. With the naked eye it is said to be possible to see about 2,500, but with the world's most advanced telescopes astronomers can find many millions. What is even more surprising is that stars too faint to be seen by any telescope will leave their record on photographic plates. The longer the exposure, the more crowded the plate becomes with 'new' stars.

Stars are balls of very hot gas which give off their own light and heat. They seem to twinkle, although in fact they give off steady streams of light. But when these light rays reach the Earth's atmosphere, areas of hot and cold air bend them. This is why the stars seem to be shimmering.

Stars are divided into 88 groups called constellations. The quickest way to recognize them is to go outside at night with your own home-made constellation viewers. You can make them after studying the diagrams above, which show six familiar groups. You can plot others by referring to star maps in your newspaper.

To prepare a viewer, trace a relevant star map on thin paper. Stick this on card and prick a hole through all the stars marking each with a cross and giving the constellations a name. On a clear night hold this card over a torch so the constellation can be seen as spots of light.

The Zodiac

When you look at star maps showing the whole sky – which many newspapers publish each month – you will recognize names such as Pisces, Leo and Aries – the Zodiac signs which are associated with particular periods of the year. Hundreds of years ago, astronomers first used the word Zodiac to describe the area of the fixed stars through which the Sun, Moon and planets passed each year. They divided the Zodiac into 12 equal parts and each part was given its own sign. The Zodiac band is shown below. The Sun's route, indicated by the broken line, is called the ecliptic.

North Star

The most important star in the Northern Hemisphere is Polaris, the North or Pole Star. You can find it on any clear evening, shining from a group of stars called Ursa Minor, the Little Bear. An imaginary line drawn through the two front stars of the Plough in the Great Bear will point almost straight at the North Star. On the other side of the North Star from the Plough is a large 'W' of five bright stars which make up Cassiopeia. When you look at the North Star through a telescope you will see that what looks like a single star to the naked eye is two stars close together.

You can find another double star much more easily by looking at the Great Bear constellation. Even without a telescope you can probably see a tiny star which seems to ride on top of the larger one which is second in the shaft.

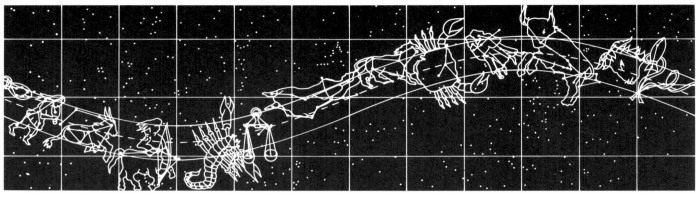

Star photography

Some stars can always be seen in Northern latitudes. They are called circumpolar because they appear to circle slowly around the North Star. You can capture this movement by photography.

Mount an ordinary camera on a stand and point it towards the sky so that the North Star is in the centre of the viewfinder. You need to choose a clear night with plenty of stars but no Moon or man-made light. Set the camera's distance at infinity, and open the shutter, leaving it open for about three hours. You will have a fascinating picture of the dark sky with the paths of the stars appearing as thin lines.

In fact, it is not the stars which are moving around the North Star. The movement is caused because the camera is attached to the surface of the Earth, which is revolving on its own axis. The photograph is just a mirror image of the Earth's rotation.

Comets

Comets produce flamboyant lighting effects, and can often be seen for months on end. The famous Halley's Comet *(right)*, which takes 76 years to travel around the Sun, will reappear in 1986. It is the only bright comet to have such a brief orbital period!

THE WEATHER

Although man has always watched the weather with interest, he did not begin to study it scientifically until the 17th century. It was natural at first to believe that the gods decided the weather, good or bad. Zeus, for example, was thought to cast thunderbolts and was lord of the winds.

It was nevertheless the Greeks who began the science of meteorology, and the earliest book on weather was Aristotle's *Meteorologica* which, written in the 4th century BC, got a lot of basic things wrong that were not disproved for some 2,000 years. From the 17th century until earlier in this century, weather predictions were based on the behaviour of barometers and on the observation of clouds. Today meteorology has become far more scientific, although cloud patterns can still provide clues. For example, the appearance of cirrus clouds, or mares' tails, high in the sky can be a good indication of the approach of a depression. And there are many old sailors' rhymes that still seem to be reliable for short periods.

But long-range forecasting is a different matter, and one that has not been conquered. Meteorologists cannot predict with the accuracy of astronomers because, while the Earth moves in a virtually unchanging path around the Sun, a current of air is acted upon by so many different forces that it behaves in a very complicated way.

It has been known since the days of the 17th-century explorers that air circulates at a low level around the world in a pattern made up of calm air near the Equator, the sub-tropical belts of the trade-winds, the zones of westerly wind in the temperate latitudes, and the polar easterlies. The measurement of upper winds by radar has shown scientists that in the higher parts of the atmosphere the winds are mainly westerly, with some narrow currents of fast-moving air called jet streams. The surface trade winds are caused by air rising near the Equator and then sinking at about Latitude 30°.

Weather prediction took a leap forward in 1855 when Admiral FitzRoy, the first director of the British Meteorological Office, deduced from studying ships' reports that there are many air currents flowing in opposite directions in the middle latitudes. The warm and humid currents came from the subtropics, while the cold and dry ones originated in the sub-polar regions. He realized that storms often formed on the boundary between these different currents. As the warm front met the cold front there was rain, and changes occurred in the speed and direction of the wind.

The alarming scene below was photographed during a night storm over Johannesburg.

Weather influences our lives in many ways. It decides what crops we can grow to eat, what we should wear, what sports we can enjoy, what sort of houses we should live in, and how often we go out or stay indoors.

People in parts of north-western Europe, and particularly the British, have a reputation for being obsessive about their weather. If they have any excuse for this, it is that their climate is so unsettled and difficult to predict. The reason for this lies in their world position in the mid-latitudes of the Northern Hemisphere, near the junction where masses of cold and warm air meet and mingle.

Because of these influences, and the uncertainty of weather conditions in certain areas, weather forecasting has become important. People in many parts of the globe now make reports at the same times each day. These are co-ordinated and plotted on charts to make a world weather pattern.

The weather forecaster uses these charts in conjunction with pictures from satellites of the prevailing weather, plus his own knowledge of why the weather behaves as it does, to predict what the weather will do next.

Having said that weather forecasting is very difficult to do with accuracy in temperate climates or at long range, there are some very simple methods that the beginner can use to observe changes in the weather and also to forecast them.

You can measure humidity, for example, by watching a piece of seaweed or a fir cone. When the air's humidity is high, the air contains a lot of moisture and it is more likely to rain. In such conditions, seaweed grows limp and the fir cone closes up. When the air is drier, the seaweed hardens and the fir cone opens its scales. The experiments below show two ways to gauge the amount of moisture in the air.

Fir-cone gauge
A slightly more scientific method of using fir cones to monitor the weather is to glue a cone on to a small piece of wood, stick a pin to one of the central scales, and then fix a short straw over it. Put this amateur weather station outdoors, but place it somewhere protected from rain.

Rig up a chart behind the fir cone to help observe the humidity. The fir cone closes its scales to protect its seeds when the air is full of moisture. When the air becomes dry the fir cone opens up and the scale carrying the straw moves it sideways, to a different place on the chart.

Hair test
You can also measure moisture in the air using a human hair. Tack a piece of card about 23 × 30 cm (9 × 12 in) to a block. Cut out a pointer from stiff paper and pin it to the card, making sure that the arrow moves about freely. Join a hair about 23 cm (9 in) long to the top of the card with tape, and then fix the other end to the arrow, making sure that the hair is stretched very tight. Start off on a dry sunny day and mark the card 'Dry' by the arrow's point.

Watch the instrument every day, marking the card to show the arrow's position. At the highest point it reaches, write the word 'Moist'. It reaches this point because the hair becomes shorter when the air is full of moisture.

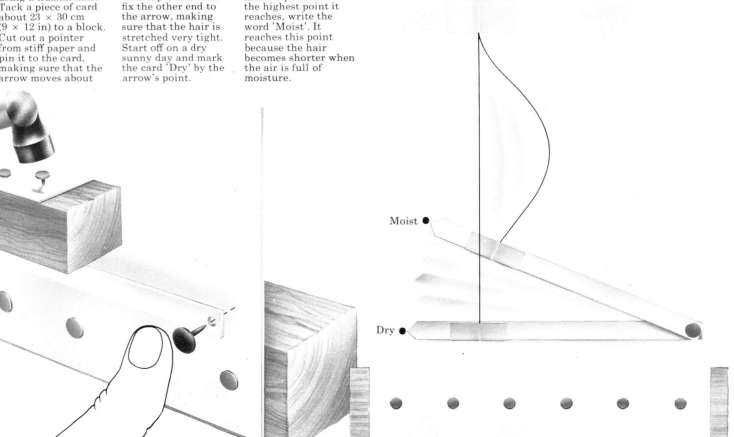

Moist

Dry

EVAPORATION

You cannot see the moisture or water in the air. But you can prove how easily the air accepts water by measuring out $\frac{1}{2}$l (1 pt) of water, boiling it for a few minutes and then measuring it again. You will find that there is less water than before. You saw some of it in the form of steam, but then it disappeared. It was absorbed into the air in the form of invisible water vapour.

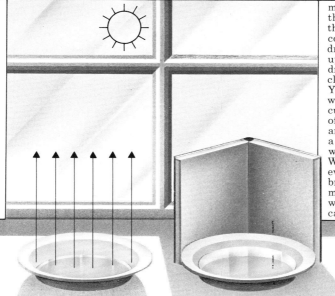

moisture rises all the time. High in the sky, where it is cooler, the small drops of water join up to make bigger drops which form clouds.

You can prove that warm air rises by cutting a few strips of thin tissue paper, and holding them over a radiator. They will flutter upwards. Wind also encourages evaporation, by bringing more and more dry air against wet things, and carrying away the air which has absorbed water vapour.

Both the Sun and the wind remove water from rivers, lakes and the sea in just the same way as they dry up puddles (and the saucers of water in our experiment). They take water from the ground too. You can prove this by filling a shallow dish with soil, pouring on water to make a mud pie and then leaving it in the Sun for a day or two. It dries out as the water is drawn off.

Heat and air
Put two plates on the windowsill, both with two tablespoons of water on them, to demonstrate the importance of Sun and shade to the evaporation process. Leave one plate in the sunshine and shade the second with a book. Check them every half hour or so, and you will find that the water in the Sun evaporates quickly, leaving the plate in the shade still wet. Warmth makes the water evaporate more quickly, which is why puddles dry up faster on a sunny day. On warm days the air carrying this

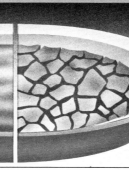

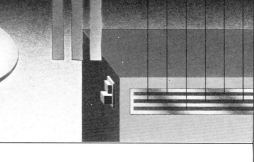

CONDENSATION

When warm air, containing a lot of water vapour, touches something cold, the small drops of water collect into drops which are large enough for you to see. This process is called condensation.

You can see this clearly on the inside of a window pane when the temperature outside is much lower than the temperature of the room. After rain, for example, the air outside cools sharply as the water evaporates. We notice a new freshness in the air if we are outdoors. But the indoor temperature will not have changed. The warm air inside the room, which contains a lot of water vapour, meets the window pane which has been cooled by the outside temperature. As the air in the room cools on the window pane, it forms water droplets, because cold air cannot hold as much moisture as warm air.

The ice experiment shown here also demonstrates the principle behind rain. When warm

Misting up
To illustrate condensation, put some ice in a glass of cold water and watch as very small drops of water form on the outside of the glass. The same thing can be seen on shiny bath taps. The hot tap remains bright, while the cold tap looks misty.

The window pane mists up on the inside because again there is a marked difference in temperature between the two sides of the window pane.

air, containing a lot of moisture, rises up to meet cold air in the sky, the small drops of water which form as the warm air cools, collect around specks of dust in the atmosphere, forming a cloud.

When the air is relatively full of water vapour, a small rise into the sky will cool it enough to cause condensation, and low cloud will form. If the air is relatively empty of water vapour, it will need to go up a long way before it is cool enough to produce small drops of water. High cloud will therefore form. The height at which cloud starts to form is known as the condensation level.

Relative humidity is an important phrase among meteorologists. Moist air which needs less cooling before it reaches condensation level, is said to have a high relative humidity. Dry air, which needs a lot of cooling and has to be pushed a long way before cloud forms, has a low relative humidity.

RAIN

Once the water has risen to make clouds, it returns to the ground in seven main ways – as rain, hail, sleet, snow, mist, dew and frost.

Rain is the most common form of condensation, and it occurs when those small drops of water join to form drops too large for the air to support. Naturally, the faster the currents of air passing upwards, the larger the drops must be before they fall. A strong up-current produces a tall, billowy cloud called cumulus. This brings showers of rain.

When the cloud goes high it can form the flat-topped cumulonimbus, which is the thunderstorm cloud. The other main type is called stratus, because it is in a flat layer. Unless it is very thick, stratus does not produce heavy rain. Because of its size however, the rain lasts longer. The highest cloud is cirrus, and forms above the freezing level as ice filaments.

So what happens inside a cloud before the rain starts to fall? The small drops of water join to produce larger drops, although no one is sure exactly how this happens.

There are thought to be three main zones in a cloud. The top zone may be so cold that the droplets have formed ice crystals; the middle zone is made up of droplets at temperatures below freezing, which are looking for crystals to freeze on to, and the bottom layer of the cloud is made up of normal water droplets.

The diagram below shows the make-up of the rain cycle. From sources on land and sea, the Sun and the wind draw evaporation up into the air where clouds form. The water droplets in the clouds are later released as precipitation, or rain. At bottom are the more common types of cloud.

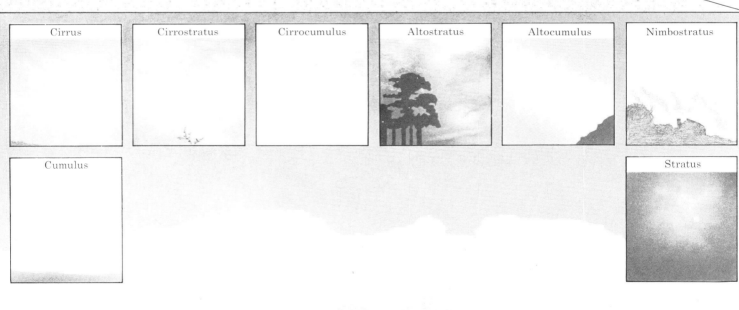

Precipitation on land

Evaporation from vegetation and soil

Evaporation from lakes and ponds

Precipitation on seas and oceans

Ground water to vegetation and soil

Ground water to lakes and streams

Evaporation from vegetation and streams

Evaporation from oceans

Ground water to vegetation

Ground water to seas and oceans

| Cirrus | Cirrostratus | Cirrocumulus | Altostratus | Altocumulus | Nimbostratus |

Cumulus

Stratus

Cumulonimbus

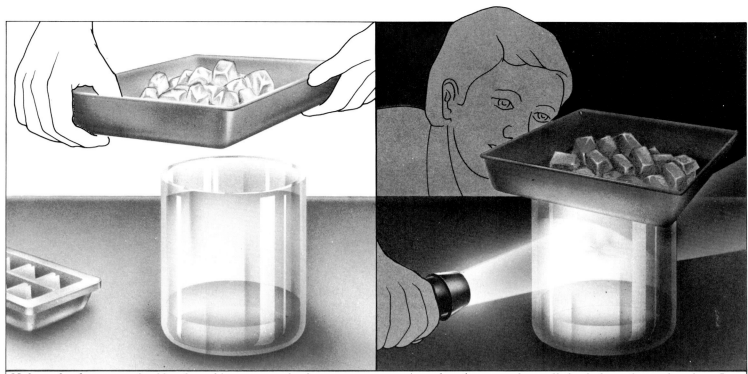

Make a cloud

Take a large glass jar and pour 2.5 cm (1 in) of hot water into it. Do not use boiling water because this will crack the jar. Put a metal baking tray on the top of the open jar, and fill the tray with ice cubes. Look at the jar in a darkened room by shining a torch. You will see that a small cloud has formed in the jar from warm air containing tiny drops of water. When that warm air eventually meets the chilled tray, it is cooled so much that still more moisture in the air condenses. Small drops of water form larger drops on the tray. These are the equivalent of raindrops.

You can make your own cloud even more easily on a very cold day. Just go outside and blow through your mouth. Your breath will look like a small, low cloud. It forms because warm, moist air from inside your body cools as it meets the cold air outside. You can also watch small clouds rising from water in a pond or lake in the early morning, when there have been low temperatures in the night. This happens because water holds heat longer than land. So during a cold night the water stays warmer than the surrounding land, and the air above it is obviously warmer too. As this warm air above the water rises, it meets colder air from the land, and a small cloud of mist is formed.

This process may be repeated later in the day, around sunset in winter. By that time the temperature of the land, in particular that beside a pond or river, has dropped below that of the water and the air immediately above it. The product is a wraith-like cloud that hovers over the land in the vicinity of the pond or river. On very cold days, when the land temperature remains low and there is little or no wind to disperse it, this mist may hang in the air throughout the hours of daylight. When you see this phenomenon, you will notice that there is always a gap between the land and the mist; this marks the meeting point of the temperature belts.

Six-sided snowflake

As the droplets in the uppermost cloud zone freeze and take on the shape of ice crystals, they eventually become heavy enough to fall through the cloud as snowflakes. Look at some through a magnifying glass and you will see that they all have beautiful six-sided shapes, like the example shown above. Usually, in temperate climates, these snowflakes sink lower and lower into the cloud, but before they can be released as snow the temperature rises; the snowflakes consequently melt, and fall as rain. But on very cold days they do not melt, and we have snow instead of rain, or there is a mixture of the two, known as sleet. This partly frozen substance can fall in isolated showers, but usually it is accompanied by a fall of either rain or snow according to the temperature prevailing.

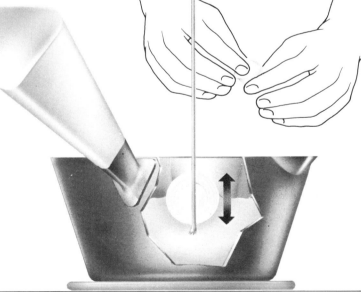

Layers in a hailstone

Hailstones have a layered structure. They are formed as strong air currents in a cloud carry a raindrop up and down several times, until it has collected a number of coatings made of snow and water droplets that freeze on to it. This process continues until the hailstone is too heavy for up-currents to support. By the time it is too heavy and falls to the ground, it will have taken on a number of clearly discernible layers rather like those of an onion.

You can demonstrate this using wax instead of ice. Melt down a wax candle, keeping the wax warm, and press a small amount into a blob around the end of a thread. Dip this in and out of the wax every few seconds. The ball will grow in size, and when you cut through it, several layers – like those of a hailstone – can be seen.

THUNDERSTORMS

When you see a cumulonimbus, a thunderstorm is probably on the way, caused by a build-up of static electricity. Hailstones and other ice crystals in the cloud collide, some taking on a positive electrical charge and some a negative charge, and then move on to different parts of the cloud. When positive and negative are separated in this way, they try to get together again, and a huge electric spark jumps from one to the other, which we see as lightning.

It is thought that lightning heats the air, producing a vacuum, and that the air rushing in to fill this vacuum causes thunder. Most lightning flashes jump from one cloud to another, but a few strike the ground causing damage. Tall buildings have lightning conductors which intercept and carry the electricity safely down to earth. The principle of the lightning conductor was discovered by Benjamin Franklin.

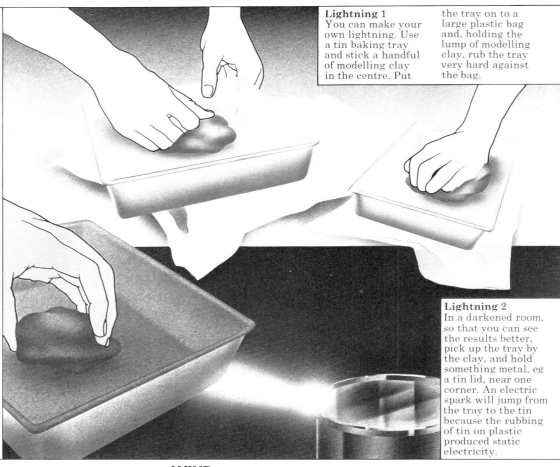

Lightning 1
You can make your own lightning. Use a tin baking tray and stick a handful of modelling clay in the centre. Put the tray on to a large plastic bag and, holding the lump of modelling clay, rub the tray very hard against the bag.

Lightning 2
In a darkened room, so that you can see the results better, pick up the tray by the clay, and hold something metal, eg a tin lid, near one corner. An electric spark will jump from the tray to the tin because the rubbing of tin on plastic produced static electricity.

WIND

Winds help to make the weather, bringing warm days and cold days, dry weather and wet weather.

You can see these changes on a small scale during a day by the sea. You will notice how a breeze blows up on some afternoons and then dies down in the evening. After dark, the breeze may blow up again, but by then it may be heading in the opposite direction.

This change happens because, although the sea temperature hardly varies, the land warms by day and cools by night, and so accentuates the temperature difference between land and sea. Air rises from the warm land during the day, and cool air from the sea comes in to take its place, giving a sea breeze. At night, when the land is cooler than the sea, the air travels in the opposite direction.

Wind vane
To make your own wind vane you will need a heavy wire coat-hanger, a narrow pill bottle, a wooden block and a piece of strong cardboard, about 15 × 5 cm (6 × 12 in). Cut an arrow shape from the cardboard and fix the pill bottle upside down on the arrow, using strong tape. Fix it about one-third the way along from the arrow's point. Cut a piece from the coat hanger, bend it into a tall L-shape, and nail the bent end to the wooden block. Put the bottle on the end of the wire and place your wind vane in a high, open place. Using a compass, mark North, South, East and West on the block. (Do not use the compass near the weather vane because the metal will affect your result.) Once the vane is working you will find that when the arrow points midway between North and East, you can expect a long period of cold weather.

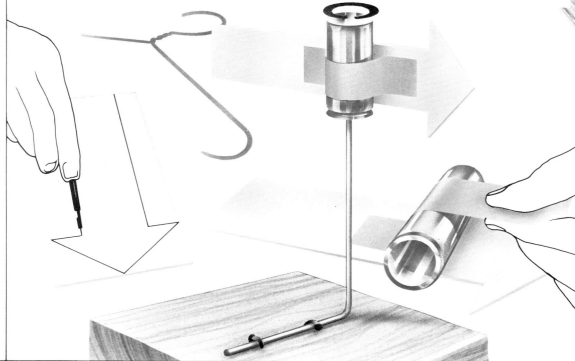

RAIN GAUGES

Thunderstorms can produce cm/in of rain in a very short time, while days of drizzle may produce very little. Farmers need to know how much rain their land is getting, and towns have to find out how much water will be available to fill their reservoirs from local rivers and streams. Rainfall is therefore carefully measured by Water Boards, local authorities and national Meteorological Offices. They all use a tall metal container, which catches the rain in a wide opening at the top. It then runs into a smaller tube that is marked in cm/in like a ruler.

You can make your own rain gauge using a glass with straight sides and a ruler. Put some water in the bottom of the glass, and fasten the ruler to the outside of the glass, making sure that the bottom of the ruler goes as far down as the bottom of the water – but not further, ie allow for the glass base and the bulge which many glasses have at the base.

Bend down so your eye is level with the water, and measure off exactly how much water is in the glass. When it is about to rain, put your rain gauge outside in an open space. After the rain, see how much water has been collected in the gauge. If you were enthusiastic enough to do this over an extended period, preferably as long as a year, you would be able to work out your average rainfall. This can vary considerably from area to area. For example, Seathwaite in the Lake District is the wettest spot in Britain, with 457 cm (180 in), while the London area gets only 63.5 cm (25 in), and Aden in the Middle East, gets less than 2.5 cm (1 in) a year (and there they have little need of rain gauges).

Anemometer

If you want to measure the wind's speed, you can make a simple anemometer. For this you will need a larger wooden block, about 30 × 15 cm (12 × 6 in), a piece of wood 45 × 5 cm (18 × 2 in) and a piece of strong card about 15 cm (6 in) square. You will also want a plastic cup which you fasten to a strip of wood about 35 cm (14 in) long and 1 cm ($\frac{1}{2}$ in) wide. Nail the block to the long piece of wood as shown, cut the card in a fan shape, mark it 'Slow' and 'Fast', and nail it to the post.

Take your plastic cup and strip of wood, and bore a hole in the wood at the far end from the cup. Make a small red arrow and fix it above the hole. Hang the stick with its arrow and plastic cup to the post by hammering a nail through the hole, near the point of the card scale. The stick must be able to swing freely.

Take your completed anemometer to an open place, and position it so that any wind blows into the plastic cup. The stronger the wind, the higher the cup will swing, making the arrow point towards 'Fast' on the scale.

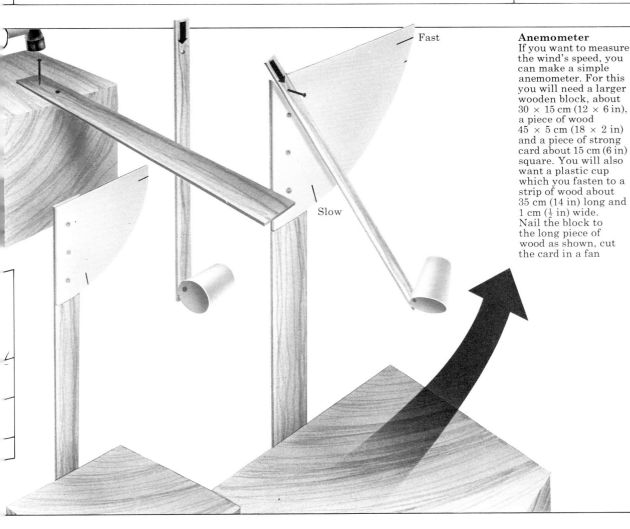

Fast

Slow

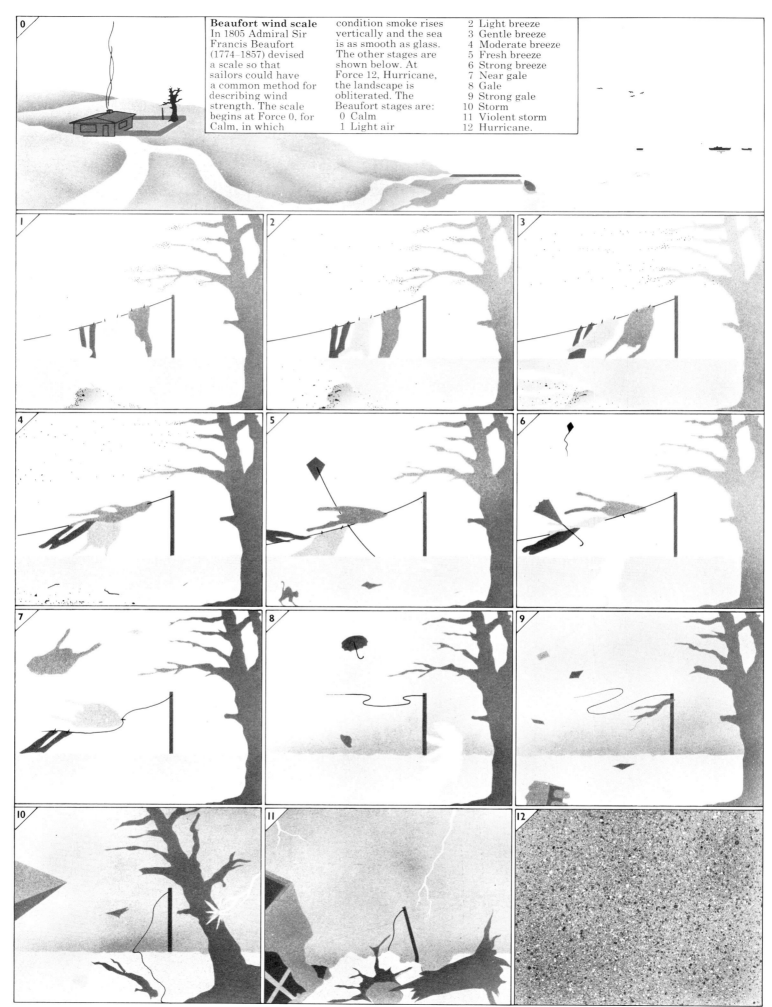

Beaufort wind scale
In 1805 Admiral Sir Francis Beaufort (1774–1857) devised a scale so that sailors could have a common method for describing wind strength. The scale begins at Force 0, for Calm, in which condition smoke rises vertically and the sea is as smooth as glass. The other stages are shown below. At Force 12, Hurricane, the landscape is obliterated. The Beaufort stages are:

 0 Calm
 1 Light air
 2 Light breeze
 3 Gentle breeze
 4 Moderate breeze
 5 Fresh breeze
 6 Strong breeze
 7 Near gale
 8 Gale
 9 Strong gale
10 Storm
11 Violent storm
12 Hurricane.

TEMPERATURE

Every weather report explains how hot or cold it is, and describes the temperature as measured in degrees by a thermometer.

The professionals use a special box, called a Stevenson Screen, housing four thermometers. There is a maximum and a minimum, showing the highest and the lowest temperatures since the last reading, an ordinary thermometer, and a wet bulb thermometer that has damp muslin wrapped around its bulb. The water in the muslin evaporates more quickly when the air is dry, and evaporation causes cooling, so this thermometer shows a lower temperature when the air is dry than when it is wet. The difference between wet and dry bulb temperatures indicates relative humidity.

You can buy your own thermometer cheaply. The bulb at the base contains alcohol mixed with a red colouring. You read the temperature by watching the red line in the tube. Centigrade measures are usually given for each 1° change, whereas those for Fahrenheit often rise or fall in stages of 2°.

The red line rises because alcohol expands when it gets warm. It drops as the alcohol shrinks in cold weather. If you put the thermometer in the freezing compartment of a refrigerator for five minutes, the red line will drop to 0°C (32°F) or less.

With the gradual conversion to metrication there is a tendency among TV and radio forecasters to read out temperatures in Centigrade only, but you can still buy thermometers that give both scales.

Use your thermometer to keep a record of daily temperatures. Remember that if you want to find the average outdoor temperature, this must be taken in the shade.

Make a thermometer
You can make a simple thermometer using a bottle about 15 cm (6 in) high, a rubber stopper with a hole in it, and a glass tube about 25 cm (10 in) long. The stopper and tube can be bought at shops stocking home wine-making materials, or from an ironmonger. Fill the bottle half full of water, add a few drops of food colouring or ink, and carefully push the glass tube through the hole in the stopper. It must be a good fit. Put the stopper in the bottle, and adjust the tube so that it reaches to the bottom of the water.

Then place your home-made thermometer in the Sun. You will see the coloured water rising in the tube. This happens because heat makes the air in the bottle expand. The air, which needs more room, pushes down on the water, and some of this water is forced up the tube.

In addition to keeping a record of temperatures, you can also use your thermometer to test the temperature of different surfaces. Try measuring those of grass, concrete, tarmac, pond water, and many others. Also experiment with one surface at different times of the day. Test concrete every hour, for example, and make a graph. Compare it to grass tested in the same way. Then test the same surfaces in the evening. You will find that those which became hottest by day are coldest at night. You will also find that water changes least of all.

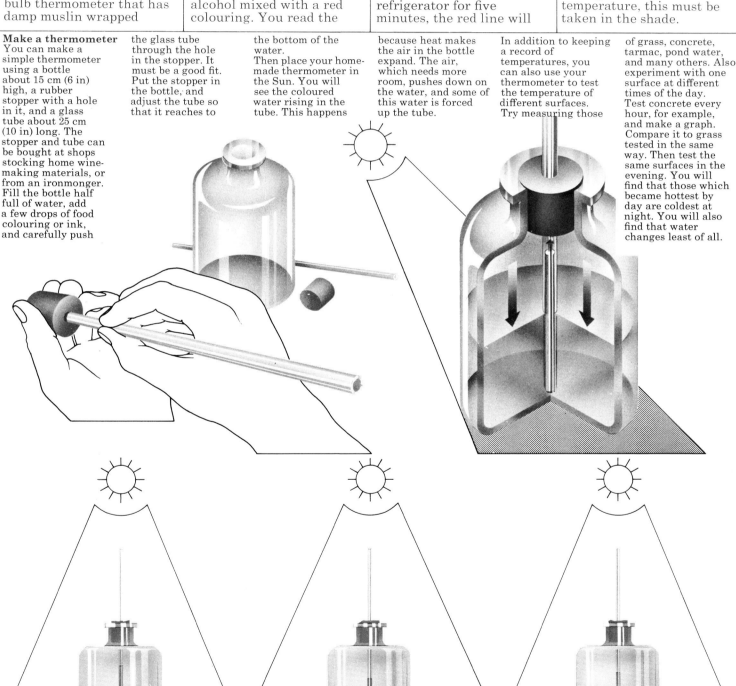

People have always been curious about the visible and invisible forces in the air, water and solids which surround us. Has the force which keeps the planets rotating round the Sun anything to do with the path travelled by a ball when it is thrown up into the air, for instance? The study of mechanics provided the answer. Are the same forces at work in the polar lights and in the shapes formed by iron filings round a magnet? And is lightning related to the crackling sparks in an electrically powered machine? These questions were answered as our knowledge of magnetism and electricity progressed.

The first step in our understanding of magnetism came when the Chinese discovered a magnetic iron ore called magnetite. They used natural magnets, or lodestones, made of this substance as compasses in their ships.

In the 13th century a French crusader called Petrus Peregrinus de Maricourt named the two poles of a magnet and found that unlike poles attract each other.

Several centuries later, Galileo praised a book about magnetism written by an Englishman, William Gilbert, in 1600. Gilbert had

6

THE SCIENCE OF PHYSICS

found that a piece of hot iron, placed exactly along the North/South axis (along which the forces of magnetic current flow) could be made magnetic simply by stroking it several times with a hammer. He also carried out experiments with a spherical lodestone which showed that this 'miniature Earth' had its magnetic North and South at either end of the axis which connected them. The magnetic forces were distributed throughout the sphere, but were weakest at the equator and strongest near the poles.

The next step came when Carl Friedrich Gauss (1777–1855), 'the prince of mathematics', became interested in magnetism and built an observatory to study it at Göttingen, in Germany. Using information which came in from all over the world, he produced an atlas and invented a refined type of magnetometer.

Scientists were also becoming interested in electricity. The early experiments involved crude machines, turned by a ball of sulphur which was rubbed in order to produce electricity. In 1729 two English scientists, Stephen Gray and Granvil Wheeler, managed to pass electricity along 89.6 m (98 yd) of thread and differentiated between good and bad conductors of electricity.

In 1746 a Dutchman called van Musschenbroek found he could store an electrical charge in a glass jar by connecting a generating machine to a nail passed through the cork in a partly filled bottle of water. The device is called a Leyden jar, after the place in Holland where van Musschenbroek conducted the experiment.

The first electrical battery was developed at the beginning of the 19th century. It was based on the discovery that it is possible to generate an electric current by placing a damp material between two different kinds of metal. The Italian physicist, Alessandro Volta (1745–

Exploring magnetism
Lodestones are natural magnets, and navigators used them to magnetize the needles of their compasses. The 17th-century example shown *(far left)* is bound in a brass case. The diagram *(near left)*, from William Gilbert's book *De Magnete*, was intended to illustrate the behaviour of a magnet at different points around the north pole of the Earth (A).

Electrical movement
A view of Gray and Wheeler's experiment of 1729 *(above)*.

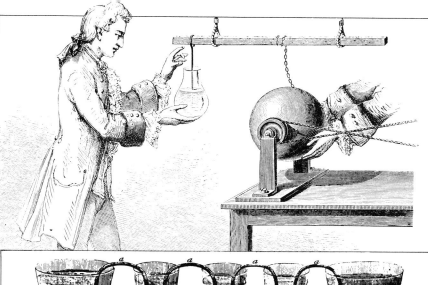

Leyden jar
The Dutch scientist Cuneus attempts to electrify water in a glass jar which is connected to a generating machine. When van Musschenbroek, Cuneus's teacher, repeated the experiment, he was thrown backwards by the shock.

Voltaic pile
The diagram shows how Volta built columns of alternating layers of copper (A) and zinc (Z). He then passed an electric current through wires connected to the ends of each column.

Early transformers
In 1831 Faraday built his first transformer (*upper drawing, below*). It consisted of an iron ring wound with two separate coils of wire. The lower drawing shows Masson and Ritchie's coil of 1842. This had a core of iron rods that formed an 'open magnetic circuit'.

Cathode ray tube
In this early tube (*bottom left*) cathode rays (electrons) which are emitted by the cathode (a) strike the end of the tube at (c). The anode (b) is cross-shaped and casts a similar shadow (d), so demonstrating that rays travel in straight lines.

1827), showed that a current would flow through wires connected to each end of a column composed of alternate discs of zinc and copper. This apparatus is called a Voltaic pile.

Our knowledge of electricity progressed enormously in the first half of the 19th century, due largely to the great English scientist, Michael Faraday (1791–1867). When electricity flows through a wire, it creates a magnetic field round it. Faraday suggested that the field round a magnet could therefore be used to produce electricity. By experimenting with an iron core, two magnets and some wires, his ideas about electromagnetism were confirmed. Faraday's work laid the foundations of our modern electrical industry. It has led to the creation of the generators which produce electricity for our homes and factories, and to the electric motors used in machines and trains.

Scientists went on to pass electricity through gases. By welding electrodes to glass tubes and then pumping the gas out, they produced the first type of fluorescent light tube. Research in this area has also led to the development of the cathode ray tube which is used in a television set.

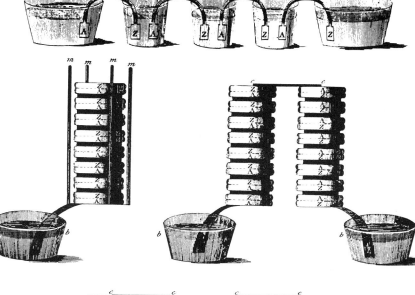

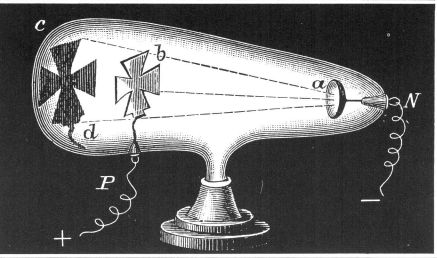

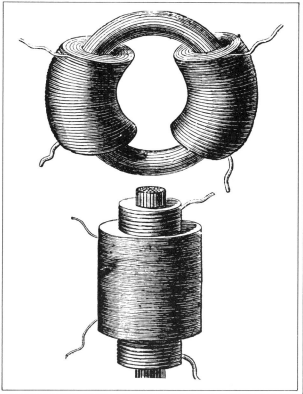

GRAVITY

Gravity at work
Stand on a box with a pencil in one hand and an orange in the other. Drop them both from the same height at the same time: they will hit the floor at

the same moment. Try this with other things, large and small, light and heavy. As Galileo discovered, all objects dropped from the same height hit the ground simultaneously. There are a few exceptions, like feathers or small pieces of paper. This

is because the air pushes against them and slows their fall. A parachute exploits this principle as it opens, bringing people down through the air slowly and safely.

When you jump up in the air, why do you come down again? And when you hold up a ruler and then let go, why does it fall to the floor? It is because the Earth pulls you and the ruler towards itself. The pull of the Earth is known as gravity.

Now think what happens when you weigh yourself on a pair of scales. If you weigh, say, 38 kg (6 stone), it means that gravity is pulling you towards the Earth's centre with a pull of 38 kg. Try weighing a few of the things you find around you, a book or a hat or a pair of roller skates. They each have a different weight. The greater the pull

of gravity on an object, the more it weighs; the smaller the pull, the less it weighs.

Over 300 years ago the famous Italian scientist, Galileo, discovered that gravity affects falling objects. He climbed to the top of the Leaning Tower of Pisa and tried dropping objects of varying weights to the ground at the same time. If you try the simple experiment on the left, you can find out what Galileo witnessed. Only when air is encouraged to push against the object does the rate of fall slow. Free-fall parachutists operate this principle to stay up in the air *(below left)*.

The pile-driver
Hold a coin about 10 cm (4 in) above a plate and let it drop. You will hear a slight clink. Now hold the coin up as high as you can and drop it again. You will hear a much louder noise. This is because the further an object drops, the faster gravity makes it fall. And the faster it drops, the harder it falls.
Machines called pile-drivers make use of this fact. They raise heavy metal weights into the air and then drop them onto pipes or logs. The impact of the falling weights drives the pipes deep into the ground *(left)*.

Low centre of gravity
By weighting an object so that its centre of gravity lies below the point of support, you can do lots of balancing tricks. For example, it is easy to balance a cup and two knives on your index finger if you cross the knives through the handle and fix them with a folded strip of

newspaper *(above)*. The heavy knife handles lower the centre of gravity to a point below your fingertip.

Peg trick
Would you believe that it is possible to balance one end of a clothes-peg, with a leather belt hung over it, on the tip of your finger? It is easy if you look at the drawings *(above and*

right) and follow the instructions carefully. Cut out a small chip from a clothes-peg, squeeze a belt into the nick, and balance the peg on the tip of your finger. The peg will lean sideways because of the slant at which the belt has been attached to it. In this way, you have moved the centre of gravity to a point below your fingertip.

If you put a ball on a table you will find that it stays there. The table is flat, so gravity cannot make the ball roll off. Now lift one end of the table: this time the ball will roll off, due to the force of gravity.

Gravity is useful to us in many different ways. Have you noticed, for instance, that our roads slant towards the kerb so that rain-water is affected by gravity and flows down towards the sewer openings? Draining-boards in our kitchens are also slanted, so that gravity pulls the water down into the sink. And fresh water flows down to our towns and cities from reservoirs which are sited on high land.

Gravity also helps children to enjoy themselves at a fair or in the playground. Gravity pulls them down the slide and enables them to fly backwards and forwards on a swing.

To understand the principle of a swing, get a piece of string and tie it round a small block of wood. Attach the other end of the string to a table so that the block can swing freely. If you give it a push it will move to and fro; when the block moves up and out, gravity pulls it down and back again.

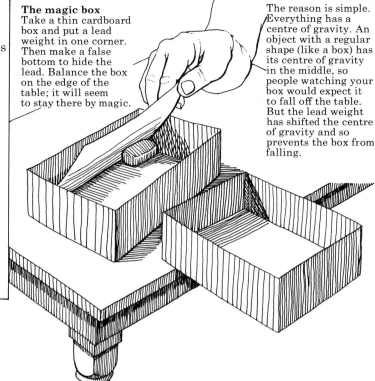

The magic box
Take a thin cardboard box and put a lead weight in one corner. Then make a false bottom to hide the lead. Balance the box on the edge of the table; it will seem to stay there by magic.

The reason is simple. Everything has a centre of gravity. An object with a regular shape (like a box) has its centre of gravity in the middle, so people watching your box would expect it to fall off the table. But the lead weight has shifted the centre of gravity and so prevents the box from falling.

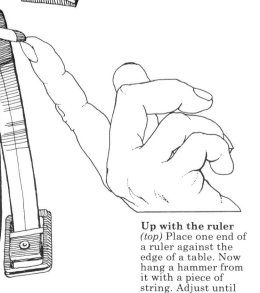

Clown on a tightrope
Take some stiff card and draw a clown like the one below. Cut it out and glue a small coin to each hand. Glue some paper over the coins to hide them and then paint the clown in bright colours on his other side – the one that will face the audience. Make him look as circusy as possible, to give your friends the feeling that they are watching a really special performance. Now surprise them by making your clown balance on his hands on almost anything from the tip of a pencil to a piece of thread, as shown. Although he may look as if he is going to fall, he does not. This is because the weight of the coins has shifted his centre of gravity to below his nose.

Up with the ruler
(top) Place one end of a ruler against the edge of a table. Now hang a hammer from it with a piece of string. Adjust until the ruler is steady. What has happened is that the hammer head put the centre of gravity below the table. The string made the hammer act as a lever and push up on the end of the ruler.

Candle see-saw
Stand a cork on some paper and push a darning needle through it, as shown. Find two identical candles and fix one to each end of the needle. Now push a knitting needle through the cork at right-angles to the darning needle and balance the apparatus on two upturned glass tumblers. At this stage, the centre of gravity of the see-saw lies exactly along the axis: this means that the apparatus is balanced. Light one candle, then the other. As they drip in turn, the centre of gravity will shift and set up a see-saw motion.

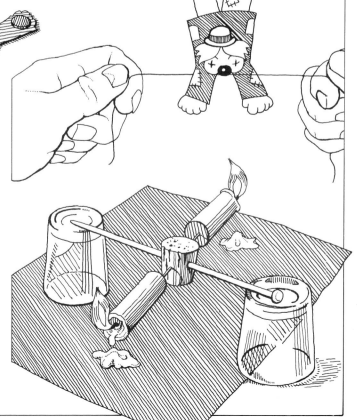

LEVERS AND PULLEYS

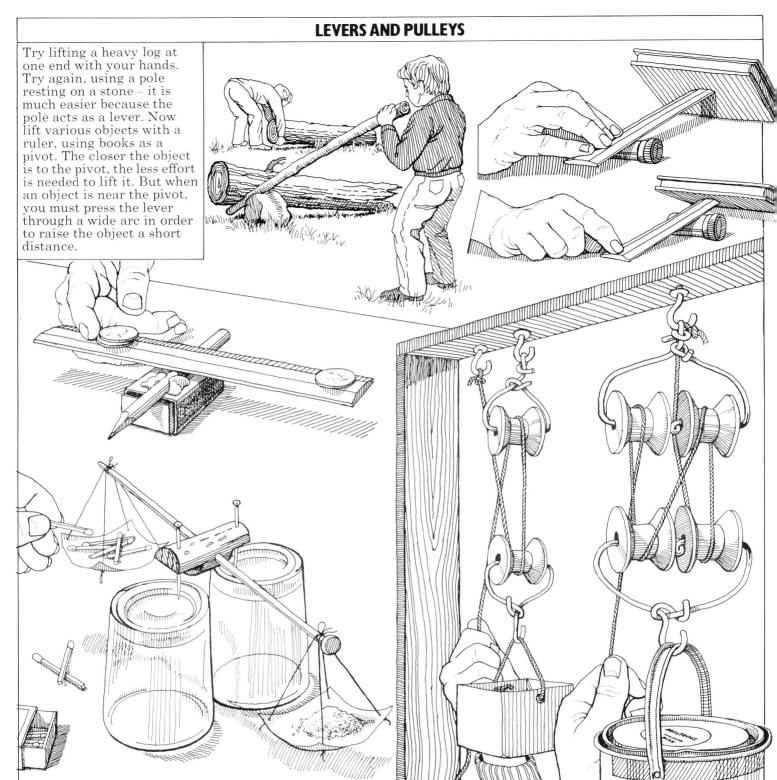

Try lifting a heavy log at one end with your hands. Try again, using a pole resting on a stone – it is much easier because the pole acts as a lever. Now lift various objects with a ruler, using books as a pivot. The closer the object is to the pivot, the less effort is needed to lift it. But when an object is near the pivot, you must press the lever through a wide arc in order to raise the object a short distance.

Using levers
Use modelling clay to fix a round pencil to the lid of a small box. Balance a ruler across the pencil, at right angles to it, and put a coin on one end of the ruler. Put two more identical coins on top of each other and slide them carefully along from the other end of the ruler until it is balanced. If you measure the distances between the centres of the coins and the pivot, you will make an interesting

discovery: the distance of the single coin from the pivot is twice that of the two coins from the pivot. A see-saw is also a type of lever and operates on the same principle as the experiment above. A light person can balance a heavier person on a see-saw if the heavier person sits nearer the pivot. A pair of scales is yet another example of a lever. You can make your own scales with a cork, a long knitting needle and two pins.

Cut two pieces out of the cork, as shown in the picture, push the needle through, and use the pins to form the pivot. Cut two equal-sized squares of thin card and hang them with cotton from the ends of the knitting needle. If you balance the cork on two glass tumblers, you can weigh light objects like grains of rice or feathers. You will find that it is a very sensitive balance.
Make a pulley system
Pulleys are often used

to help us lift things. You can see them in cranes and over lift doors, hauling up heavy loads. You also find them in the racks used to dry clothes in old-fashioned kitchens. Pulleys have always been used to haul up the sails in sailing ships, and modern ships still use them to load and unload cargo. Although a single pulley will lift a load, a double pulley makes the job much easier. You can make your own model pulley

from two large cotton reels, some thick flexible wire, and some string. Take two pieces of wire, each about 30 cm (1 ft) long. Bend them through the reels and make a hook for each reel, as shown in the picture above. Attach one reel to the top of a doorway, using a strong hook. Now take a long piece of string. Tie one end to a hook about 5 cm (2 in) away from the first hook and thread the rest round the two reels, as shown. Finally,

hang a weight on the lower pulley. You will find that the pull needed is only about half the weight you lift, though for every 30 cm (1 ft) you lift the weight, you have to pull 60 cm (2 ft) of string through the pulleys. The more pulleys you use, the easier it is to lift the weight. Try making even more ambitious models with four or eight pulleys.

MAGNETISM

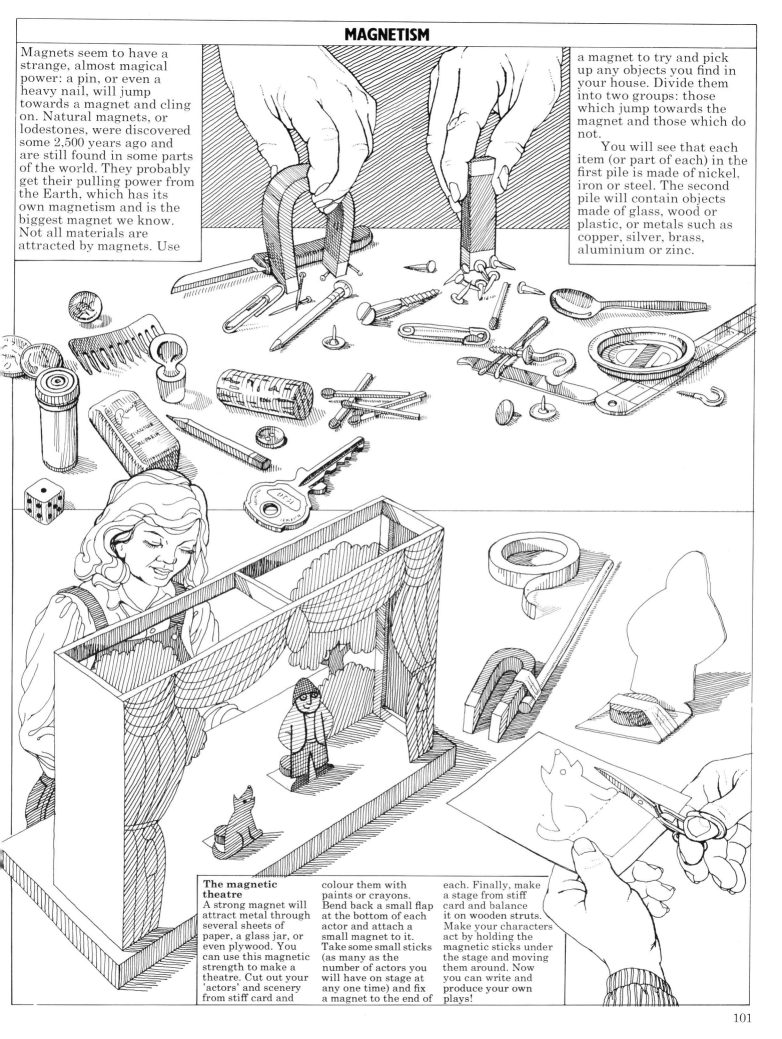

Magnets seem to have a strange, almost magical power: a pin, or even a heavy nail, will jump towards a magnet and cling on. Natural magnets, or lodestones, were discovered some 2,500 years ago and are still found in some parts of the world. They probably get their pulling power from the Earth, which has its own magnetism and is the biggest magnet we know. Not all materials are attracted by magnets. Use a magnet to try and pick up any objects you find in your house. Divide them into two groups: those which jump towards the magnet and those which do not.

You will see that each item (or part of each) in the first pile is made of nickel, iron or steel. The second pile will contain objects made of glass, wood or plastic, or metals such as copper, silver, brass, aluminium or zinc.

The magnetic theatre

A strong magnet will attract metal through several sheets of paper, a glass jar, or even plywood. You can use this magnetic strength to make a theatre. Cut out your 'actors' and scenery from stiff card and colour them with paints or crayons. Bend back a small flap at the bottom of each actor and attach a small magnet to it. Take some small sticks (as many as the number of actors you will have on stage at any one time) and fix a magnet to the end of each. Finally, make a stage from stiff card and balance it on wooden struts. Make your characters act by holding the magnetic sticks under the stage and moving them around. Now you can write and produce your own plays!

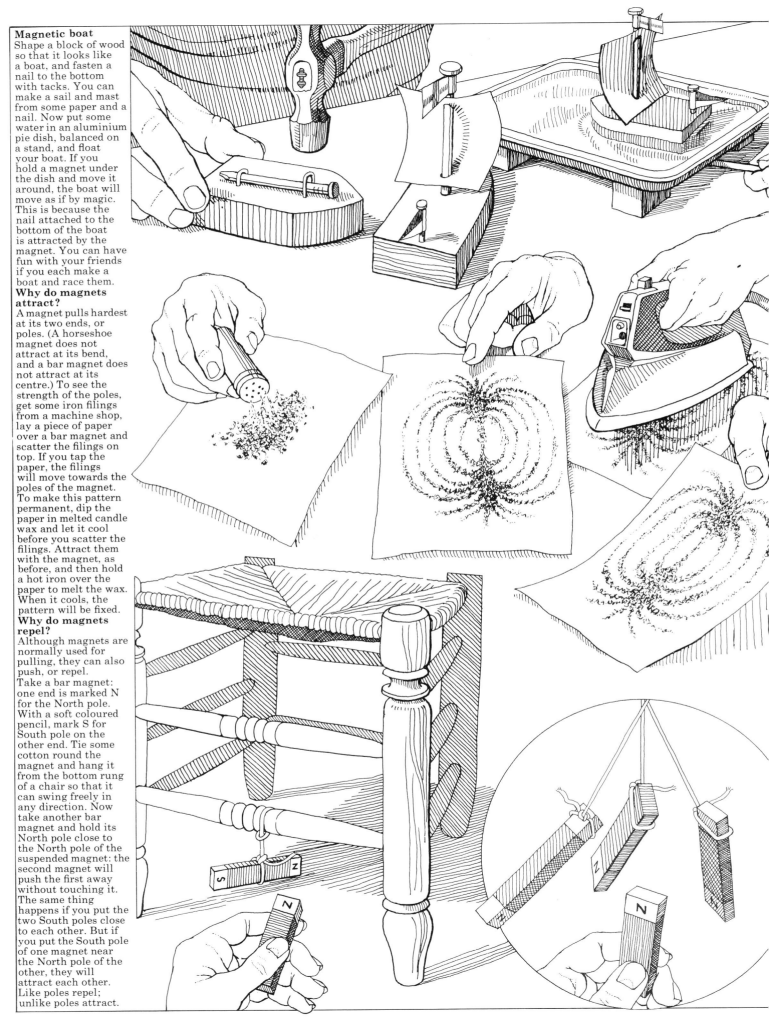

Magnetic boat

Shape a block of wood so that it looks like a boat, and fasten a nail to the bottom with tacks. You can make a sail and mast from some paper and a nail. Now put some water in an aluminium pie dish, balanced on a stand, and float your boat. If you hold a magnet under the dish and move it around, the boat will move as if by magic. This is because the nail attached to the bottom of the boat is attracted by the magnet. You can have fun with your friends if you each make a boat and race them.

Why do magnets attract?

A magnet pulls hardest at its two ends, or poles. (A horseshoe magnet does not attract at its bend, and a bar magnet does not attract at its centre.) To see the strength of the poles, get some iron filings from a machine shop, lay a piece of paper over a bar magnet and scatter the filings on top. If you tap the paper, the filings will move towards the poles of the magnet. To make this pattern permanent, dip the paper in melted candle wax and let it cool before you scatter the filings. Attract them with the magnet, as before, and then hold a hot iron over the paper to melt the wax. When it cools, the pattern will be fixed.

Why do magnets repel?

Although magnets are normally used for pulling, they can also push, or repel.
Take a bar magnet: one end is marked N for the North pole. With a soft coloured pencil, mark S for South pole on the other end. Tie some cotton round the magnet and hang it from the bottom rung of a chair so that it can swing freely in any direction. Now take another bar magnet and hold its North pole close to the North pole of the suspended magnet: the second magnet will push the first away without touching it. The same thing happens if you put the two South poles close to each other. But if you put the South pole of one magnet near the North pole of the other, they will attract each other. Like poles repel; unlike poles attract.

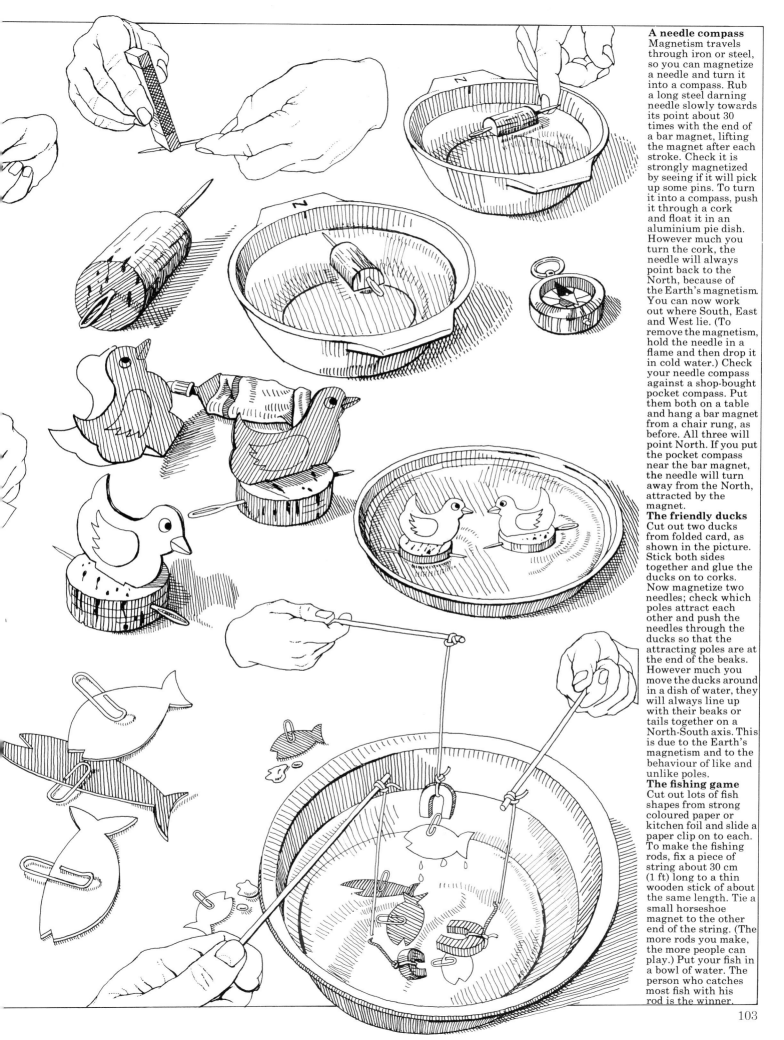

A needle compass

Magnetism travels through iron or steel, so you can magnetize a needle and turn it into a compass. Rub a long steel darning needle slowly towards its point about 30 times with the end of a bar magnet, lifting the magnet after each stroke. Check it is strongly magnetized by seeing if it will pick up some pins. To turn it into a compass, push it through a cork and float it in an aluminium pie dish. However much you turn the cork, the needle will always point back to the North, because of the Earth's magnetism. You can now work out where South, East and West lie. (To remove the magnetism, hold the needle in a flame and then drop it in cold water.) Check your needle compass against a shop-bought pocket compass. Put them both on a table and hang a bar magnet from a chair rung, as before. All three will point North. If you put the pocket compass near the bar magnet, the needle will turn away from the North, attracted by the magnet.

The friendly ducks

Cut out two ducks from folded card, as shown in the picture. Stick both sides together and glue the ducks on to corks. Now magnetize two needles; check which poles attract each other and push the needles through the ducks so that the attracting poles are at the end of the beaks. However much you move the ducks around in a dish of water, they will always line up with their beaks or tails together on a North-South axis. This is due to the Earth's magnetism and to the behaviour of like and unlike poles.

The fishing game

Cut out lots of fish shapes from strong coloured paper or kitchen foil and slide a paper clip on to each. To make the fishing rods, fix a piece of string about 30 cm (1 ft) long to a thin wooden stick of about the same length. Tie a small horseshoe magnet to the other end of the string. (The more rods you make, the more people can play.) Put your fish in a bowl of water. The person who catches most fish with his rod is the winner.

ELECTRICITY

Nowadays we tend to take electricity for granted, yet it is one of the most versatile and widely used sources of power we know. Wherever you look, you can see electricity at work. It is used to ring doorbells and milk cows; it brings us television and lights our streets at night. Even the paper used for this book was produced by electrically powered machines.

Electricity is one of the most mysterious sources of power. Here is a simple explanation of how it works. Everything in the world is made up of millions of tiny atoms. At the centre of each atom is a nucleus which contains minute particles called protons. Circling round the nucleus are even smaller particles called electrons. There are always as many electrons as protons. Each electron has a negative electrical charge, shown like this: ⊖, while each proton has a positive electrical charge, shown as: ⊕. A material which allows electricity to pass through it easily has one 'free' electron which orbits outside the others and can be separated from its atom, as demonstrated in the upper drawing below. Such materials are called good electrical conductors.

The pictures below show some of the ways in which electricity helps us. It powers domestic objects and railway locomotives, and, in battery form, a short-range type of car.

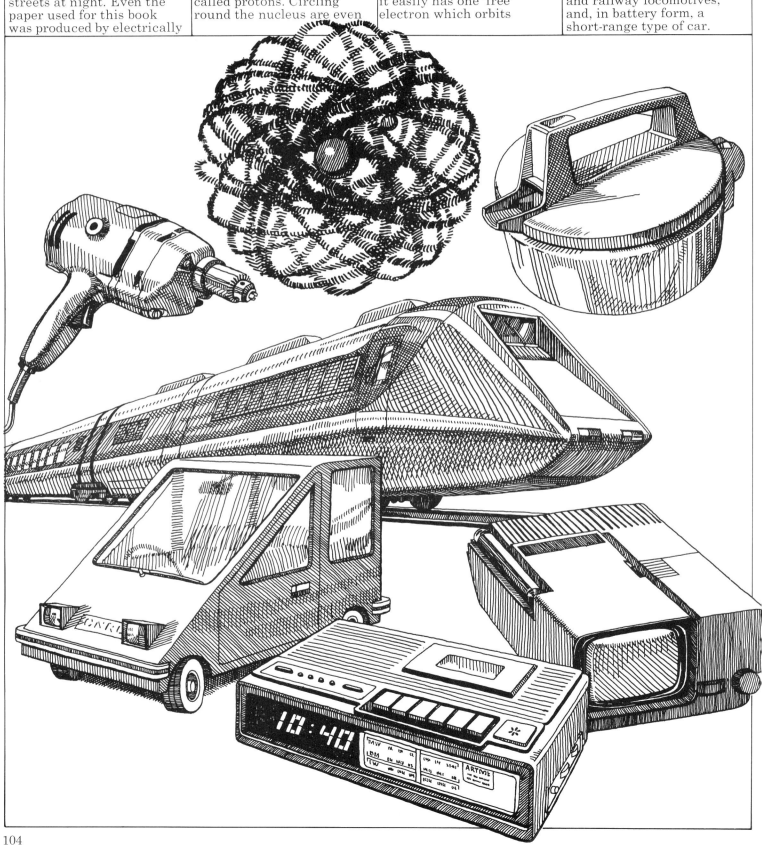

Complete the circuit
Graphite (the 'lead' in a pencil) is a good conductor of electricity. You can see this for yourself by trying a simple experiment. Connect a torch bulb and a battery, using a pair of scissors and a pencil, as below. As soon as everything is connected, the bulb will light up. The electrical current from the battery flows through the metal of the scissors, lights up the bulb, and then flows back to the battery through the graphite shaft in the pencil. Being a good conductor, the graphite completes the circuit.

Electric current
When a metal wire is connected to a battery, the free electrons of the atoms in the metal pass from one atom to another. This movement of electrons is called electric current. Although these free electrons only move a few millimetres a second, electricity is instantly produced. A simple experiment will help explain this. Line up some marbles between two heavy books. If you push one of the end marbles, the others will move too. In just the same way, electrons all start to move as soon as an electric current is produced.

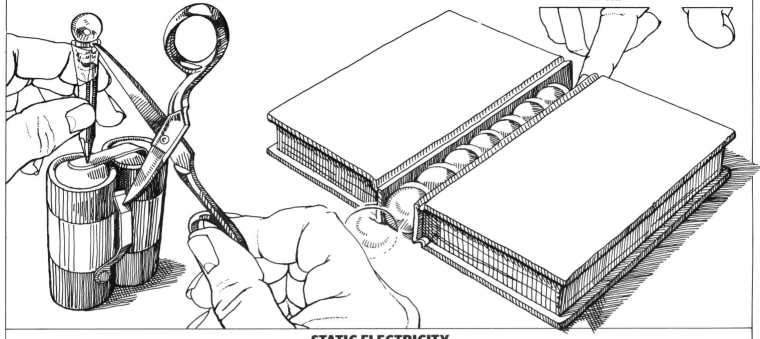

STATIC ELECTRICITY

Sometimes you can hear electricity on your body. If you stroke a cat, comb your hair on a cool, dry day, or pull off clothes made from man-made fibres, you often hear a crackling sound. It comes from static electricity. You can see and feel static electricity if you shuffle your shoes on a thick pile carpet or rug and then reach out with one finger for the metal doorknob in a dark room. Just before you touch the knob, a tiny spark will jump from your finger to the metal, and you will feel a small, tingling shock.

Lightning is another phenomenon caused by static electricity. The experiment on page 92 shows that it is also due to friction, or the effect of rubbing one thing against another.

Electric tricks
As the teeth of a comb pass through the strands of your hair, electrons are transferred across and the comb becomes charged with static electricity. Comb your hair, then immediately hold the comb near some small pieces of tissue paper. They will jump up and stick to the comb, attracted by its static electricity. They will remain attracted for a short time, until the electricity in the comb has leaked away through your body. When a comb is charged with static electricity, it can also be used to bend water. Turn on a tap so that a gentle stream of water flows into the sink. If you hold the charged comb near it, the water will bend towards the comb. (Do not let the comb get wet, or its static electricity will leak away.)

You can create static electricity in another way. Put a piece of paper on the table and rub it with a pencil. Then lift up one end of the paper and let it go again. It will immediately jump back to the table and you will hear the crackle that was caused by the static electricity.

The magic balloon

Tie a blown-up balloon on a long string. Rub it on a wool sweater for 30 seconds and let it go; it will stick to the ceiling or wall, held there by static electricity. It becomes electrically charged when rubbed because it removes negatively charged electrons from the sweater. Because charged bodies attract uncharged bodies, the balloon clings there until the charges become equal. (In a dry atmosphere this can take hours – the electrons flow slowly into the ceiling, which is a poor conductor.) Next, rub two balloons on a sweater and hold them up in one hand. They will repel each other because both are negatively charged.

Salt and pepper trick

If you scatter ground pepper and coarse salt on the table, you can use static electricity to separate them. Rub a plastic spoon with a woollen cloth so it becomes electrically charged. Hold it over the mixture. It will first attract the pepper, which is lighter. To pick up the salt which remains, hold the spoon lower and it too will be attracted.

The snake-charmer

You can be an Oriental snake-charmer by using a plastic pen as your flute! Cut out a spiral coil from some tissue paper and draw a snake's head at one end. Bend the head up and lay your snake on a tin lid. Rub a pen on something made of wool and hold it over the coil. It will rise up like a living snake. This is because the pen takes electrons from the wool and so attracts the uncharged paper. When the paper touches the pen, it takes part of the electricity and passes it on to the metal lid, which is a good conductor. The paper is then uncharged once more and so stays unattracted as the pen loses its charge.

Fast-moving breakfast

Fill a dish with any breakfast cereal which is made of puffed rice. Next rub a plastic spoon on something made of wool until the spoon is electrically charged. If you hold it over the dish, the pieces of puffed rice will jump up and stick to the spoon and then suddenly shoot off in all directions. Why does this happen? The puffed rice is attracted to the spoon until some of the electrons have passed from the spoon to the rice. Once the rice and the spoon have the same electrical charge, the rice shoots off. This is because – as we have seen on previous pages – like charges repel each other.

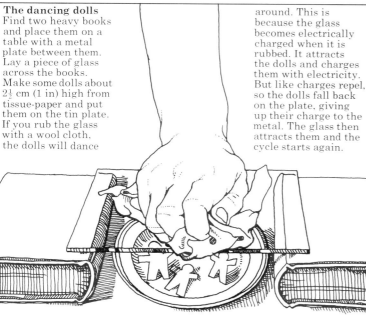

The dancing dolls

Find two heavy books and place them on a table with a metal plate between them. Lay a piece of glass across the books. Make some dolls about 2½ cm (1 in) high from tissue-paper and put them on the tin plate. If you rub the glass with a wool cloth, the dolls will dance around. This is because the glass becomes electrically charged when it is rubbed. It attracts the dolls and charges them with electricity. But like charges repel, so the dolls fall back on the plate, giving up their charge to the metal. The glass then attracts them and the cycle starts again.

Jumping silver balls

Rub a long-playing record with some wool and stand it on top of a glass tumbler. Make some small balls of silver paper and toss them on to the record. They will jump around, repelled and attracted by each other. This is because the electricity on the record is distributed in irregular fields and the balls take up different charges. Some repel each other, while others are attracted to each other.

CURRENT ELECTRICITY

It is fun to play around with static electricity but – because it stays in one place and does not travel along wires – it cannot run machinery or bring light to our homes. To do these jobs we need current electricity, which travels along the wires from power plants and is fed directly into our towns and cities.

The wires from power plants are called transmission lines; they are normally made of copper because it is an excellent conductor. They have to be insulated so that the electricity stays in the wire and keeps on the right path. Materials which are poor conductors are used as insulators. If you look at the broken end of an old lamp flex and scrape off some of the covering, you will find two copper wires, each wrapped in rubber in order to insulate it and make it safe.

The next few pages suggest some simple experiments you can do with current electricity. Many of the objects shown below will already be within reach of your home laboratory, such as the hammer and nails. But you may need to go to an electrical shop to buy 3.5-volt torch bulbs and a bulb-holder, a 4.5-volt battery, and lengths of flex and florist's wire.

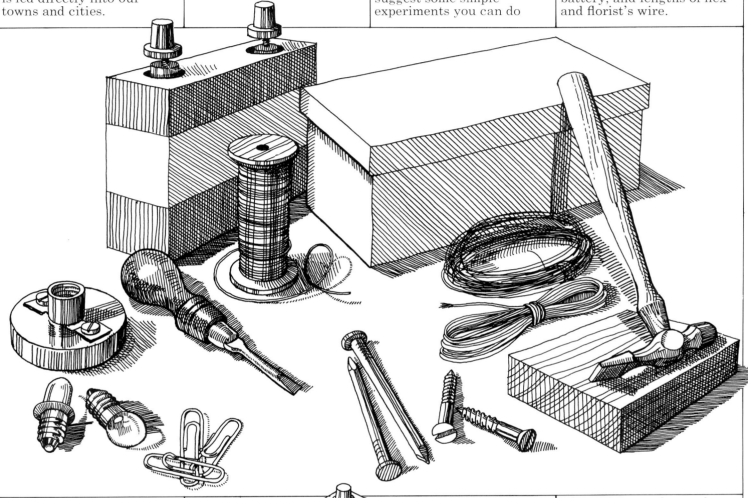

How a battery works

Electrons will not move along a wire by themselves. A force is needed to push them along and thus create the electric current. This electro-motive force is produced by a battery. Its strength is measured in volts, named after Count Alessandro Volta (1745–1827), the Italian electrical pioneer who invented the battery. Batteries are not as powerful as the electricity supplied to our homes, but they are portable and safe. On no account experiment with the plugs and sockets in your house; this is very dangerous.

The picture shows that a battery is composed of a large number of cells. It is full of a liquid called the electrolyte, made up of billions of positive and negative particles. Two rods called electrodes are submerged in the electrolyte. A chemical reaction in the liquid sends positive particles to one electrode and negative particles to the other. When a wire is connected to the electrodes, electric current flows along the wire and lights up a bulb. The current stops flowing only when the chemicals in the electrolyte are used up. Liquids spill easily, so dry batteries are used in things like torches. They still have two electrodes – a carbon rod and a zinc case – but the cell has a paste electrolyte sealed inside a case.

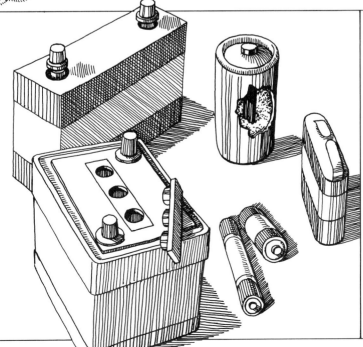

107

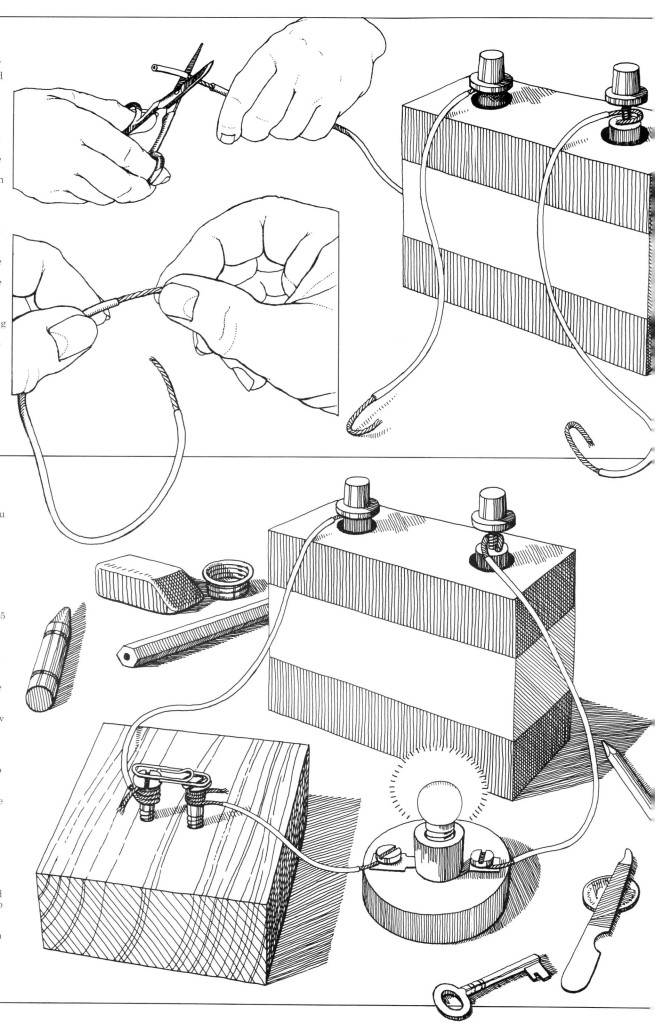

How to make a circuit

With a pair of scissors, strip off about 1.5 cm (½ in) of plastic from each end of two pieces of flex. Be careful not to sever the wires. Twist the wires together to make a neat end. To connect the pieces of flex to the battery, hook the bare wires round the terminals and tighten them by turning in a clockwise direction. To wire up the bulb holder, undo the screws slightly, hook the wires of the flex round, tighten the screws and put in the bulb. The battery is now connected to the bulb holder, so the light will go on. The electric current from the battery runs along the flex, through the bulb, and back to the battery. Its path is called a circuit. If you cut the flex, the circuit will be incomplete and the light will not go on. But if the cut wires touch once more, the bulb will light up again.

Conductors and insulators

Use a battery to find out which materials conduct electricity and which do not. You will need: a block of wood about 15 cm (6 in) square, 1 m (3 ft) of flex, a torch bulb and holder, and two flat-headed screws about 4 cm (1½ in) long. Partially sink the screws into the wood, with the tops 1.5 cm (½ in) apart. Cut a piece of flex 25 cm (10 in) long, remove the insulating plastic as in the experiment above, and wind one end tightly round one of the screws; fasten the other end to the battery terminal. Now do the same with a second piece of flex, but this time fasten it to the bulb holder. Connect the holder to the terminal with a third piece of flex. Attach the bulb to the holder: it will not light up. (Wood is a poor conductor, so the block breaks the circuit.) To complete the circuit, close the gap between the screws. First try a paper clip: it is a good conductor, so the bulb lights up. Now test other objects in the same way. Try coins, a pencil, a key, a bottle top, a nail file, a crayon, a comb, a tin can, a nail, a piece of card and a pair of scissors.

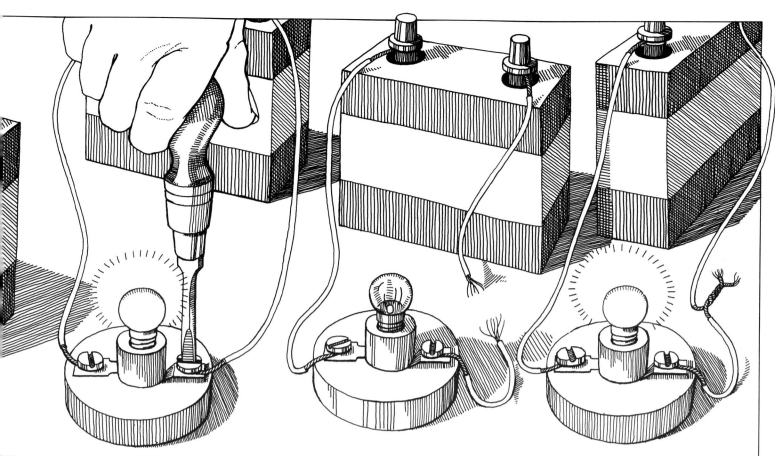

Electric light

How does electricity make a torch bulb light up? The explanation lies in the very fine wire inside. The American scientist, Thomas Edison (1847–1931), made the first electric light bulb in 1879. He sealed a cotton thread inside a glass bulb, pumped out the air, and passed an electric current along the thread until it glowed. The thread was so fine that the electrons passing through bumped into the atoms of the thread, making it get very hot. Edison's revolutionary incandescent light bulb glowed for some 40 hours before it finally burned out.

A modern light bulb works on exactly the same principle. The wire is so fine that it resists the flow of electricity. It gets very hot and starts to glow. It cannot actually burn because there is no air inside the bulb. In most light bulbs, the wire is made of a tough metal called tungsten, which can glow for hundreds of hours before it breaks. It has been calculated that, when a light is switched on, about 3 trillion free electrons pass through the bulb filament every second.

Switches

Light switches are used to make and break circuits. You can make a simple switch to add to your circuit. Take the wooden block with two screws in it that you used for the experiment on page 108. Find a strip of tin about 1.5 cm ($\frac{1}{2}$ in) wide, and 1.5 cm ($\frac{1}{2}$ in) longer than the distance between the two screws. Use a hammer and nail to make a hole in one end of the tin strip. Then take one of the screws out of the wood and put it back with the tin fixed firmly underneath it. The loose end should be bent up so it does not touch the other screw. Now connect your light and battery to the switch by pressing the strip down on the screw. You have now completed the circuit: electricity travels from one terminal of the battery through the wire and the tin strip to the light and the second terminal. The bulb will not light up if the tin is not touching the second screw. Thus the strip acts as a switch.

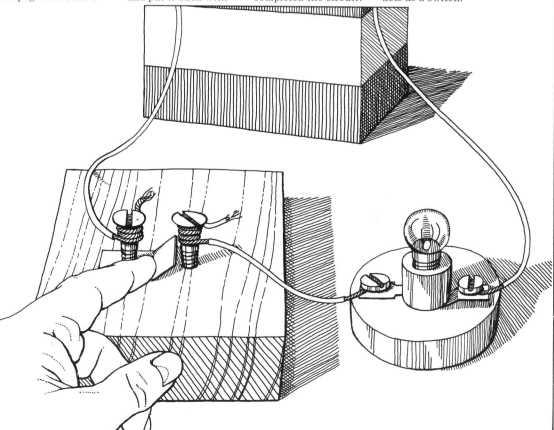

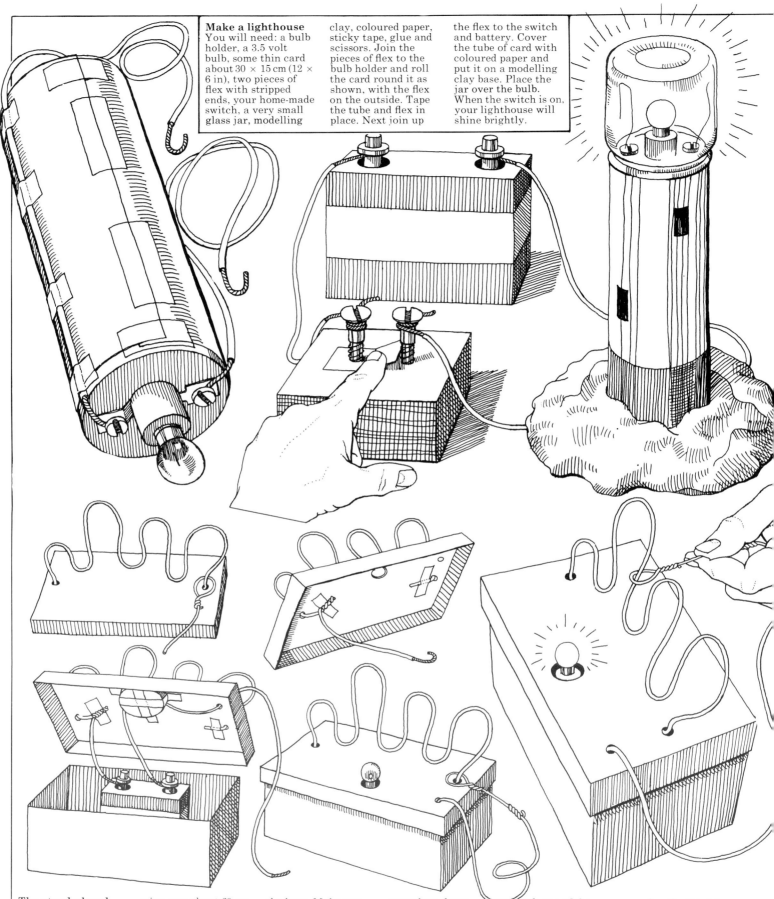

Make a lighthouse

You will need: a bulb holder, a 3.5 volt bulb, some thin card about 30 × 15 cm (12 × 6 in), two pieces of flex with stripped ends, your home-made switch, a very small glass jar, modelling clay, coloured paper, sticky tape, glue and scissors. Join the pieces of flex to the bulb holder and roll the card round it as shown, with the flex on the outside. Tape the tube and flex in place. Next join up the flex to the switch and battery. Cover the tube of card with coloured paper and put it on a modelling clay base. Place the jar over the bulb. When the switch is on, your lighthouse will shine brightly.

The steady-hand game

To make this game, you need: a bulb holder; a cardboard box with a lid; a 3.5 volt bulb; a 4.5 volt battery; three pieces of flex with stripped ends; two pieces of florists' wire, one about 60 cm (2 ft) long and one about 30 cm (1 ft) long; scissors and sticky tape. Make a loop in one end of the shorter wire. Make lots of bends in the other wire, as shown, and thread it through the loop. Make two holes in the top of the box lid and push the ends of the bent wire through. Bend back one end and tape it to the lid. Twist one end of a piece of flex round the other end of the wire and tape them down. Attach the bulb to the holder. Make a hole in the box lid and push the bulb up through it. Keep the holder in the box and attach two pieces of flex to it. Make a hole in the lid and push one of these pieces of flex through, twisting it round the end of the wire with a loop in it. Join the other flex to one terminal of the battery. Connect the second terminal to the end of the bent wire, using the third flex. Place the battery in the box beside the bulb holder. Put the lid on and try to pass the loop along the bent wire without lighting up the bulb. The more bends, the harder the game.

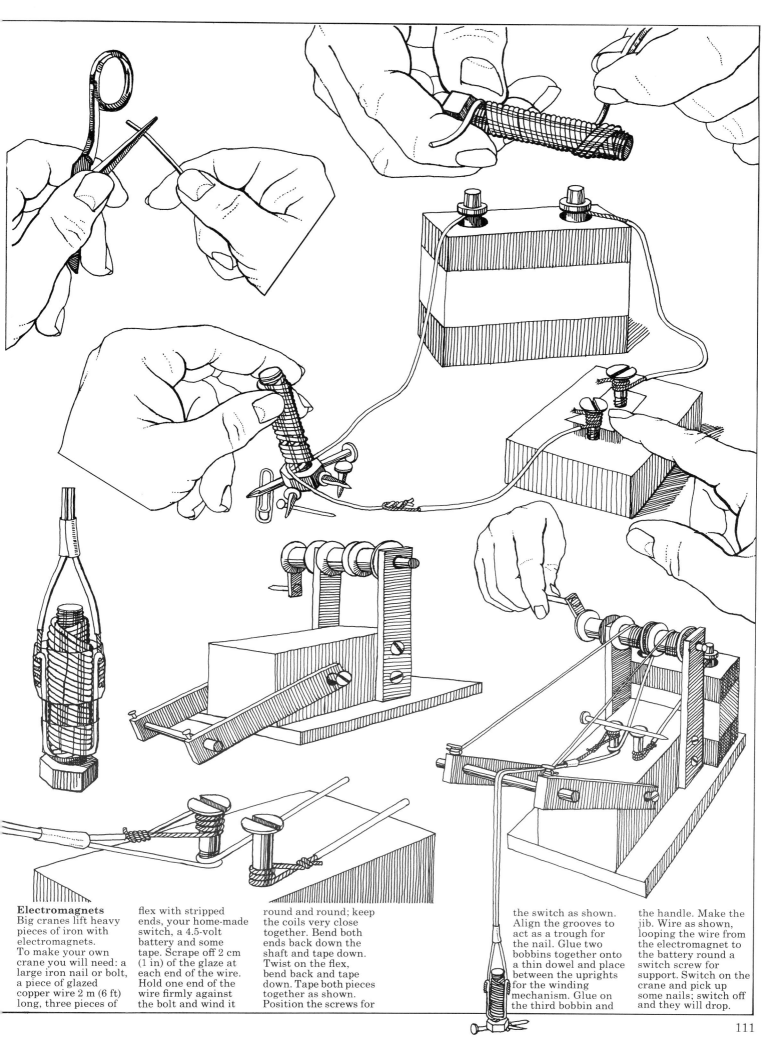

Electromagnets

Big cranes lift heavy pieces of iron with electromagnets.

To make your own crane you will need: a large iron nail or bolt, a piece of glazed copper wire 2 m (6 ft) long, three pieces of flex with stripped ends, your home-made switch, a 4.5-volt battery and some tape. Scrape off 2 cm (1 in) of the glaze at each end of the wire. Hold one end of the wire firmly against the bolt and wind it round and round; keep the coils very close together. Bend both ends back down the shaft and tape down. Twist on the flex, bend back and tape down. Tape both pieces together as shown. Position the screws for the switch as shown. Align the grooves to act as a trough for the nail. Glue two bobbins together onto a thin dowel and place between the uprights for the winding mechanism. Glue on the third bobbin and the handle. Make the jib. Wire as shown, looping the wire from the electromagnet to the battery round a switch screw for support. Switch on the crane and pick up some nails; switch off and they will drop.

Chemistry has always played an important part in our lives. For centuries, men have made dyes from the indigo plant, extracted and made use of gold, and known about the healing properties of certain plants.

In pre-Christian times in Greece, Egypt and East Asia, an early form of chemistry, known as alchemy, was widely practised. It continued to be important for some 2,000 years. It was not until 1661 that a young Irish nobleman, called Robert Boyle, challenged the unproved theories of the alchemists. In his book, *The Sceptical Chymist*, Boyle argued that chemistry must become more critical; it should be based on experiment, rather than on theory.

The ancient Greeks believed that the entire world was composed of four elements: earth, fire, air and water. Using his suggested experimental approach, Boyle set out to discover the true elements. One of his findings was that there is a part of the air which is necessary for both respiration and combustion. Thanks to Boyle, research has continued in this field and we now know that the world is composed of about 90 elements.

Towards the end of the 18th century various scientists, including Henry Cavendish and Joseph Priestley, discovered compounds within air, thus proving that it is not a single element. The study of gases then began in earnest. Cavendish showed that hydrogen is distinct from other combustible gases, and also succeeded in separating nitrogen from the other elements in air. He then discovered that water, too, is a compound of different substances. In 1766, he heated hydrogen with oxygen in a closed test tube under electric sparks, and found that this produced a quantity of water equal in weight to that of the gases used for the experiment.

Another field in which important developments were made was that of organic chemistry. Although this term was originally used to describe

7

THE SCIENCE OF CHEMISTRY

work on the substances found in living animals and plants, it was later realized that most of these substances are compounds of the element carbon. So 'organic chemistry' came to be used to describe the chemistry of all compounds of carbon, of which there are very large numbers.

By the late 19th century, people had begun to build chemistry laboratories on an industrial scale. Illustrated here is an example of a dye factory in Paris at that time. In order to manufacture dyes on a large scale, chemical equipment had changed radically since the early days. The mortar used by the first chemists had grown into a stone-crushing machine, and the retort had become a huge boiler.

The science of chemistry has grown out of the study of chemical changes. When a change of this kind takes place, a single substance turns into one or more new substances, each with different properties. There are numerous examples of such changes in the world around us: iron rusts, wood chars, milk turns sour, and fruit and vegetables rot, all as a result of chemical change.

Developments in the field of chemistry are constantly changing our lives. Our homes are now more comfortable than before, we can travel faster, and many illnesses can be cured – all because of new materials which were unknown to our grandparents. Even the clothes we wear are

Chemical code (*above*)
The table of 'chymical' and other 'characters' shows how the scientists of earlier times developed a language of symbols to represent a range of substances, here from acid to zinc. Some employ letters of the alphabet, and others are diagrammatic, such as that for sand with its grains. The sign for Mercury, on the other hand, adopts the ancient symbol used by astrologers.

Die factory (*left*)
Workers are shown making die at the 19th-century works of Poirier & Chappat in St Denis.

bleached, dyed and finished by chemical processes. And rayon is a synthetic material, made chemically out of wood chips.

Our bodies are only able to function because of chemistry. The food, air and water we take in are transformed by complicated chemical changes, and so form our bones and flesh, supply us with energy, and ultimately keep us alive. We also use chemistry in the kitchen. When we cook, vinegar, baking-powder, and the starch in foods like potatoes are simply the ingredients in a chemical process.

Atoms and molecules
The four most important words to any chemist are: atom, molecule, element and compound. When a house is being built, you can watch the materials being moved, as the bricks or stones are put into place. During a chemical reaction, on the other hand, you cannot actually see everything that happens. The materials moved around are such small units that they cannot be seen with the naked eye. But scientists have long known that there must be some mechanical shifting of materials in order to build the new substances which are produced.

Elements are made up of tiny particles, called atoms. These are so small that the diameter of an atom has been calculated to be less than one four-millionth of a centimetre (one ten-millionth of an inch). If 30,000 atoms were piled up, one on top of the other, the height of the pile would only be equal to the thickness of a piece of paper. Atoms do not exist alone

The changing pepper
Chemical changes happen all around us every day. Here a pepper was stood on a shelf and left to rot. The fruit's source of nourishment was removed when it was picked from the parent plant. From that moment it was dead, and automatically began to decay. The chemical changes that occurred to it were then recorded every so often by the camera. In due course the pepper shrivelled as it dried out, and split open to expose the seeds from which new plants might grow.

Many gardeners profit from this natural process to keep up their stocks of plants without having to buy fresh packets of seed each year. You can do the same after the broad bean plants in your garden have flowered and fruited. Select one plant and leave it until the pods wither and turn black. Then uproot the plant and hang it upside down over a sheet of newspaper in a shed or garage. The ripe beans, suitably dried, will drop onto the paper and can be stored in a cool dry place ready for planting out the following season.

Atom system
This model shows the make-up, much enlarged, of a molecule composed of just two atoms. Atoms can join with others of their own kind or with atoms of other elements.

for long. They prefer to join up with other atoms to form part of a larger grouping, called a molecule. They may join with other atoms of the same kind as themselves, or with atoms of other elements. Some molecules contain only two atoms, while others contain a great many. Any substance whose molecules contain more than one kind of atom is called a compound.

Elements and compounds
A chemical compound can be separated into its component parts. You can break down water, for example, into hydrogen and oxygen. But no matter how hard you try, you cannot break down hydrogen or oxygen by chemical processes. Basic substances like these are called chemical elements. Scientists do not usually write out their full names; they use standard, internationally recognized abbreviations, on the model of the early versions illustrated opposite.

The simplest way of naming a compound is to refer to the elements of which it is composed. For example, water is made up of two parts of hydrogen to one of oxygen, so the chemical formula for water is H_2O.

The only way to learn more about chemistry is to go on experimenting. Over the centuries, chemists have discovered more than 500,000 different substances – and the list is still growing. You can conduct your own chemical experiments if you follow the suggestions on the next few pages. You will find it fun, and you will also learn more about the world we live in.

Water is one of the most important compounds on Earth. It is composed of two elements, oxygen and hydrogen. It is not difficult to make water from these two elements. For example, whenever a substance containing hydrogen is burned, water is formed. It appears first in the form of a vapour, and this then cools down into the liquid water. As another example, when petrol burns in an engine, the hydrogen in the fuel combines with oxygen in the air to form water. Each 4½ l (1 gal) of petrol a car uses produces about 4 l (7 pt) of water.

Water is vital to us all because it forms solutions with many other important substances. It is also important as a solvent, and figures in many of the experiments demonstrated in this book.

There are many other solvents besides water, though none of them can dissolve as many substances. However, some will dissolve things that water cannot touch. For example, carbon tetrachloride and naphtha will dissolve oil and grease, which water cannot do.

Look around your house and see how many different solvents you can find. (The picture on the right will give you some ideas.) Check which substances will dissolve in each other, and whether any of them will dissolve in water.

It is also interesting to see whether hot or cold solvents are more effective. A race between two cubes of sugar will enable you to find the answer. Take two cups: fill one with boiling water and the other with cold. Drop one cube of sugar into each cup at the same time, and stir both equally. You will see that the sugar will dissolve much faster in the hot water than in the cold. Hot solvents are usually more effective than cold, and heat is important in chemical experiments.

Salt and water are an exception, however. When these two are mixed, the salt dissolves just as quickly whether you add it to hot water or cold.

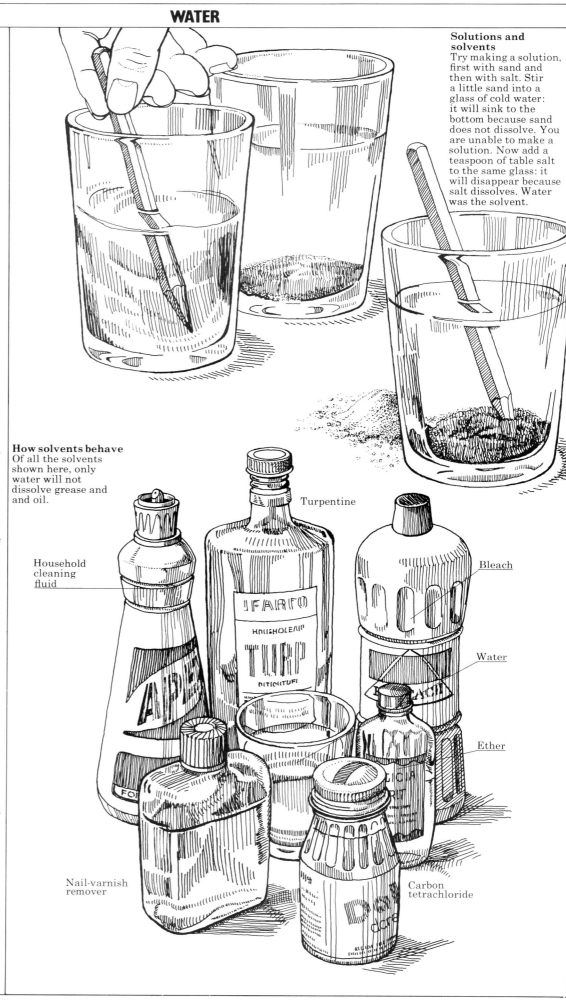

Solutions and solvents
Try making a solution, first with sand and then with salt. Stir a little sand into a glass of cold water: it will sink to the bottom because sand does not dissolve. You are unable to make a solution. Now add a teaspoon of table salt to the same glass: it will disappear because salt dissolves. Water was the solvent.

How solvents behave
Of all the solvents shown here, only water will not dissolve grease and and oil.

Turpentine

Household cleaning fluid

Bleach

Water

Ether

Nail-varnish remover

Carbon tetrachloride

CRYSTALS

When liquids evaporate, there is often an interesting result; something seems to appear from nowhere, as if by magic. There is a scientific explanation, of course. A solid which has dissolved in a liquid, and thus become invisible, will become a solid once more when the liquid evaporates. This process is called crystallization.

The solid sometimes forms itself into a pattern known as crystals. Every crystal has its own distinct symmetric geometrical shape, which often helps you to identify it.

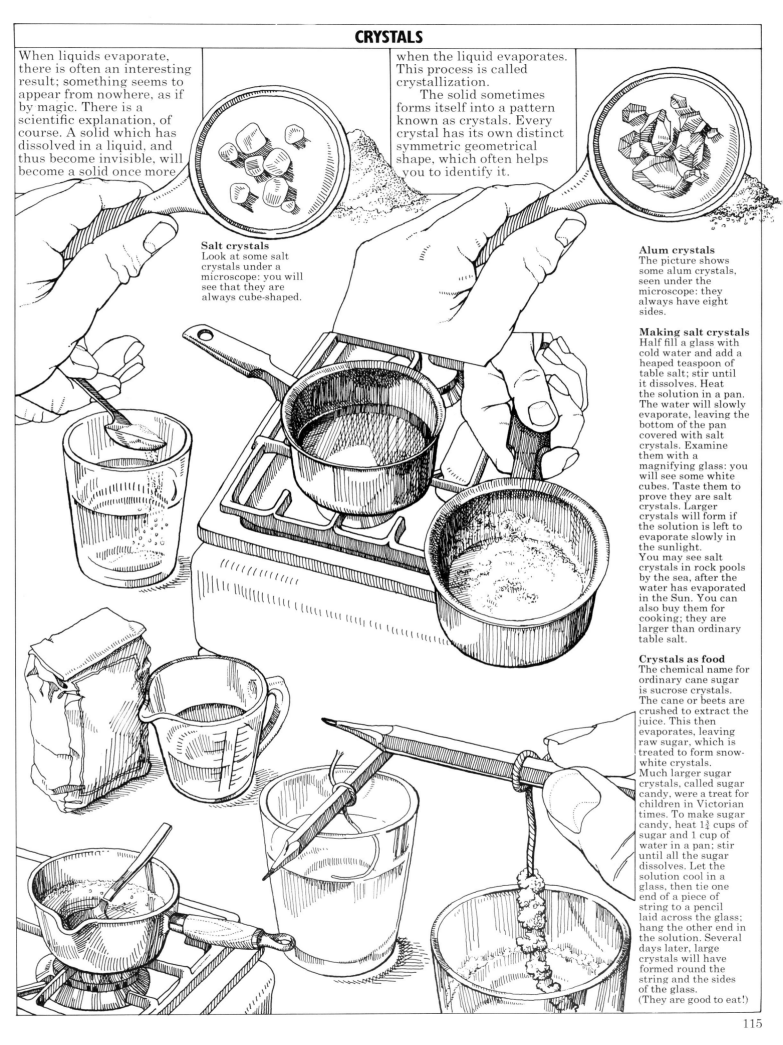

Salt crystals
Look at some salt crystals under a microscope: you will see that they are always cube-shaped.

Alum crystals
The picture shows some alum crystals, seen under the microscope: they always have eight sides.

Making salt crystals
Half fill a glass with cold water and add a heaped teaspoon of table salt; stir until it dissolves. Heat the solution in a pan. The water will slowly evaporate, leaving the bottom of the pan covered with salt crystals. Examine them with a magnifying glass: you will see some white cubes. Taste them to prove they are salt crystals. Larger crystals will form if the solution is left to evaporate slowly in the sunlight.
You may see salt crystals in rock pools by the sea, after the water has evaporated in the Sun. You can also buy them for cooking; they are larger than ordinary table salt.

Crystals as food
The chemical name for ordinary cane sugar is sucrose crystals. The cane or beets are crushed to extract the juice. This then evaporates, leaving raw sugar, which is treated to form snow-white crystals. Much larger sugar crystals, called sugar candy, were a treat for children in Victorian times. To make sugar candy, heat $1\frac{3}{4}$ cups of sugar and 1 cup of water in a pan; stir until all the sugar dissolves. Let the solution cool in a glass, then tie one end of a piece of string to a pencil laid across the glass; hang the other end in the solution. Several days later, large crystals will have formed round the string and the sides of the glass. (They are good to eat!)

Crystals are useful as well as beautiful. The hardest substance known to man is diamond *(right)* which consists of a crystal of carbon. Industry uses diamonds to cut and polish other hard substances. Quartz is another widely used hard crystal. Quartz crystals help keep radio receivers and transmitters tuned; they are also used to send many different telephone conversations over one channel at the same time.

Crystallization is used

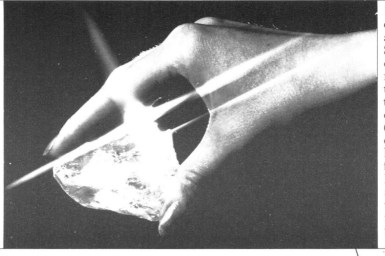

by chemists to separate one substance from another and to purify compounds. Sometimes the crystallization process is repeated many times with the same batch of material, to obtain a completely pure compound. Marie Curie (1867–1934) worked for eight months to separate half a teaspoon of radium from 8 tonnes of impurities. For her research on radium and its compounds, she won the Nobel Prize. To understand the process, try the experiment below.

Separate salt and sand
Put a teaspoon each of dry sand and salt into a glass, half fill it with water and stir well to dissolve the salt. Pour the salt solution off into a pan, leaving the sand at the bottom of the glass. Wash the sand through several times to remove all trace of salt. Heat the salt solution till crystals form. You have used crystallization to separate salt and sand.

Make a chemical garden
This experiment is based on the fact that the salts of most metals combine with a substance called sodium silicate. This substance dissolves in water to form a solution known as water-glass.
To make your garden, you will need some water-glass, a large glass jar – a ½ kg (1 lb) size will do – and crystals of as many of the following compounds as possible: ferrous sulphate, copper sulphate, nickel sulphate, calcium nitrate, manganese sulphate, iron alum, potash alum, cobalt chloride, ferric chloride and zinc sulphate.
Half fill the jar with water-glass and top it up with water. Put a layer of sand about 6 mm (¼ in) thick in the bottom of the jar and drop in the crystals, one by one. Some will immediately start to produce shoots, while others will take longer. Changes will take place over several days; at the end you will have a many-coloured chemical garden.
If you want to prevent further changes, siphon off the liquid and replace it with fresh water.

ELECTROLYSIS

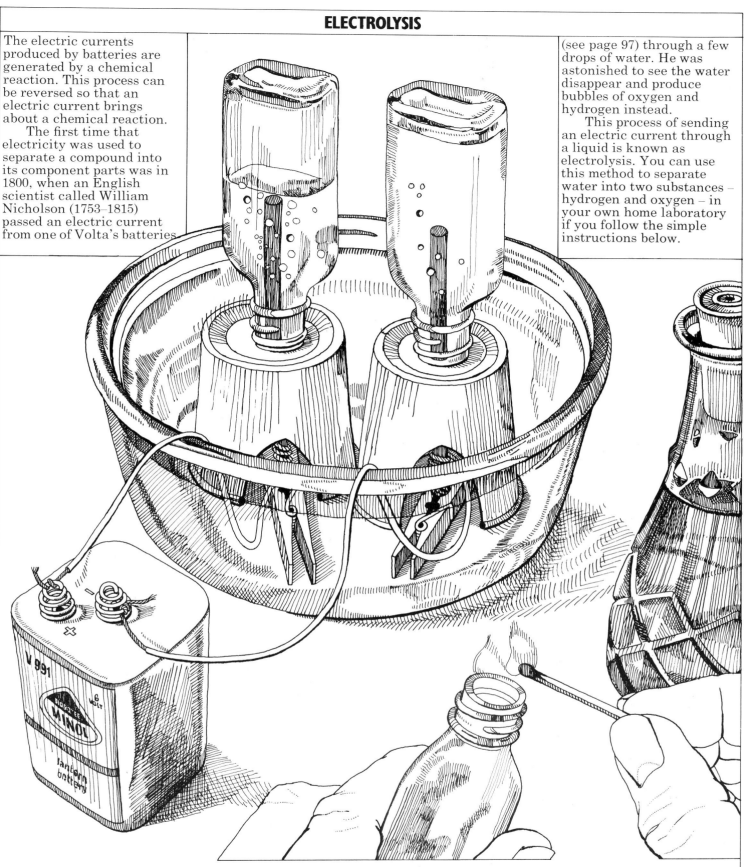

The electric currents produced by batteries are generated by a chemical reaction. This process can be reversed so that an electric current brings about a chemical reaction.

The first time that electricity was used to separate a compound into its component parts was in 1800, when an English scientist called William Nicholson (1753–1815) passed an electric current from one of Volta's batteries (see page 97) through a few drops of water. He was astonished to see the water disappear and produce bubbles of oxygen and hydrogen instead.

This process of sending an electric current through a liquid is known as electrolysis. You can use this method to separate water into two substances – hydrogen and oxygen – in your own home laboratory if you follow the simple instructions below.

Separate water into oxygen and hydrogen

You will need: two carbon electrodes from old dry batteries, two yoghurt cartons, two small glass bottles, two lengths of flex, a large bowl, a battery, two clothes-pegs, a nail and some vinegar.

Make a small hole with the nail in the bottom of one of the yoghurt cartons, push a carbon rod through the hole, and cut out a small nick from the rim. Do exactly the same with the other carton. Fix a piece of flex to each carbon rod with a clothes-peg, as shown.

Now almost fill the bowl with water and lie the bottles in it so they are completely full of water. Invert the cartons in the bowl and slip a bottle over each carbon rod. (Make sure the bottles are still full of water.) Connect the free ends of the flex to the battery terminals: you will see bubbles coming off the rods. Add some vinegar to the water; this makes water a better conductor of electricity, so more bubbles are produced. The electricity splits the water into two substances: oxygen and hydrogen. There is twice as much hydrogen as oxygen, and it collects at the negative carbon rod, or cathode. The oxygen collects at the positive rod, or anode. Test the gases like this. Take the bottle at the cathode out of the bowl and turn it upright. Before the gas has time to escape, hold a lighted match to the mouth of the bottle. The gas will burn with a loud pop, showing it is hydrogen. Hold a glowing match over the top of the other. The match will relight, thus proving the gas is oxygen.

Invisible inks

You can make invisible ink from lemons, milk or onions. Cut a lemon in half and squeeze out the juice. Write a message in the juice, using a toothpick or a pen with a nib. If you let the writing dry, it will become invisible. Give it to a friend. When he wants to read it, all he has to do is warm the paper carefully over a candle flame; the writing will soon appear in light brown ink. This happens because a substance must be heated to its ignition temperature before it will burn. The citric acid in lemon juice has a lower ignition temperature than that of paper, and so it burns before the paper does. The heat makes the citric acid join with the oxygen in the air. (We say that the citric acid has been oxidized.) You can make ink from milk or the juice of an onion in just the same way.

Do you remember reading about the secret, invisible black spot in R L Stevenson's book, *Treasure Island*? You can make your own black ink by mixing half a teaspoonful of alum with some water in an egg cup. If you write with this solution and let it dry, it will become invisible. Then warm it over a candle flame and it will turn black. The ink oxidizes before the paper is affected by the heat.

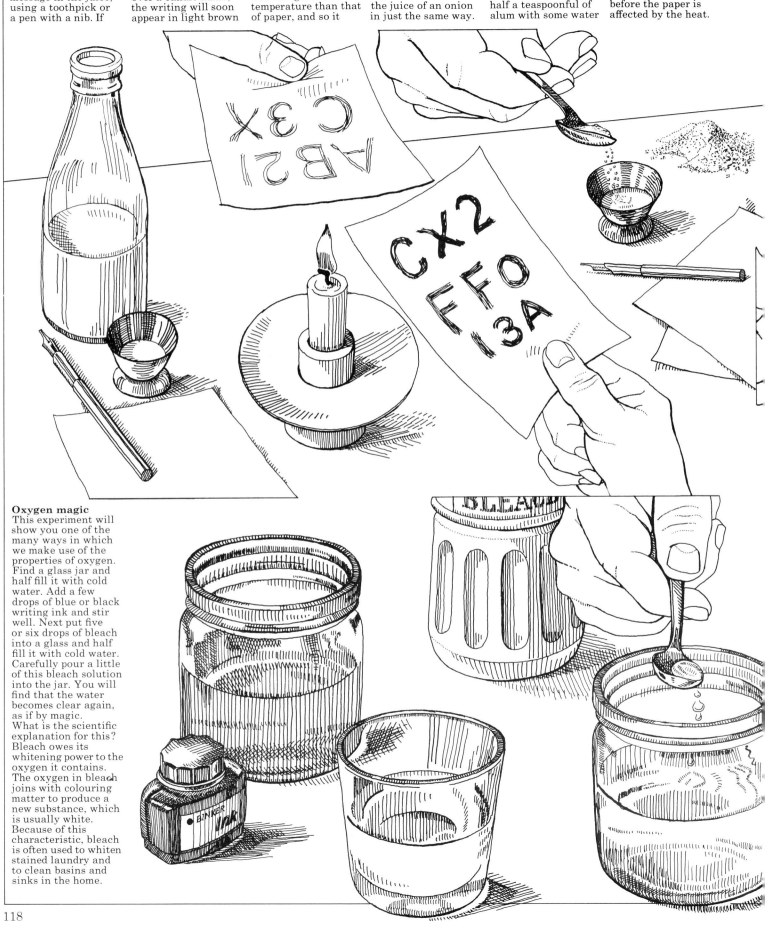

Oxygen magic

This experiment will show you one of the many ways in which we make use of the properties of oxygen. Find a glass jar and half fill it with cold water. Add a few drops of blue or black writing ink and stir well. Next put five or six drops of bleach into a glass and half fill it with cold water. Carefully pour a little of this bleach solution into the jar. You will find that the water becomes clear again, as if by magic.

What is the scientific explanation for this? Bleach owes its whitening power to the oxygen it contains. The oxygen in bleach joins with colouring matter to produce a new substance, which is usually white. Because of this characteristic, bleach is often used to whiten stained laundry and to clean basins and sinks in the home.

Flame tests

When a scientist wants to discover what elements a particular substance contains, he will often use a flame test. You can do your own tests if you make a small loop in the end of a piece of wire from a coat-hanger and test your chemicals on it. (If you carry out these experiments in a darkened room, they look far more exciting.) Dip the loop in water, light your home-made spirit burner, and clean the wire by burning the loop in the flame. Next dip the clean loop in some salt and hold it in the flame. The salt will burn with a bright yellow flame, which means that sodium is present. (Salt is simply sodium chloride.) Burn the loop clean and dip it in water again before you test these other chemicals: copper sulphate, chloride of lime, boric acid and cream of tartar. Check your results against the chart.

Flame colour	Element
bright yellow	sodium (salt/sodium chloride)
lilac	potassium (cream of tartar)
red	calcium (chloride of lime)
green-blue	copper (copper sulphate)
green	boron (boric acid)

Titration

During a chemical reaction, the chemicals can react vigorously on each other. Health salts, for example, are made from an acid and a base which react together in water and produce lots of bubbles.

You can test solutions for the presence of acids and bases by using an 'indicator'. Litmus is one of the most common; it will change from blue to red in an acid, and back to blue again in a base. Make your own indicator by pouring the liquid from some pickled red cabbage into a small glass jar with some water. Add a base like washing soda: the indicator will turn green. Then add a household acid like vinegar: it will change back to red. A chemist uses this process to measure the amount of acid or base in a solution. To help him, he has standard acid and standard base, or alkali, which are of known strengths. He adds an indicator to a set volume of the acid solution whose strength he wants to know, and then adds just enough standard base from a burette to react completely with the acid and change the colour of the indicator. (A burette is a graduated tube which lets out an accurate, measured volume of the base.) This process is called titration. It is a common method of analyzing solutions.

Colorimetry

You can often tell how strong a solution is by its colour. Dark brown tea is strong, for example, while a paler colour means it is weak. This way of measuring strength by colour is also used by chemists. It is known as colorimetry, which means the comparison of the colour of a particular solution with the colours of previously prepared standard concentrations.

You can do your own colorimetry. Weigh a few crystals of copper sulphate and dissolve them in $\frac{1}{4}$ l ($\frac{1}{2}$ pt) of water. The solution will be bright blue. Then take a teaspoon of this solution and add enough water to make it up to $\frac{1}{4}$ l ($\frac{1}{2}$ pt) again. The colour will now be much weaker, in proportion to the amount that you have diluted it.

By weighing the copper sulphate and measuring the volume of water used to dissolve it, you have made a known concentration of copper sulphate. If you then make a series of different, known concentrations, you can take any other solution of copper sulphate and find its strength by comparing it with the colours of your known concentrations. You can use this same principle to discover the strength of many other solutions too.

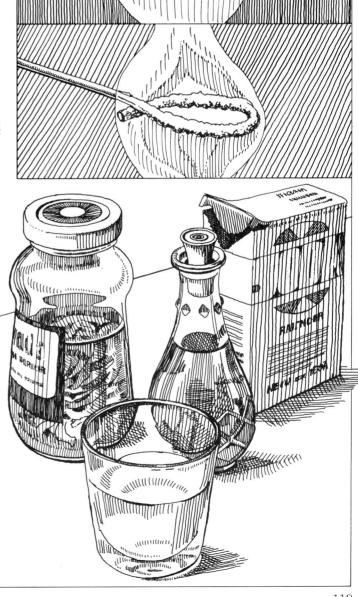

Secret printing press
To be a successful spy, you will need to pass secret messages to other agents. You can do this if you set up a printing press. For printing fluid, mix a cup of water, half a cup of turpentine and a little washing-up liquid in a jar. Now cut out an interesting newspaper article, with a photograph and a big heading, and put it up face up on a table. Cover it with printing fluid and put a sheet of white paper on top. Press it down with a block of wood. You will find a copy of your article printed on the sheet of paper, but you will need a mirror to read it because your print is a mirror image of the cutting.

How does this work? Turpentine is a good solvent. It wets the printing ink of the newspaper so that the print comes off and is transferred to the white sheet of paper.

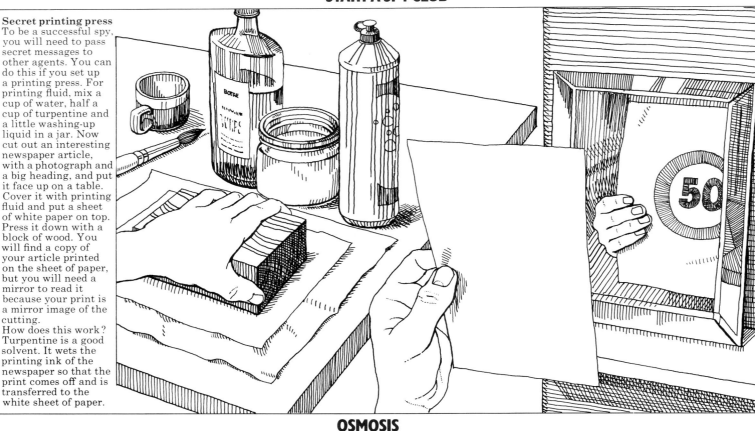

OSMOSIS

All living things depend on a process called osmosis; it also plays an important part in chemistry. Osmosis occurs whenever two liquids containing different concentrations of dissolved matter are separated only by a semi-permeable membrane. (This is a thin wall, through which liquids can pass.) Fluid passes from one solution to the other, through the membrane. The next few experiments will show you that the movement of fluid is always from the weaker to the more concentrated, or stronger, solution.

Osmosis causes the food we eat to pass through the walls of the intestines to the blood, and then on to the cells of the body, where it is used to make the energy we need. Living cells of all kinds, including all the cells of the human body, are surrounded by a semi-permeable membrane. Through this membrane the cells are able to absorb water and substances that have been dissolved through the process of osmosis.

The experiments on this page and the next will help you understand how osmosis works.

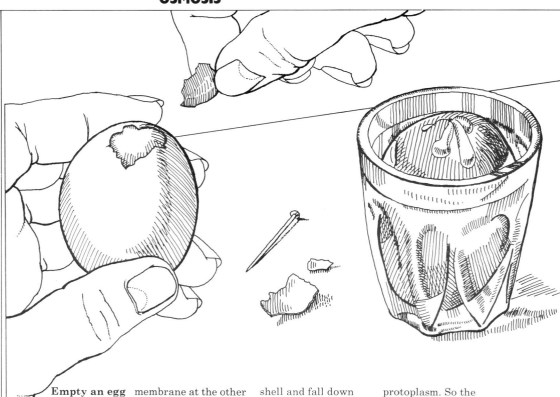

Empty an egg
It is easy to show your friends how osmosis works; all you need is a glass of water and a raw egg. Carefully break or file away a small patch of shell at the broad end of the egg, without puncturing the white membrane underneath. Make a small hole with a pin through the shell and membrane at the other end. Then stand the egg in the water so that the exposed membrane is submerged. Although the inside of the egg is separated from the water by the membrane, the water will still find its way through. After about half an hour, the inside of the egg will have started to rise up out of the shell and fall down the outside as a sticky overflow. This is because the egg membrane is semi-permeable, like the cell walls in our bodies. It contains minute pores which allow tiny water molecules to pass through freely, but act as a barrier to the larger molecules of egg albumen or cell protoplasm. So the water can pass through into the egg, but the contents of the egg (or, similarly, of one of the cells in the human body) cannot escape. The water passing in by osmosis forces the contents of the egg out of the hole you have made at the other end. In time only water will remain in the egg.

Fingerprinting

Did you know that your thumb print is unique? To see a print of it, press your thumb down on a sheet of white paper and then light your spirit burner. Pour a few drops of iodine into a tin lid, hold it with a wooden clothes-peg and gently warm it over the flame. With your other hand, hold the paper in the vapour: your thumb print will appear, as if by magic. This is because the iodine evaporates when heated; the vapour then cools back and produces the print.

Vanishing ink

To make your ink eradicator, you need to prepare two solutions. For the first, mix an egg-cupful of lemon juice with an equal amount of cold water. For the second, mix three egg-cupfuls of water with one of bleach. When you want to get rid of a secret message written in ink, carefully apply the lemon solution, wait a few minutes, and then apply the bleach. The ink will gradually disappear because the oxygen in the bleach joins with the ink to produce a new, white substance.

Secret pathways

This is another example of osmosis at work. Dissolve a teaspoon of salt in a glass of warm water and allow it to cool. Seal the top with parchment paper, secured with an elastic band. Add some dye or food colouring to a bowl of cold water and stand the glass upside down in it. As you watch, the water will become the same colour in the bowl and in the glass. This happens because the parchment paper acts as a semi-permeable membrane. The tiny molecules of water and dye pass through the invisible pores in the paper, and into the more concentrated salt solution in the glass. As we saw in the egg membrane experiment, the fluid always passes from the weaker to the stronger solution.

Expanding peas

Put a handful of dried peas into a small glass jar, fill the jar with cold water, and stand it on a metal lid. As the peas gradually absorb the water through osmosis, they will swell and so take up more and more space. Eventually they will become too big to fit into the jar; they will jump out and clatter on to the lid, making a strange, ghostly noise. The noise will go on for as long as the osmosis continues – probably for hours.

A large part of the bodies of animals and plants is made up of water. This water penetrates the walls of the cells, through osmosis, and thus stretches them. If a plant cannot get enough water, its cells become flabby and it wilts, and eventually dies.

8

THE SCIENCE OF FOOD AND COOKING

Early man did not give a lot of thought to food, he just ate what he could find – plants, roots, birds' eggs and fruit. At first the animals he caught were only what he could kill with his bare hands. He tried to trap snakes, insects, shellfish and small game, and learned by experience which were harmful and which safe.

But as man developed he was able to make simple weapons, and by the Stone Age he had become a hunter. Later, when he had invented hooks and harpoons, he fished too,

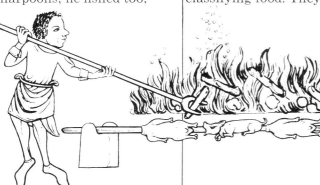

and then extended his range of action by using bows and arrows. We do not know when fire was first used for cooking, but roasting, and later boiling, greatly extended the range of animals and plants that man could digest. Cooking also helped survival because heat destroys harmful bacteria in meat and poisonous elements in some plants.

Man then settled down to farming and in the late Stone Age produced the first earthenware kitchen utensils. Grinding of flour also began. Tribes learnt about food preservation; so granaries were built, fish was dried or smoked, and meat was salted.

Magical notions became associated with food. There is, for example, the ancient belief that a man's soul can 'escape' through his mouth when he is eating. For that reason some primitive tribes still cover their faces during meals. Beetroot juice, probably just because it is red, was thought to cure anaemia, and celandine flowers were said to cure jaundice. There may be some truth in a few of these old wives' tales. For

example, fish is still thought by some people to improve our brains, and it certainly does contain phosphorus, which the brain needs.

The Greeks, who liked to apply philosophy to everyday life, devised their own strange way of classifying food. They thought in terms of their four elements – air, water, fire and earth. The coolness of air, moisture of water, heat of fire and dryness of earth were attributed to food. Foods were combinations of these elements and the Greeks felt that different people needed different foods, according to their health and circumstances. Therefore, a patient with 'hot' blood needed 'cool' food. Even the Romans believed this, and the idea persisted in Europe until the 17th century.

Scientists did not begin to examine the effect of food on our bodies until the 18th century. Nutrition is one of the newest branches of science. Before food, our body's fuel, could be investigated, we had to understand how our organs work. As you saw on pages 38–9, the study of the human body was delayed until long after the Reformation.

The famous French chemist, Antoine Lavoisier (1743–94), studied the way that the body turns food into energy, and the energy value of food began to be expressed in calories – units of heat. Two other terms,

now very familiar, emerged. Justus von Liebig (1803–73), a German biochemist, analysed proteins and carbohydrates. Proteins are organic compounds containing carbon, oxygen, hydrogen and nitrogen. We obtain proteins by eating meat, eggs, milk, cheese and some vegetables. Carbon, hydrogen and oxygen are contained in carbohydrates, but in different proportions than in proteins. Carbohydrates are found in starch and sugar. Butter, oil and fatty meats provide fat, which is also an important part of our diet.

In the 19th century scientists began to realize the importance of extra inorganic and mineral substances, like iron, calcium and potassium. But there were still great gaps in their knowledge. Sailors, for example, had died from scurvy for hundreds of years. Captain Cook was one of the first to recognize scurvy as a dietary deficiency, and eventually citrus fruit juice was ordered by the British Admiralty for all its ships. The need to have vitamins in food was accepted, although even in the 1930s over half the population of Britain lived on a vitamin-deficient diet. Nowadays we understand which vitamins we must eat and why.

A great change in kitchen design came when coal replaced wood as a

common fuel in the 19th century. Hearths could be made smaller and eventually the kitchen range was conceived. The man who designed the prototype of the enclosed range was Count Rumford (1753–1814), the statesman, scientist and founder of domestic science. This range was the forerunner of our modern stoves and was used during the 1800s.

Rumford had the first scientifically constructed kitchen range installed in a Munich house in 1789. Robert Southey, the English writer and historian, saw it and described it: 'The top of the fire is covered with an iron plate, so that the flame and smoke, instead of ascending, pass through bars on the one side, and there heat an iron front, against which food may be roasted as well as by the fire itself; it passes on heating stoves and boilers as it goes, and the smoke is not suffered to pass up the chimney till it can no longer be of any use. On the other side is an oven heated by the same fire, and vessels for boiling may be placed on the plate over the fire. The smoke finally sets a kind of wheel in motion in the chimney, which turns the spit. I could not but admire the comfort and cleanliness of everything about the kitchen.'

Gas and electric cookers began to replace ranges at the end of the last century. The Science Museum in London has an early gas cooker (c1850) which is made of wood, and their golden age arrived in the 1880s, when all manner of stoves, heaters and geysers adorned the ironmongers' catalogues. Electric cooking only became very popular in the 1930s, when electric

The 14th-century kitchen

In the first picture (opposite) you can see a pig and a pair of fowl being roasted on a spit. Two people were needed for this job: one to stoke up the fire and one to turn the spit by hand. The second picture shows large jars of boiling liquid, and a cook using a strainer to test the consistency of the mixture being prepared. Below and on the right two more cooks prepare meat for the pot. One man is chopping or 'smiting' the meat into small pieces, while the other uses a pestle and mortar to pound meat and herbs together. The illustration is from the *Luttrell Psalter* (c 1340). Cooking on such a grand scale was usually the preserve of the great house and its lord. The less wealthy still found it hard to keep food fresh, and made increasing use of cookshops – special shops where pies and cooked meats could be bought, and to which people could take their own cuts of meat to be cooked to order.

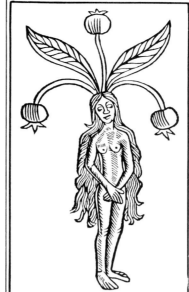

kettles, grills and spits were introduced.

We now understand the physical and chemical changes produced by cooking, which make raw food easy to chew and digest. The connective tissues around the muscle fibres of meat are softened. Starch grains swell and burst their walls so that our digestive juices can work on them easily, and the cellulose fibres and cell walls of vegetables become tender. Even the smell of cooking food helps. It stimulates the glands which produce saliva, the fluid which helps mastication.

Few people think of food and cooking as a science. It has usually been regarded as an artistic activity. There have been few exceptions amongst famous cooks. But one was Mattieu Williams, who wrote his book *The Chemistry of Cookery* at the end of the last century. He said: 'The kitchen is a chemical laboratory in which are conducted a number of chemical processes by which our food is converted from its crude state to a condition more suitable for digestion and

CHEMISTRY.   Plate XI.

Lavoisier and La Place's calorimeter

The heat energy of food was measured in the calorimeter. The sectional view on the right shows the wire cage in which the substance to be measured was placed; surrounding it is a cavity for lumps of ice, and outside this is an outer cavity for crushed and pounded ice, which was also used in the lid. The illustration is dated 1802.

nutrition, and made more agreeable to the palate.'

He wanted science to elevate cooking, so that the kitchen was a more interesting place. He wrote about various experiments, including the one on the next page about cooking eggs.

Magical notions

The roots of the mandrake plant, which slightly resemble the human body, were thought to increase sexual powers. Above is a 15th-century representation of male and female mandrakes.

Gas cooking

(below) One of the early gas stoves: the Eureka gas stove was made by John Wright & Co, Birmingham in the 1890s. This stove included a water heater on one side. Its ancestor in the modern period is Count Rumford's kitchen range, first installed in 1789.

Perfect eggs

Mattieu Williams believed that we spoil eggs by boiling them. You can try his experiment to prove this *(right)*.

Put some raw egg white into a test-tube with a thermometer. Place the test-tube in a pan of water to heat. Williams found that at 56°C (134°F), white fibres began to appear in the egg white. At 71°C (160°F), it had all become white and almost opaque. But the white was still tender, and in his view more easily digested. When another sample of egg white was heated to 100°C (212°F) for four minutes, the normal way to boil an egg, the egg white became dryer and tougher. Williams next devised a simple new way of cooking eggs.

Cook one egg in simmering water for four minutes. Take it out, and put in a second egg, but this time take the pan off the heat and leave the egg in the hot water for 10 minutes. The white of the egg boiled for four minutes is solid, while the egg left to cook slowly in hot water has a softer white, which many people prefer.

Air pressure

The boiling point of water depends on the air pressure at its surface, as this experiment *(right)* shows.

Use a small-necked, heat-proof glass coffee jug with a cork stopper, and a large cube of ice. Boil about 10 mm (½ in) of coffee in the jug until the steam drives out all the air. Stopper it immediately the steam subsides. When it stops boiling, invert the jug and put the ice cube on the bottom. The coffee boils again until it is almost cold. This is because the pressure has been reduced by the ice condensing the steam, thus producing a partial vacuum in the pot. The boiling temperature has therefore been lowered because it depends on the air pressure.

Boiling point

Water will not boil any faster by turning up the heat. This can be simply proved. Turn up the edges of a small card about 10 cm (4 in) by 7.5 cm (3 in) and pour water into it. Hold a lighter flame underneath; the water soon boils without the card scorching. This is because water cannot be heated above its boiling point – 100°C (212°F). Above this temperature, all further heat is used to turn the water into steam. The water cools the card to its own temperature. The card never reaches its burning temperature, so the flame does not affect it. It is important to use just enough heat to simmer water. Anything higher is a waste of fuel and money.

Food contains water

The food we eat contains a lot of water, which can be shown by testing an onion in the following way *(see right)*.

Take your home-made spirit-burner and tripod stand, an old metal plate, a tin lid and a small supply of sand. Using the metal plate as a chopping-board, chop a large onion finely. Weigh it at this stage and make a note of the figure.

Now put the plate covered in sand on the tripod over the burner, place the onion on the tin lid and position the lid on the sand. Heat the onion until it looks dried out, turning the pieces constantly with a knife so that they do not burn. You can actually see the water vapour as it joins the vapour already in the air.

Then turn off the burner, and when the onion pieces have cooled look at them closely. They take up much less space because their water has been driven off by the heat. The onion pieces are dehydrated, and when you weigh them again, you will find they are much lighter. Try this experiment with other foods, including lettuce which contains more than 95 per cent water. Because dehydrated vegetables take up less space, many food manufacturers produce dried vegetables and fruit. They can be stored easily in the kitchen for cooking at a later time. You can buy dehydrated onions, peppers and mixed vegetables. In the same way herbs are dried for winter use, and some people dry apple rings and mushrooms.

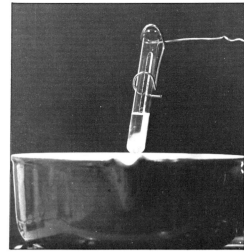

Heat energy

Heat can be measured in various different ways. In food, the amount of heat energy is measured in calories. Scientists work out the number of calories in different types of food by putting a sample of each into a calorimeter, which has an internal chamber for burning food. This chamber is surrounded by a weighed amount of water contained in the outer wall of the calorimeter.

As the food in the inner chamber is burned, its value in terms of calories is measured by the temperature rise in the surrounding water. It was soon found that some foods, particularly carbohydrates like sweets, cakes and potatoes, give off a lot of heat energy when eaten. Other foods, like vegetables and fruit, contain few calories. They keep our bodies healthy, without producing large amounts of heat energy.

If you eat more calories than you need, those extra calories are used to build fat, because fat is one way the body has of storing energy for future use.

How many calories?

The amount of calories we need varies according to our age, sex, height and daily physical activity. Children need more calories relatively to maintain their growth

CALORIE CHART

Fruit juices (per glass)
Grapefruit, fresh	56
Orange, fresh	88
Tomato, canned	56

Beverages (per cup or glass)
Coffee or tea, plain	0
Orange squash	40
Tonic water	50

Dairy foods (per 100 g)
Milk, fresh	66
Milk, skimmed	35
Butter	226
Cheese, Cheddar	424
Cheese, cottage	116
Egg, 1 medium	110

Bread and cereals
Bread, white, 1 slice	69
Bread, wholemeal, 1 slice	65
Cornflakes, 1 helping	100
Doughnut, 100 g	200
Macaroni cheese, 100 g	200
Rice, boiled	120

Fruit (1 medium-sized)
Apple	40
Banana	65
Orange	50
Peach	50
Pear	45

Vegetables (per 100 g)
Beetroot, boiled	44
Broccoli, boiled	14
Carrots, boiled	21
Corn on the cob, canned	77
Peas, fresh, boiled	49
Potatoes, mashed	120
Potato crisps	550
Spinach	26
Tomato, raw	14

Meat, fish and poultry (per 100 g)
Beef, sirloin steak, grilled	297
Lamb chop, grilled	418
Pork chop, grilled	333
Ham, boiled	302
Bacon, fried	607
Veal chop, fried	219
Chicken, roast	185
Tuna	217
Salmon, canned	170
Luncheon meat, canned	335
Pork sausages, fried	450

Desserts (per helping)
Blancmange	150
Fruit salad	100
Gooseberry pie	300
Jam roll, baked	450
Mince pie	150
Treacle tart	400
Yoghurt, fruit	150
Chocolate, milk, 115 g (4 oz) bar	660

Miscellaneous (per tablespoon)
Mayonnaise	110
French dressing	132
Assorted jams	74
Sugar, white	112

Beers and ciders
Bitter, 1 pint	180
Light ale, bottled	90
Stout, bottled	100
Cider, dry, 1 pint	200
Cider, sweet, 1 pint	240

Wines (per glass)
Champagne	105
Beaujolais	95
Sauternes	130

Fortified wines (per glass)
Port	130
Sherry, dry	100
Sherry, sweet	115

Spirits
Whisky, single	58
Gin, single	55
Gin and tonic	67
Rum, single	75
Vodka	63
Vodka and tonic	75
Brandy	75

than an adult who works at a desk throughout the week. Manual workers need more than desk-workers, and considerably more than old people whose metabolism has slowed down.

Calorie chart (left)

Use this list to check approximately how many calories are in your daily diet. Don't forget the little extras – the milk or sugar in your tea, the odd piece of chocolate, etc. If your intake is larger than your likely need, you could well be overweight. This is not the place to launch into a slimming guide, but obvious areas in the diet to cut down are bread, potatoes, butter, cream, hard cheeses, eggs, and sweets. Eat plenty of fresh fruit and vegetables.

Daily averages

Below are some average calorie requirements. The peak for active men may be as high as 3,600, and for women 2,700. These figures decrease with advancing age. In their teens, boys burn up more calories per day than girls.

1,700 – 2,600
Child from age 5 – 15

3,200
Man aged 25

2,300
Woman aged 25

2,500
Man aged 70+
(2,200 for woman)

STARCH TEST

We know that food is made up mainly of fats, proteins and carbohydrates. Because they contain a high proportion of calories, they have to be avoided in many diets. You can do the following test to see which foods contain starch. Remember that starch is made up of chains of sugar units; it is broken down into these during the food's passage through our digestive system.

Choose about a dozen foods of different kinds – perhaps a cereal, bread, onion, carrot, cooked rice, apple, raw meat, fish fingers and sugar. You will also need old saucers, a medicine dropper, tincture of iodine, starch powder, a glass jar and an old spoon. First make an iodine solution by putting five drops of iodine in the jar, adding water to a depth of about 5 cm (2 in) and stirring with the spoon. This is your iodine solution for the experiment. So that you know what to look for when you test for starch, put some starch powder in a saucer, add a few drops of iodine solution and it turns blue/black – the correct starch reaction. If no starch is present, the solution keeps its original reddish-brown colour.

Now test all the foods for starch, cleaning the saucer between each one. It is best to slice the food and soak it in water for a short time. Then add a few drops of iodine solution. Make a chart showing which foods contain starch.

You could turn it into a game with friends, seeing who scores most points for guessing which foods contain starch.

In general you will find that cereals such as oats, rye, wheat, maize, etc., have a high starch content (with maize it is 92 per cent). It is also found in roots and tubers, and in pulses – the edible seeds of the pea and bean family. Among the fruits, few apart from bananas and plantains contain much starch.

YEAST

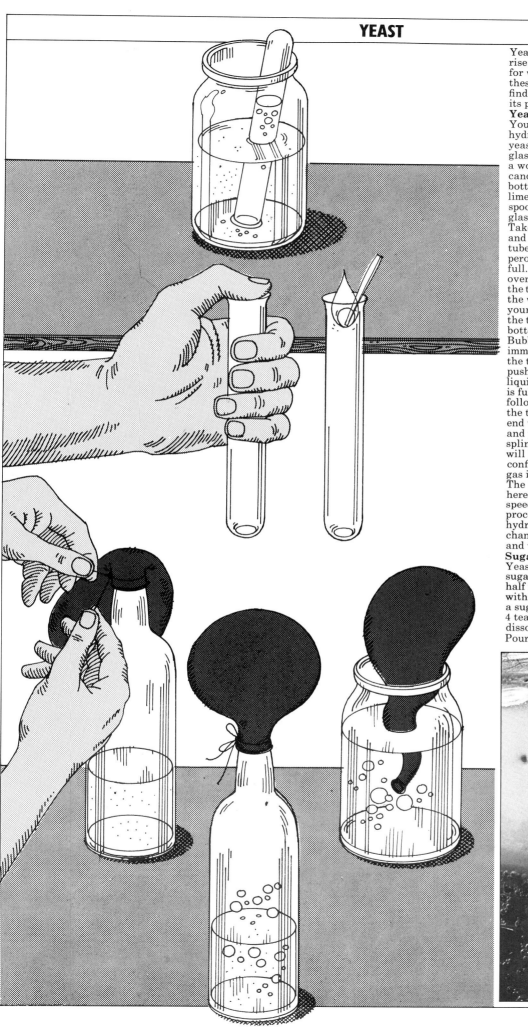

Yeast makes bread rise and is essential for wine-making. Do these experiments to find out more about its properties.

Yeast as a catalyst

You will need hydrogen peroxide, yeast powder, two glass jars, a test-tube, a wooden splint, a candle, string, a litre bottle, sugar, a balloon, lime-water and an old spoon. Half fill one glass jar with water. Take a pinch of yeast, and put it in the test-tube, adding hydrogen peroxide until it is full. With your thumb over the end, invert the tube and put it into the water. Remove your thumb and leave the tube resting on the bottom of the jar. Bubbles of gas will immediately form in the top of the tube, pushing down the liquid. When the tube is full of gas, do the following test. Remove the tube, covering its end with your thumb, and push a glowing splint into it. It will burn brightly, confirming that the gas is oxygen.

The yeast is acting here as a catalyst, speeding up the process when hydrogen peroxide changes into oxygen and water.

Sugar and yeast

Yeast also reacts with sugar. To test this, half fill a glass jar with water, and make a sugar solution from 4 teaspoons of sugar dissolved in the water. Pour this solution into the bottle. Wash the jar and in it mix 1 teaspoon of yeast with a little water. Add this mixture to the solution in the bottle. Loosen a balloon by blowing it up several times, then fix the deflated balloon tightly to the neck of the bottle with string. Put the bottle in a warm place. Within an hour you should start to see bubbling and notice a characteristic sweet smell. The balloon will eventually be blown up by the gas made by the yeast acting on the sugar. Test the gas by carefully removing the balloon without letting the gas escape. Put some lime-water in a glass jar and hold the neck of the balloon under the surface. The lime-water gradually turns milky as the gas is released – the standard test for carbon dioxide.

This happens because yeast is made up of minute fungi. It is alive, and will grow and multiply when it has air, water, warmth and food. Sugar is the food that yeast fungi need. This is why recipes for beer and wine include sugar. As yeast grows, the fungi form chemicals called enzymes. These break down the sugar into alcohol and carbon dioxide. Below, bubbles form as yeast acts on grape juice during the fermentation stage of making wine.

Carbon dioxide in the kitchen

Carbon dioxide is important in drinks. It is the gas which gives your drink its 'fizz'. To make your own fizzy drinks, you will need citric acid, icing sugar, sodium bicarbonate and a shallow glass jar with a screw lid. Mix together 3 tablespoons of citric acid, 7 of icing sugar and $1\frac{1}{2}$ of sodium bicarbonate in the glass jar. Grind the mixture finely. When it is mixed well you have dry sherbert, which can be stored for a long time in the screw-topped jar. It can also be made into a refreshing drink by mixing it with water. This is because the citric acid and sodium bicarbonate make carbon dioxide when they are mixed with water. Baking powders, which make cakes rise, are often made of sodium bicarbonate and a solid acid like citric acid. Mix a teaspoon of baking powder with about three of water. You will soon see a froth of bubbles which are carbon dioxide gas. This substance plays an essential part in producing light sponge cakes.

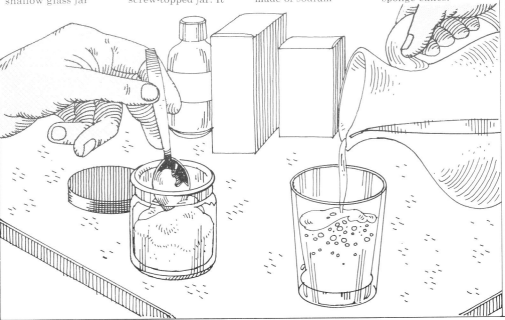

Sugar is carbon and water *(right)*

You can find out more about sugar when you use it in cooking. Try making caramel, after first asking for help from your parents. Put half a cup of sugar into a frying-pan. Stir the sugar over a medium heat until it melts and then boils. When it turns dark brown, take it off the heat to cool. You have produced caramel, which is sugar strongly heated, but not burnt. The sugar loses its oxygen as water at about 200 C (392 F). Sugar is made of hydrogen, oxygen and carbon, and therefore turns into caramel, which is sugar's carbon.

Put some of this caramel in an old pan which you do not mind wasting, and heat it more strongly. Some of the carbon joins with the gases to form carbon dioxide and sharp-smelling acrolein. What is left in the pan is just black, hard-to-remove carbon.

Sugar magic *(far right)*

Sulphuric acid has such a strong affinity for water that it can often remove it from other compounds. It can be used in a spectacular stunt, which also demonstrates the basic composition of white sugar – black carbon plus hydrogen and oxygen in the same proportion in which they occur in water. But do this experiment, or any others using concentrated acid, in the presence of an adult. Half fill a small glass with sugar, and using a glass rod stir in enough sulphuric acid to wet it well. Then watch carefully. The sugar soon darkens, boiling begins and then a coke-like column of carbon rises out of the glass to a great height, accompanied by clouds of steam.

Utensils in the kitchen

If you use aluminium cooking pans, you will have noticed how some foods make them go dark, while others do not. That dark discoloration may be due to a swapping of metals after cooking oatmeal or some other food containing iron. Since aluminium is more active chemically than iron, part of the cooking pan went into solution, while the iron from the oatmeal was deposited on the pan.

Most cooks scour away deposits like this after cooking. But there is another, more scientific way. Cook acid foods like tomatoes in the pan, and the iron will be automatically removed *(below)*. Aluminium may also be darkened by cooking foods containing baking soda or alkalis, because an impure form of aluminium oxide forms on the pan. Again, this can be removed scientifically by the counteracting method of cooking acid foods.

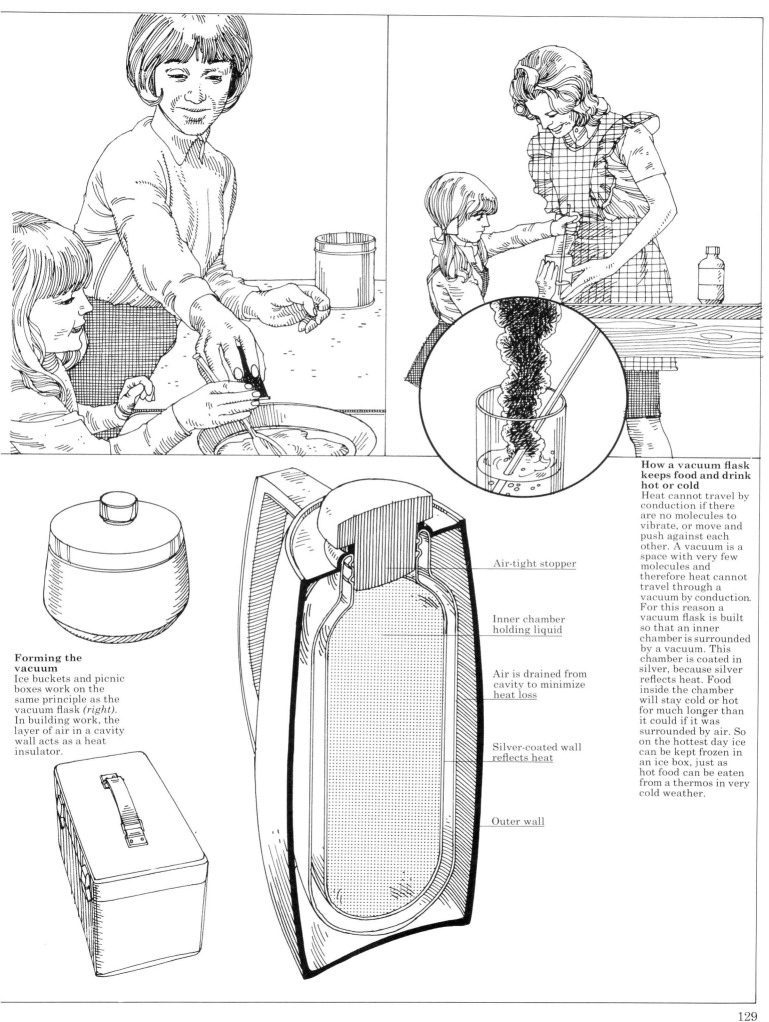

Forming the vacuum
Ice buckets and picnic boxes work on the same principle as the vacuum flask (right). In building work, the layer of air in a cavity wall acts as a heat insulator.

Air-tight stopper

Inner chamber holding liquid

Air is drained from cavity to minimize heat loss

Silver-coated wall reflects heat

Outer wall

How a vacuum flask keeps food and drink hot or cold
Heat cannot travel by conduction if there are no molecules to vibrate, or move and push against each other. A vacuum is a space with very few molecules and therefore heat cannot travel through a vacuum by conduction. For this reason a vacuum flask is built so that an inner chamber is surrounded by a vacuum. This chamber is coated in silver, because silver reflects heat. Food inside the chamber will stay cold or hot for much longer than it could if it was surrounded by air. So on the hottest day ice can be kept frozen in an ice box, just as hot food can be eaten from a thermos in very cold weather.

Early man's knowledge of light came from his observations of the Sun. He saw that the Sun offered the most accurate means of measuring time. The Sun was also reliable, rising each morning and setting at night, dividing the day in two. Man noticed too that the height of the Sun in the sky differed according to the time of year. From these observations, early man went on to discover the relationship of the Sun's movements to the

Some remote peoples, in Borneo for example, still use gnomons for measuring time.

Even the world could be measured using a gnomon. A man called Eratosthenes,

contemporary school of Democritus thought, on the other hand, that objects exposed to light sent out their own small particles of light material towards the eye.

operations of nature.'

The German poet and amateur scientist J W Goethe (1749–1832) also thought Newton's efforts odd, but laughably so. A hundred years after Newton's discovery of the spectrum he wrote, 'The idea of white light being composed of coloured lights is quite inconceivable, mere twaddle, admirable for children in a push-cart.' Despite opposition like this, Newton's theory was gradually accepted after

Speed of light
In Fizeau's apparatus *(right)*, light enters the tube from above and is bounced along it and back by mirrors. The time this takes is measured by a system of rotating cogs; a detail is shown below right.

Measuring Sun shadows
Tribesmen in Borneo *(below)* use a gnomon or stake to measure the noon shadow. They applied this knowledge to make a seasonal clock. The photo was taken in about 1910.

seasons of the year.

Measurements were made by driving a stake into the ground and calculating the length of the shadow cast by the Sun at various times of the year. The stake was our earliest form of sundial, and it was called a gnomon. Our ancestors found that the stake's shadow was shorter at midday, and that the length of the midday shadows varied according to the seasons. At the hottest times of the year, the Sun was higher and therefore the shadows were shorter.

a pupil of the Greek mathematician Archimedes, found a way of doing it as early as 200 BC. With a gnomon, he measured the angle of the Sun at Alexandria when it was directly overhead at a place called Syene. From this he worked out the difference in latitude between the two places, and then he paid a man to pace between Alexandria and Syene, measuring the distance between them. He used this information to calculate the circumference of the Earth. This result, 38,624 km (24,000 miles), is close to today's accepted figure of 39,912 km (24,800 miles).

The earlier Greek school of Pythagoras (6th–4th century BC) was one of the first to examine the behaviour of light. They put forward the idea that sight could be explained by the light in the human eye. According to them, the eye sent out a kind of beam to the object being viewed, which then streamed back, bringing with it information about the object's colour and shape. The

This muddle began to be sorted out by the geometric theories of Euclid (c 300 BC), who was first to decide that light rays travelled in straight lines, and that the behaviour of light was regular enough to be expressed numerically and geometrically. While the laws affecting reflection (see page 135) were set out by Euclid, it was not until much later that René Descartes (1596–1650) determined the laws of refraction (see page 133).

After Descartes, Sir Isaac Newton (1642–1727) found out that white light is in fact composed of seven spectral colours. In his now-famous experiment (see page 144), Newton placed a triangular glass prism in a beam of sunlight passing through a small hole in a window blind. He found that the white light split up into coloured rays.

Realizing what an important step forward he had made, he said, 'It is in my judgment the oddest, if not the most considerable, detection which hath hitherto been made in the

Fizeau's cogs
The speed of the returning beam of light is calculated according to how far the toothed wheel has rotated since the beam first passed through it.

his experiments were repeated by one scientist after another.

During the 19th century, many scientists performed successful experiments to measure the speed of light more accurately than ever before. Most experiments involved passing a beam of light between the teeth of a wheel turning at high speed. (The apparatus of the French physicist Armand Fizeau (1819–96) is illustrated above.)

The speed of rotation of the cogged wheel was known, and the experiment was set so that light passed first between two teeth. It was then reflected from a distant mirror, and passed back between the next two teeth on the wheel, the shaft having turned exactly the distance between two teeth in the intervening period. Some scientists measured the speed of light in a north-south direction, and then in an east-west direction. They were surprised to find the results the same,

Hooke's microscope
The engraving below shows one of Robert Hooke's microscopes and a condenser for concentrating the light. Below right is an engraving of a flea, one of the highly detailed drawings in Hooke's *Micrographia*, which was published in 1665.

believing that the speed of the Earth's rotation would affect the east-west speed of light. Other scientists measured the speed of light in a vacuum, in glass, and in water, all the while adding to their knowledge about light.

The fact, for example, that light travels more slowly through glass is the reason why it is bent or refracted by a glass lens. All kinds of scientific possibilities were opened up once lenses and other optical devices had made their first appearance, about 300 years ago. Scientists used clear and accurately made pieces of glass to perform experiments, and in one important application developed the ability to help people with defective sight.

In the 17th century, glasscutters probably working in Holland assembled the first lenses suitable for small telescopes and microscopes. They extended our vision far out into the universe, and down to the minute living things that can now be studied in a drop of water.

Two men in particular pioneered lens development. They were the British scientist Robert Hooke (1635–1703) and the Dutchman Anton von Leeuwenhoek (1632–1723). Hooke used microscopes to study living things. He was the first scientist to use the word 'cell' to describe the smallest parts of plants and animals. An engraving of one of the fine drawings in

Leeuwenhoek's tiny microscope
Although only about 2.5 × 5 cm (1 × 2 in), this single-lens microscope *(right)*, made 300 years ago, could magnify up to 400 times. Van Leeuwenhoek used it to observe bacteria years before their medical importance was known.

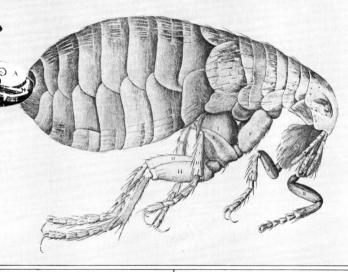

his book *Micrographia* (1665) is shown in the centre of this page.

Van Leeuwenhoek made very small lenses, and built a tiny single-lens microscope. Although the entire microscope measured not much more than 2.5 × 5 cm (1 × 2 in), it could magnify up to 400 times and gave clearer pictures than earlier microscopes with double lenses. Using his microscope held up to the eye, with the object to be examined fixed on a small pin, van Leeuwenhoek made several important discoveries. He found bacteria, for example, in scrapings taken from his teeth – long before bacteria and their role in diseases were accepted by doctors.

Photography – another highly significant application of our understanding of light – became a possibility after the work of Louis Daguerre (1787–1851) and other pioneers. They took the *camera obscura*, a box with a lens at the front which was in essence a drawing machine used by artists to improve their perspective. Light from the scene passed through the lens and was reflected by a mirror onto

a glass screen. The artist then copied from the image formed on the screen.

The great advance was to substitute a light-sensitive material for the mirror and so obtain a permanent image. In 1839 Daguerre broke through when he invented a method of making pictures on silver-plated copper sheets, which became known as daguerreotypes. In Britain, Henry Fox Talbot also advanced photography by

taking pictures on light-sensitive paper using a short exposure. As scientific knowledge has progressed, we have found ways of taking photographs both under the microscope and in outer space. The various branches of optics are uniting.

'Painting with light'
Early photographers were said to blend the sciences of chemistry and optics when they 'painted portraits with light'. The illustration is from T Eckardt's *Physics in Pictures* (1882).

HOW LIGHT TRAVELS

There is never any light unless something is there to generate it. During the day that something is the Sun. If we did not have light from the Sun we would live in almost total darkness, and extreme cold. We would also soon die because without light most plants, and other forms of life we use for food, would wither away.

After sunset there is little natural light. The stars offer some, and the Moon periodically provides light also. The Moon itself does not generate light, but acts as a giant mirror, reflecting light from the Sun. For the most part, we have to produce our own artificial light. Usually this is provided by electricity. We use many different types of electric light, some dim and others bright. Most are white but some are coloured; and some send out strong beams along definite paths, while others send out their light equally in all directions.

All light, however, has one thing in common. It travels in straight lines, moving from its source to an object, and from there to the eye. In the picture on the right, the light from the lamp shines down on the book and bounces off into the boy's eyes, enabling him to see what is written there.

Straight-line test

To prove that light travels in straight lines, take three pieces of card about 15 cm (6 in) square. Cut a hole about 2.5 cm (1 in) square in each. Fold over 2.5 cm (1 in) at the foot and stand the three pieces in a line, with weights to keep them from falling over. The holes must be in a straight line. Put a lighted candle at one end and you will be able to see it through the holes. Now move one piece of card 2.5 cm (1 in) to one side. You cannot see the candle at all now.

Wave motions

Light is made up of waves, and this allows a little of each ray to break up or diffract outwards along slightly different straight paths. Throw a stone into a pond, and you will see it send out waves in a circle. But the water disturbed by the waves does not flow along with them; instead it goes up and down at right-angles or transversely to them.

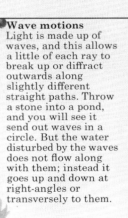

Light lines

Once the light waves are broken up, they will be seen as strips of bright and dark lines.

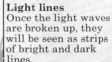

Breaking up the waves

As the wavelength of visible light is about one two-thousandth part of a millimetre, the distances it can diffract sideways are so small that we do not notice them. But if you look at a fluorescent striplight through a very narrow slit between two books – holding them in front of just one eye – the thin slit of light becomes a fine series of dark and light lines. This happens because the slit is small enough to diffract the light waves. When they reach the eye, some are added together to give bright lines and others cancelled out to give dark ones.

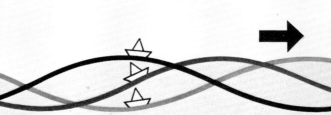

Transverse paths

Rays of light follow a path similar to that of ripples on water, moving up and down in transverse waves.

REFRACTION

Refraction is the bending of light rays when they pass from one medium to another. The reason for this is that the speed of light differs from one optical medium to another.

The speed of light is highest in space or in a vacuum, the latest accepted figure for this being 299,727 km (186,242 miles) per second. When we look at an object as distant as the Sun, therefore, the light from it

is taking about eight minutes to make the journey.

Many stars are very much farther away, and astronomers measure their distances in light years. A light year, the distance light travels in one year, is 9,945,745,000,000 km (5,878,500,000,000 miles).

While light travels fastest in space or in a vacuum, it is far slower in water, glass, and other

transparent substances. The speed of light through water, for example, is only 224,708 km (139,000 miles) a second. Water slows light rays in much the same way as it slows down your legs and feet when you walk through it in the sea or a swimming pool. And it is because water slows down the light rays that they bend or refract when they reach water, penetrating the new medium at a

greater angle.

In a similar way, rays of light coming up to the eye from an object under water; perhaps resting on the bottom, bend when they pass through the surface. This is what makes swimming pools and clear rivers seem shallower than they really are. Primitive peoples, who shoot fish with bows and arrows, soon learnt to aim off-target to allow for refraction.

Seeing refraction
Fill a glass about two-thirds full of water. Put in a straw and you will see that the light rays make it look slightly bent at the top of the water. Now half fill a glass with concentrated salt solution and top it up slowly with pure water, using a spoon.

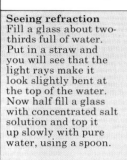

Hold a straw to one side of the glass and it will seem to be broken into three pieces. Because salt solution has a different composition from water, the angle of refraction is different and the light rays bend twice.

Refraction in the dark
Take an empty bottle and fill it with water and several drops of milk. Cap the bottle and lay it down on a sheet of paper. Cut a slit in a piece of card and hold it over the front of a torch so that a thin ray shines through. When you darken the room, you will see the ray bending as it meets the water.

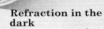

Seeing invisible gases
Refraction can also be used to see gases which are normally invisible, eg carbon dioxide. Make up some gas by pouring a little bicarbonate of soda and some vinegar into a small jar. When the mixture foams, tilt the jar in front of a light background, preferably in sunlight. You will see the carbon dioxide leaving the jar in light and dark clouds. These form because air and carbon dioxide have different optical densities, and light rays passing through them are bent in different directions.

LENSES

Lens is the Latin word for a type of seed that curves rather like a glass lens. One of the most important applications of the refraction principle is found in the lenses used today in almost every optical device, ranging from binoculars, microscopes, eye glasses and magnifying glasses to complicated cameras and telescopes.

Although lenses are now used in many different combinations, there are only two basic types. Concave lenses give a reduced image of a large area, just like a convex mirror.

Convex lenses are far more common. They are thicker in the middle than at the edge, eg a magnifying glass, and they behave like a concave mirror, giving an enlarged view of a small area. Remember that you should *never* look at the Sun through any kind of lens.

The distance from a lens to the point where rays of light from a distant object passing through it converge, is known as the focal length. You can test lenses taken out of old spectacles or magnifying glasses. The most common are convex, which vary greatly in thickness.

Measuring focal length
Fix your lens on to the end of a ruler using modelling clay. Aim it at a window and hold a piece of white paper on top of the ruler. Move it until a sharp image of the window can be seen on the paper. Measure the distance between the lens and the paper, and that will be the lens's focal length.

Make a convex lens
Fill a glass jar with water and several drops of milk. In a darkened room, shine a torch through a piece of card with two slits in it. When the two rays of light arrive at the glass jar, it acts as a lens and makes the rays converge.

Convex
A convex lens makes a close object look larger than it really is. This type is used in magnifying glasses.

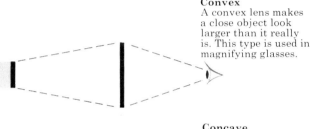

Concave
A concave lens makes objects look smaller.

Make a projector
Cover a torch with tissue-paper and stick a piece of film over it, upside down. In a dark room, shine the torch through the lens from about 1.5 × focal length. This will produce an enlarged image on a facing wall.

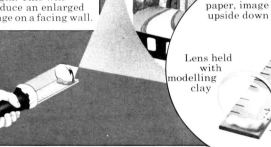

Film taped to tissue paper, image upside down

Lens held with modelling clay

1.5 × focal length of lens

A 'burning glass'
The Sun's rays can be made to converge through a convex lens to produce a very bright, hot point of light. On a sunny day you can scorch paper, or in time light a bonfire. This is why a convex lens is sometimes called a 'burning glass'.

Make a microscope
Take two convex lenses. One lens close to the object forms an enlarged image, which is magnified again by a second lens. The ideal bottom lens is thick, with a focal length of 5-7.5 cm (2-3 in). Fix it at one end of your ruler, with a thinner lens (focal length 10-12.5 cm/4-5 in) about 20 cm (8 in) away. It is the thinner lens that goes nearer the eye.

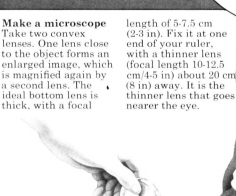

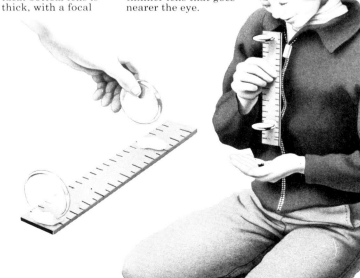

A drop microscope
Take a strip of metal and make a small hole in the centre. Then bend it so that it can be taped about 10 mm ($\frac{1}{2}$ in) above the upturned base of a thin glass. Put a small mirror inside, resting aslant. A drop of water, inserted in the hole, magnifies like a convex lens. A small insect, placed on the base of the glass beneath the drop of water will be magnified up to × 50 when you look through.

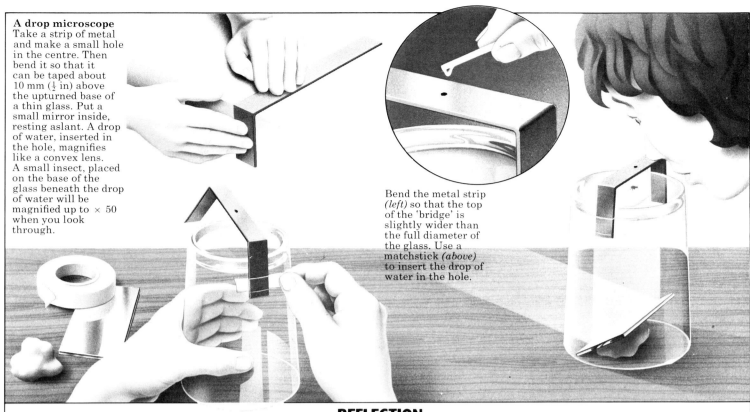

Bend the metal strip *(left)* so that the top of the 'bridge' is slightly wider than the full diameter of the glass. Use a matchstick *(above)* to insert the drop of water in the hole.

REFLECTION

We see objects because of reflected light. Go into a dark room and try to read this book. Impossible, of course, because the book has no light of its own. Turn on the light, and the book will reflect light from the bulb on to your eyes.

A book reflects light well because it is white. Dark objects, however, reflect very little light. You can test this simply with a piece of white paper, and a torch. Switch it on in a dark room and shine it towards the paper. Hold your hand about 30 cm (12 in) above the paper, and you will see a lot of light reflected towards your hand. When you do the same with black paper, much less light is reflected and your hand is darker.

The mirror was the first piece of optical equipment used by man. Mirrors then were of polished metal. They were not good reflectors of light because the metal could not be made flat enough. Today's mirrors are much more finely profiled and can produce a near-perfect image. Compared with them, any reflection in a metal mirror will be fuzzy.

Powers of reflection
You can test the reflecting efficiency of various surfaces with the following experiment. Take a flat mirror and place it face upwards on a table in a darkened room. Shine a torch on it and you will produce reflected light that is almost as bright as the torch beam.
Now lay down a smooth piece of foil. Shine the torch and the foil, if it is flat enough, will reflect about half as much light as the mirror. For the third stage of the experiment, take another piece of foil and crumple it up into a ball and then open it out still full of crinkles. Shine your torch on it, and the light will bounce off in all directions because rough surfaces do not reflect light as well and evenly as smooth surfaces.

Concave and convex mirrors
While a flat, or plane, mirror produces an image the same size as the object in front of it, curved mirrors will change an object's size.
A concave mirror takes in light from something small and sends out a big reflection. This type is used for shaving, to show up the details of a stubbly chin and ensure a good, close shave.
A convex mirror bulges outwards. You sometimes see circular ones hanging in people's houses which give a reflection on a reduced scale of all that is in the room. A driving mirror is another example of the convex type: this takes in light from a large area of the road, and sends a smaller reflection back to the driver's eyes.

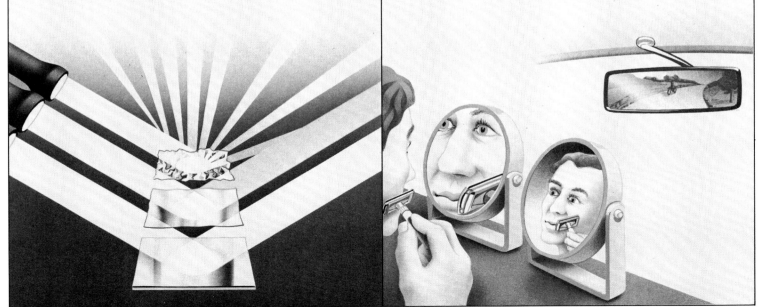

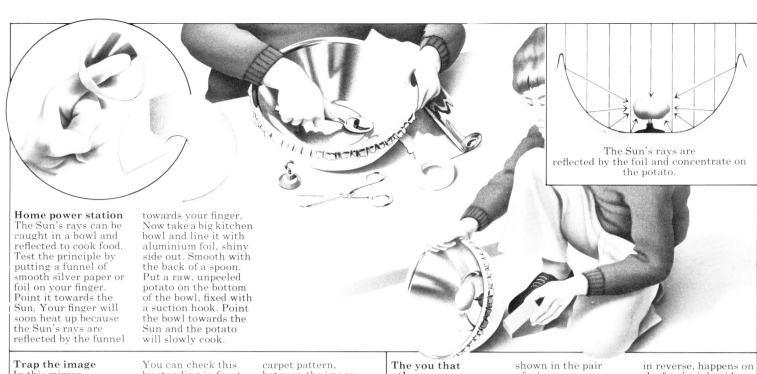

The Sun's rays are reflected by the foil and concentrate on the potato.

Home power station

The Sun's rays can be caught in a bowl and reflected to cook food. Test the principle by putting a funnel of smooth silver paper or foil on your finger. Point it towards the Sun. Your finger will soon heat up because the Sun's rays are reflected by the funnel towards your finger. Now take a big kitchen bowl and line it with aluminium foil, shiny side out. Smooth with the back of a spoon. Put a raw, unpeeled potato on the bottom of the bowl, fixed with a suction hook. Point the bowl towards the Sun and the potato will slowly cook.

Trap the image

In this mirror experiment you can locate the exact position of a reflected image.

Stand an object in front of a plain sheet of glass, which substitutes for an ordinary mirror. Then, watching the reflected image, manoeuvre an inverted jar behind the glass/mirror until the image appears to be inside the jar (see drawing). Now that you have trapped the image, you can measure its exact position in a line perpendicular to the plane of the glass. Wherever the object has been placed, you will find that the image is just as far behind the glass as the object is in front of it.

You can check this by standing in front of a long mirror and looking down. You will see exactly the same number of floor tiles, or amount of carpet pattern, between the image of your feet and the base of the mirror, as there is between your real feet and the mirror.

The you that others see

When you look in a mirror, the reflection shows you the opposite way round. To see yourself as others do, set up two ordinary mirrors at right-angles.

No part of your image shown in the pair of mirrors comes originally from the single mirror in which it is seen. The image of the face's left side is caught by the left mirror and reflected on to the right mirror, which reflects it back to your eye. The same, in reverse, happens on the face's right side.

Look into infinity

Hold a small mirror so you can look past it into a larger mirror. You will see a never-ending series of mirrors. As they recede, so their definition fades.

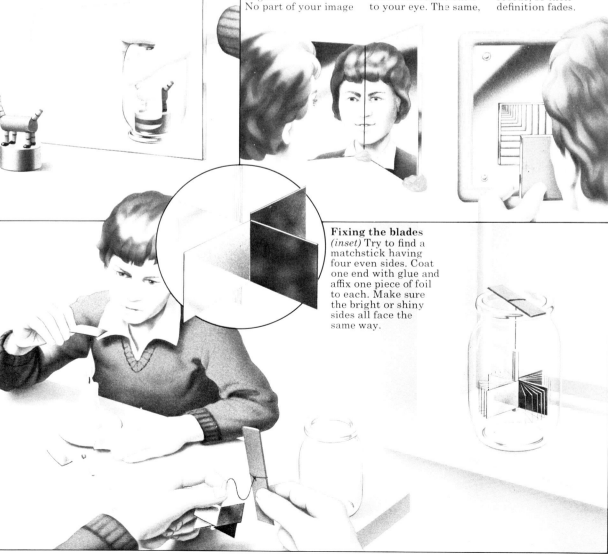

Make a light mill

Light mills rely on bright reflecting surfaces working alongside dark absorbing surfaces. Make one with four pieces of foil, 2.5 × 3.5 cm ($1 \times 1\frac{1}{2}$ in) in size, stuck on a used matchstick, the bright sides facing the same way (inset). Darken the matt sides of the foil with a candle flame. Suspend the light mill in a glass jar, using fine thread stuck with glue to one end of the matchstick. The mill starts to spin round when it is put in the Sun. This is because the dark sides of the foil absorb the Sun's rays, and get far hotter than the light-reflecting bright sides. The imbalance starts the mill rotating.

Fixing the blades

(inset) Try to find a matchstick having four even sides. Coat one end with glue and affix one piece of foil to each. Make sure the bright or shiny sides all face the same way.

The family periscope

You can make your own periscope by forming a tube from a piece of stiff card measuring about 30 × 20 cm (12 × 8 in). You will also need two small mirrors about 6 cm (2½ in) square. With a pencil, mark off the card along its length into four panels of equal width, and score along the lines. Cut square holes at the ends of two sides (see drawing). Near the ends of the other two panels cut angled slits at 45°, as shown; these are to hold the mirrors in position. Bend the panels and join up the tube with sticky tape. Then push the mirrors into position through the angled slits. Your periscope is ready. Test it by viewing an object from below table-level, as shown.

Why it works
The periscope works because light from the object hits the top mirror, is reflected down into the lower one, and travels on towards your eyes.

The family kaleidoscope

A kaleidoscope also works because of reflection. It was invented in the 19th century by Sir David Brewster. He named it from two Greek words meaning 'beautiful' and 'form', and added the word 'scope' to signify something that you look at. To make a kaleidoscope, first cut out a piece of stiff card about 23 × 15 cm (9 × 6 in). With a pencil, mark off the card along its length into four panels of equal width, and score along the lines.

Stick foil over three of the panels with the shiny side up, as shown, and a strip of black paper over the fourth. Then bend and stick the card into a triangular tube shape with the foil facing inwards. Close both ends by gluing on pieces of clear plastic, and at one end also stick white paper over the plastic, and insert small strips of coloured plastic or beads between the two surfaces; leave enough space for them to move about freely.

To use your kaleidoscope, hold it over a light and look through at the patterns caused by reflections in the foil mirrors.

SHADOWS

A shadow forms when light hits an opaque object. The light, unable to pass through the object, is stopped, and a shadow is thrown out on the side of the object facing away from the light.

Objects are generally classified as opaque or transparent according to whether or not they act as barriers to light. Clear water, most glass, and many plastics are transparent.

Seawater and coloured glass are examples of translucent materials, sending out very little light of their own. But most materials form a total barrier to light, and are known as opaque.

Tree shadows

By watching and measuring the shadow formed by a tall tree, you can get some idea both of the time of day and of the time of year. The shadow is at its shortest midway between sunrise and sunset, when the Sun is shining down from almost overhead at a very shallow angle.

The tree's shadow moves as the Sun moves. In the afternoon, when the Sun is in the west, the shadow points eastwards. In the morning the shadow is on the west side of the tree.

Shadows also vary at different times of the year. At midday in winter the Sun is lower in the sky than at midday in summer, and forms a longer shadow.

To measure tree shadows, choose a tall thin tree, and use pegs to plot the movement of its shadow. Note the different shadow

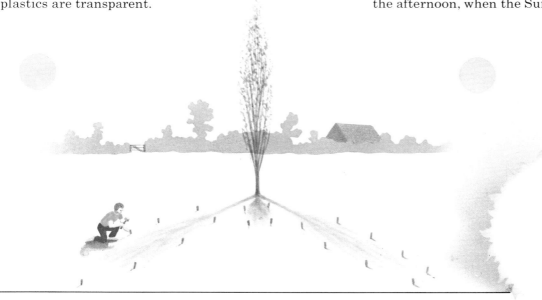

THE HUMAN EYE

The human eye works in much the same way as a camera. Both rely on scientific principles such as refraction, and the fact that light travels in straight lines.

Both can distinguish colours, focus for far or near vision, and, in general, make use of light to find out what is happening in the world. The size of the camera's aperture, and the eye's pupil, are controlled by the iris, which also gives colour to the eye. In both, the iris regulates the size of the hole which lets in rays of light, depending on the state of the weather. And behind the hole, both the camera and the eye have a lens which helps to focus light on the film or the retina at the back of the eye. Like a photographic plate, the retina contains chemical substances that are changed by light of different wavelengths. Because light travels in straight lines, rays from the top part of

Iris
The iris controls the amount of light coming through the central hole into the eye or camera. The iris regulates the hole size according to the light conditions outside.

Lens
Just behind the pupil or camera aperture is a lens. This helps to bend light so that it focuses clearly on the film, or the retina at the back of the eye.

Receptive area
The camera and the eye both have a receptive area. Like the photographic plate, the retina contains chemical substances which are changed by light of varying wavelengths.

Pupil
Both the eye and the camera have a dark hole in the centre which lets in light. If you look closely at a human eye, you will see that the hole, or pupil, enlarges when it is dark and becomes very small in bright light.

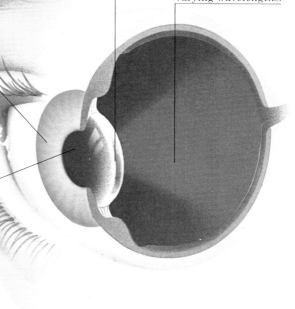

sizes and positions at different times of the day and year. Plot these on a graph and compare the morning curves with each other and with the afternoon ones.

Lunar eclipse
An eclipse of the Moon usually lasts for several minutes, and takes place when the Moon, Earth and Sun are in a direct line, and the Moon is completely covered by the cone of shadow cast by the Earth. Solar eclipses occur when the Moon passes between the Earth and the Sun, and casts its shadow on the Earth's surface.

You are likely to see several eclipses of the Moon in your lifetime, but eclipses of the Sun are rarer. The next one is due to occur on 11 August 1999.

Definition and colour
There are many different types of shadow. In general, if the source of light is big, the shadows will have blurred edges. If the source is small and bright, the shadows will have clear, sharp edges.

Make animal shadows with your hand between a lamp and a white wall. The shadows you make grow bigger the closer your hand is to the light. The frosted bulb on the left produces a grey, blurred shadow, but the clear bulb, with its pinpoint light source, gives a hard black shadow.

Although most shadows are black or grey, this is because the light source is usually a neutral colour. But if the source is coloured, this will be conveyed in the shadow. Prove this by placing coloured filters over your light source. Note how the red and blue mix as magenta (see also pages 146–7).

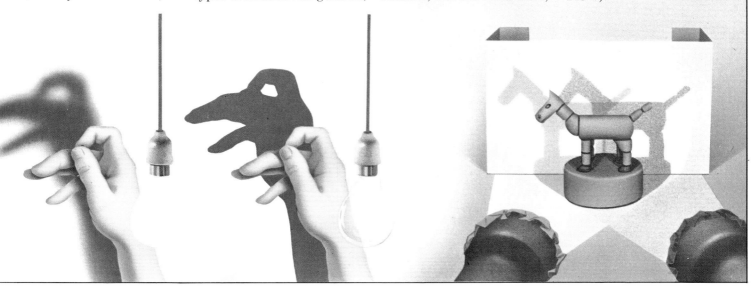

AND THE CAMERA

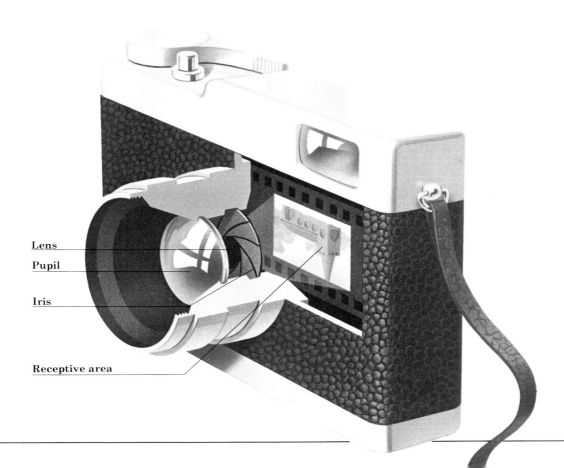

Lens

Pupil

Iris

Receptive area

the scene pass through the camera aperture or pupil and strike the bottom part of the film or retina. For this reason the image is then upside down and the wrong way round. To get a picture that is the right way round, the image on the film, or negative, must be transferred onto photographic paper. In the case of the eye, our brain does the inversion for us.

It is refraction which makes the lens work. Light bends when it passes from a dense medium to a less dense medium, and vice versa. We have seen this by looking at a straw in a glass of water. The camera lens, with its basically biconvex shape, works like a magnifying glass. The rays of light are bent by refraction and are then concentrated in one spot. On page 134 we saw the bright spot of light projected by the glass onto paper. The lens in an eye or camera does a similar job.

THE PINHOLE CAMERA

The simplest camera is the pinhole type demonstrated here. You can make one at home that will take real if rather primitive photographs, like the one shown opposite. The image may be a bit blurred, but it should be perfectly 'readable'.

The basic machine is a light-tight box loaded with a piece of film fixed to the end wall facing the aperture. Most of the differences between this camera and sophisticated modern versions have to do with the pinhole itself. As a means of focusing the image, the pinhole diaphragm is not very efficient. This is because when the rays of light from the object being photographed pass through the hole and form an image on the film, they arrive in the shape of tiny elliptical spots of light; these merge with adjacent ellipses and so produce blurring.

More advanced cameras avoid this problem by having a lens that focuses and concentrates the image as a series of points on the film. The image is thereby much sharpened. But for our experiment you can reduce the amount of blurring if you keep the size of the pinhole small: in other words, don't wiggle the needle or pin about when you pierce the box initially. A small, symmetrical hole is what you should aim for.

The pinhole camera's other drawback is its low light-transmitting power, or 'speed'. The pinhole lens can only admit a relatively small amount of light and has to be kept open (exposed) for a long time if a sufficiently dense image is to form on the film. The family scientist will probably need to experiment a little before he or she hits the best exposure time. In caption 4 below, we suggest 15 minutes as a reasonable period to begin with. This is a guide; you could need rather more or less, depending on the weather and the brightness of the natural light in your area.

For all its primitive imperfections, the pinhole camera is fun to make and very clearly illustrates many of the photographic processes. If the business of developing the film proves irksome, you can always take it to a pharmacy and let a professional do the job.

In the end, though, provided you are reasonably patient, your pinhole camera should provide you with a small gallery of photographs. Once you have conquered the basic art, try taking wide-angled pictures using two or more apertures and pieces of film, side by side.

1 Take a rectangular cardboard box and line the inside with black paper. Cut a rectangular hole in one end-wall, and cover it with a piece of opaque paper. Pierce the centre of this paper with a fine needle or pin. This is the pinhole aperture through which light is admitted to form an image on the film.

2 Make a light-excluding shutter from a strip of sticking plaster. This should have a pad in the middle to cover the pinhole. Place it in position.

3 Buy some photographic film. In a darkened room, fix a piece of film on the end-wall of the box facing the pinhole aperture. The dull or emulsion side should face outwards. Put the lid on the box and tape it round to exclude all light.

4 The camera is now ready. Put it on a table facing a window, peel off the shutter and leave it off for 15 minutes or so. When the exposure time is up, stick the shutter back in place.

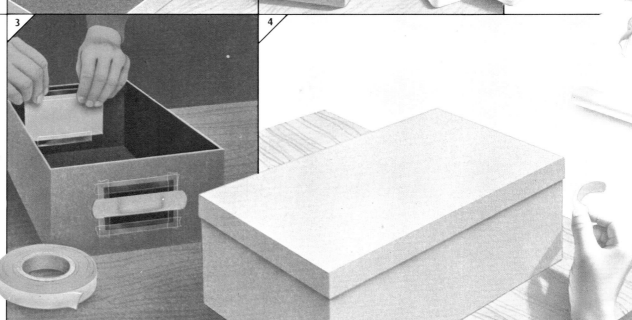

A finished print, produced with the *Family Scientist*'s resident pinhole camera.

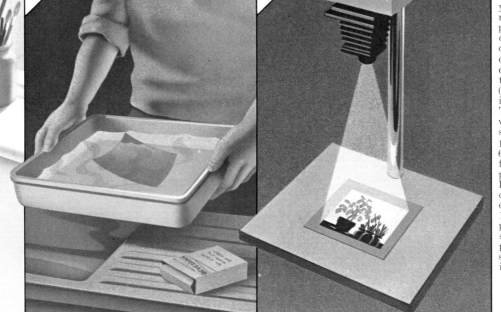

5 Take the box to your darkened room, remove the film, and place it in a dish of photographic developer. Agitate the dish to ensure an even coverage. After about three minutes at 20°C (68°F), a negative image should appear. Take out the film and wash it in water to stop the developing process.

6 Place your negative face down on photographic paper. In normal room conditions shine an enlarger or a clear 100-watt bulb on the paper for 30-90 seconds. When the positive image looks satisfactory, place it in a dish of fixer.

MOVING PICTURES

Modern movie film depends on an optical illusion. Every strip and spool of film is really just a series of still pictures, each recording the scene a fraction of a second apart from its neighbours. When the film is projected, it is wound through the projector at just the right speed to suggest natural movement. As the sample piece of edited film on the opposite page shows, there are sprocket holes along the edge of the film. These hold each frame in exactly the right place in the projector.

Moving pictures were first produced by Eadweard Muybridge in the 19th century. He took a series of still photographs by setting up 12 cameras fitted with high-speed shutters. As the subject (below we show a horse) raced past, it broke a series of strings which set off each camera in turn.

Pictures that appear to move can be made very simply. Take a notebook, and draw a clown with his arms by his sides. Then prick the paper at various key points to mark his position on subsequent pages; it is essential to draw him exactly the same size and in the same place each time. Then draw him again on the following right-hand page. In this second drawing, alter the position of his arms a little, moving them up or down to convey the idea of a gesture unfolding. Then draw the clown again on the next right-hand page, and continue through the notebook, developing the sequence as you go. When the pages of the finished book are flicked through, the clown's arms will seem to move. (If, like most

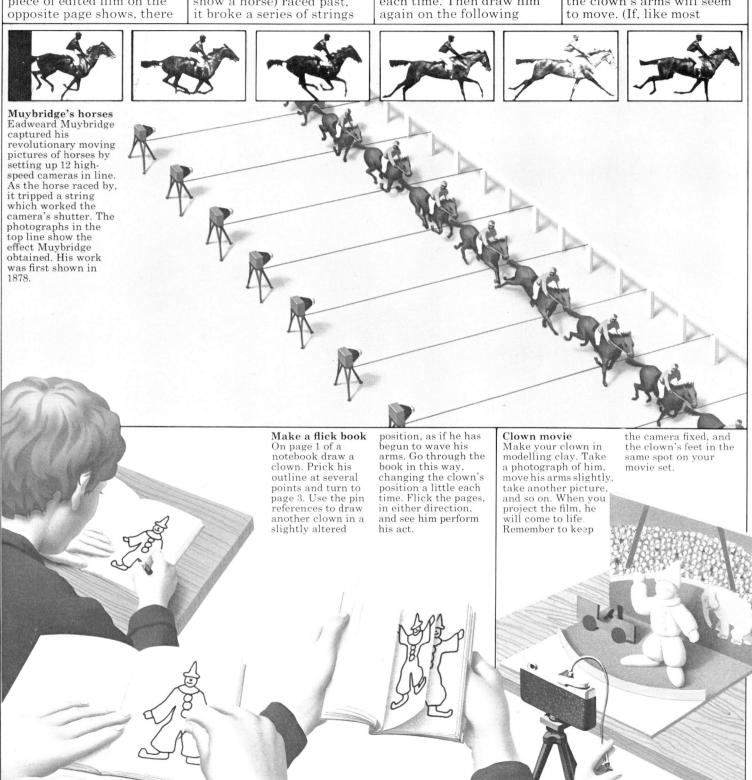

Muybridge's horses
Eadweard Muybridge captured his revolutionary moving pictures of horses by setting up 12 high-speed cameras in line. As the horse raced by, it tripped a string which worked the camera's shutter. The photographs in the top line show the effect Muybridge obtained. His work was first shown in 1878.

Make a flick book
On page 1 of a notebook draw a clown. Prick his outline at several points and turn to page 3. Use the pin references to draw another clown in a slightly altered position, as if he has begun to wave his arms. Go through the book in this way, changing the clown's position a little each time. Flick the pages, in either direction, and see him perform his act.

Clown movie
Make your clown in modelling clay. Take a photograph of him, move his arms slightly, take another picture, and so on. When you project the film, he will come to life. Remember to keep the camera fixed, and the clown's feet in the same spot on your movie set.

people, you flick the book from back to front, the clown's movements will appear in reverse order.)

It is, of course, an optical illusion. The image of each slightly different clown is formed on the retina of the eye, and stays there for a fraction of a second. When the pages of the notebook are flicked, the images overlap and the clown seems to move continuously. Cinema cartoons may use as many as 25 different pictures, or frames, per second, to ensure that the movement looks smooth and natural. You too can make this more sophisticated kind of moving picture using a fixed camera. Follow the instructions in the bottom right-hand picture on the opposite page. The Victorian praxinoscope, patented in 1877, was a device for showing sequences of photographs of humans and animals as moving pictures. Reynaud's original 'wonder' cylinder adapted Muybridge's series of photographs for the home viewer. Although apparently a complicated box of tricks, the praxinoscope was basically simple and consisted of a drum whose inside was lined with a series of photographs. When it was spun quickly, the spectator looking through a slit (see illustration below) saw the figures in motion. You can apply this principle to make the viewer below.

Make a praxinoscope
Draw a sequence of clown pictures and stick them in order round the outside of a circular baking tin. Put a stick attached to a suction pad in the base of the tin to serve as a spindle. Now float the tin in a larger dish. Make a pinhole in a piece of card and hold it close to one eye. Spin the baking tin and the figures will pass your eye so quickly that they merge as one.

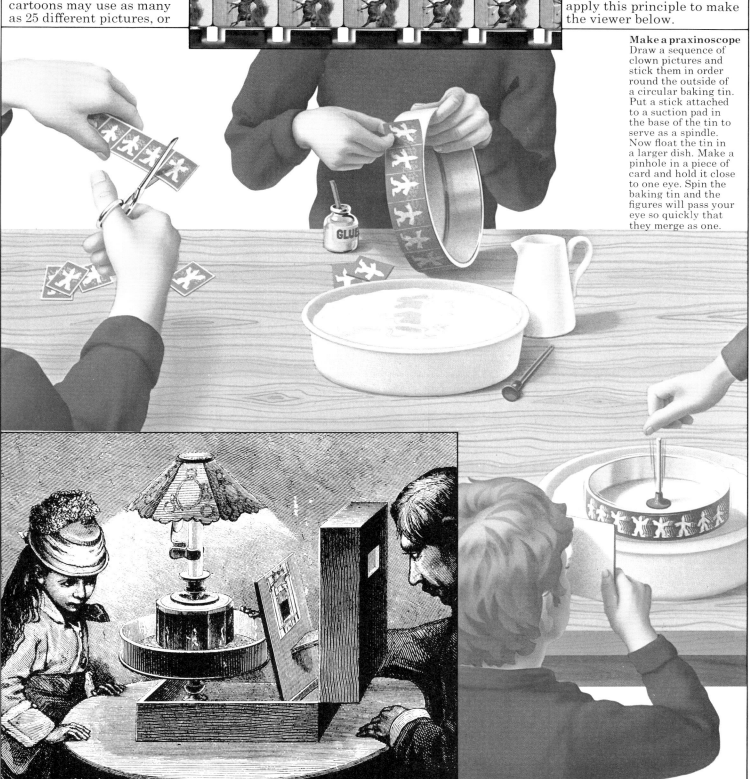

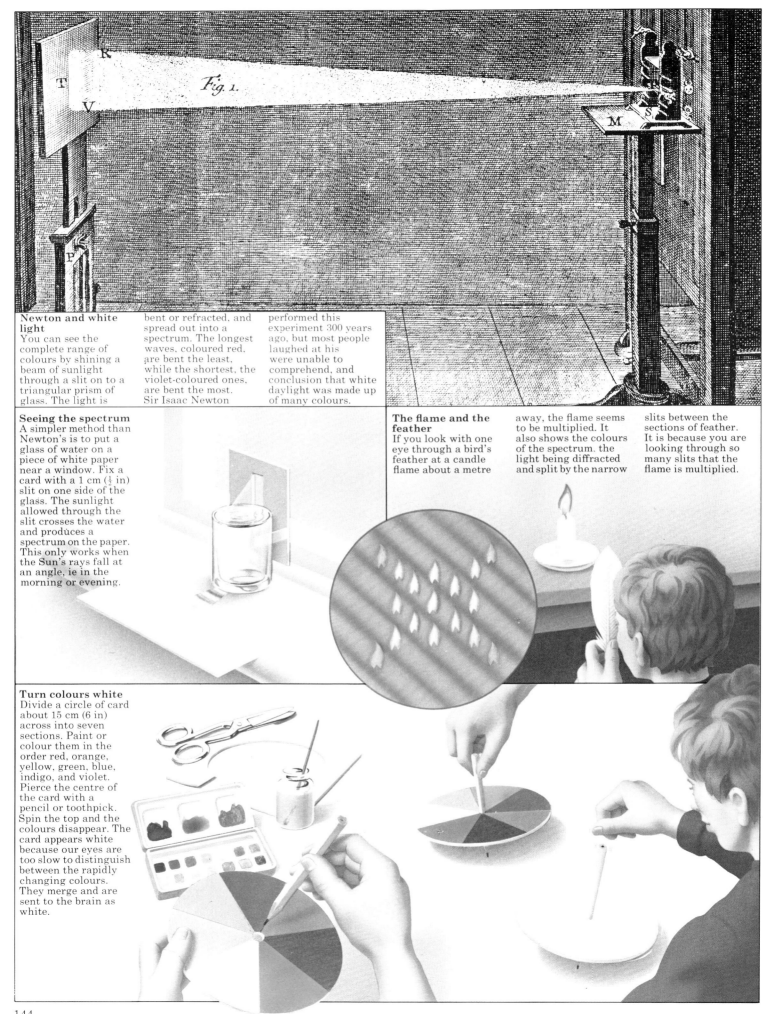

Newton and white light
You can see the complete range of colours by shining a beam of sunlight through a slit on to a triangular prism of glass. The light is bent or refracted, and spread out into a spectrum. The longest waves, coloured red, are bent the least, while the shortest, the violet-coloured ones, are bent the most.
Sir Isaac Newton performed this experiment 300 years ago, but most people laughed at his were unable to comprehend, and conclusion that white daylight was made up of many colours.

Seeing the spectrum
A simpler method than Newton's is to put a glass of water on a piece of white paper near a window. Fix a card with a 1 cm ($\frac{1}{2}$ in) slit on one side of the glass. The sunlight allowed through the slit crosses the water and produces a spectrum on the paper. This only works when the Sun's rays fall at an angle, ie in the morning or evening.

The flame and the feather
If you look with one eye through a bird's feather at a candle flame about a metre away, the flame seems to be multiplied. It also shows the colours of the spectrum. the light being diffracted and split by the narrow slits between the sections of feather. It is because you are looking through so many slits that the flame is multiplied.

Turn colours white
Divide a circle of card about 15 cm (6 in) across into seven sections. Paint or colour them in the order red, orange, yellow, green, blue, indigo, and violet. Pierce the centre of the card with a pencil or toothpick. Spin the top and the colours disappear. The card appears white because our eyes are too slow to distinguish between the rapidly changing colours. They merge and are sent to the brain as white.

One of the most important properties of light is colour. Colour exists because the waves of most kinds of light do not all have the same length. Some are spaced about one half-millionth of a centimetre apart; these cannot be seen, and are called ultra-violet rays. They derive from the part of sunlight that turns our skin brown. Many scientists now say that too much ultra-violet light wrinkles and ages the skin, and may also encourage skin cancer.

Infra-red rays are invisible too, but are much coarser, being as much as 0.2 mm in wavelength. Infra-red rays are hot and they now have many uses. They are employed in special cameras to take pictures in the dark or in fog without the help of bright lights. Long-focus cameras are used in spy planes to pierce the clouds and scan land beneath the flight path. Back at base, the photographs are developed and fitted together into a map. A more peaceful application is shown in the map of Washington below. Infra-red film is of special value because it can pick out differences that cannot be seen at visible-light wavelengths. It can spot variations in crops, for instance, and diseases in trees.

Between infra-red and ultra-violet are all the wavelengths making up visible light. The infra-red waves give way to dull red then bright red. This turns into orange, then yellow, green, turquoise, blue, indigo, and violet. This gradually fades out leaving just ultra-violet.

Aged skin
This Greek peasant woman has a heavily wrinkled face caused by a lifetime of exposure to the Sun's ultra-violet rays. These not only accentuate wrinkles and ageing in the skin but may encourage skin cancer.

Infra-red photography
This view of Washington DC taken from a NASA aircraft picks out aspects of the land not observable using ordinary colour film. The red areas depict densely populated regions, the pink, vegetation.

145

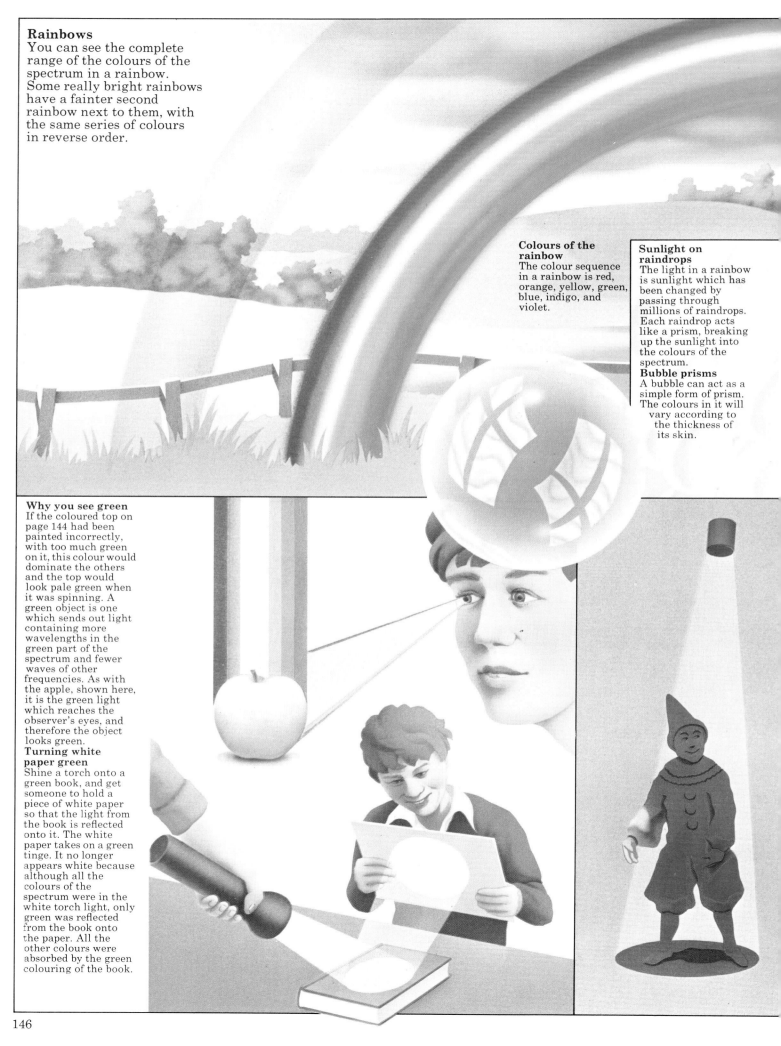

Rainbows

You can see the complete range of the colours of the spectrum in a rainbow. Some really bright rainbows have a fainter second rainbow next to them, with the same series of colours in reverse order.

Colours of the rainbow
The colour sequence in a rainbow is red, orange, yellow, green, blue, indigo, and violet.

Sunlight on raindrops
The light in a rainbow is sunlight which has been changed by passing through millions of raindrops. Each raindrop acts like a prism, breaking up the sunlight into the colours of the spectrum.

Bubble prisms
A bubble can act as a simple form of prism. The colours in it will vary according to the thickness of its skin.

Why you see green
If the coloured top on page 144 had been painted incorrectly, with too much green on it, this colour would dominate the others and the top would look pale green when it was spinning. A green object is one which sends out light containing more wavelengths in the green part of the spectrum and fewer waves of other frequencies. As with the apple, shown here, it is the green light which reaches the observer's eyes, and therefore the object looks green.

Turning white paper green
Shine a torch onto a green book, and get someone to hold a piece of white paper so that the light from the book is reflected onto it. The white paper takes on a green tinge. It no longer appears white because although all the colours of the spectrum were in the white torch light, only green was reflected from the book onto the paper. All the other colours were absorbed by the green colouring of the book.

Make a rainbow
Take a garden hose and stand on a stool in the late afternoon with your back to the sun. Spray a fine shower from the hose and a circular rainbow will appear. Only the shadow of your body briefly breaks the circle.

Adding and subtracting colours
Take a torch and cover it with a piece of coloured plastic. Shine this on a brightly coloured object in a darkened room and note which colour appears. The object will absorb some of the wavelengths of the torchlight, and will appear the colour of the wavelengths that are left. This process is known as colour subtraction.

Quite different things happen when lights of different colours are added together. We have already seen that the spinner appeared white when spun. This is an example of colour addition. The important primary colours of light are red, green and blue, and they can be mixed to make any other colour. A red light makes the clown on the far left look red, but if the red light is mixed with a green one, the clown looks yellow. Blue and red light mix to make magenta. Green and blue make cyan blue. And when all these primary colours are mixed together, they make white light.

White objects reflect back all the seven colours of the spectrum that make up white light. Inhabitants of hot countries wear white clothes and live in white houses to protect themselves from the hot sunlight. By reflecting part of the rays' intensity back into the atmosphere, people help to keep their bodies relatively cool. The illustration above shows a Tunisian street scribe at work; the white robes and whitewashed walls are appropriate to that country's hot climate.

Black clothes, on the other hand, absorb heat and can keep you warmer in cold weather. For this reason, the solar panels now used to absorb the Sun's rays and heat buildings, are always painted black. The upper-right photograph shows a prototype solar collector set into the roof of a house in Wandsworth, London. The absorber plates are made of copper, and painted matt black.

The colour of the sky

Few people stop to ask themselves why the sky normally looks pale blue. It does so because our eyes receive more light of this blue wavelength than any other when we look up at the sky. This light comes from the Sun, but on the way it is scattered by minute particles of dust in the atmosphere.

If you climb up through the atmosphere in an aircraft, the sky appears a darker blue, and to astronauts in space the sky looks completely black. This is because, beyond the Earth's atmosphere, there is no dust to scatter the sunlight.

Why does the setting Sun look red? The reason is that we see it after it has passed at an angle through thousands of kilometres of atmosphere and dust. The tiny particles scatter away most of the blue and violet light during this journey, leaving a red sky at night. When the Sun is overhead, however, the scattering of light by dust is much less, and the Sun appears its natural yellowish-white colour.

Light and life

At the beginning of this chapter, the importance of the Sun's light for life and growth was explained. Animals live on plants, and the plants themselves need light to survive. This is easily proved by carrying out the experiment on the opposite page.

Light is needed by all plants when they perform what is called photosynthesis (see also page 22). This literally means 'building with light'. Plants take water vapour and carbon dioxide from the

How black absorbs heat

You can prove that black absorbs more heat than white or shiny surfaces with a simple experiment. Take an empty metal can and smoke half of it, inside and out, by holding one side over a candle flame. Then suspend a 100–watt bulb in the can so that it hangs as near the centre as possible. Cup your hands around both sides of the can and you will find that the black side is much hotter. The reason is that it has absorbed more heat than the shiny side.

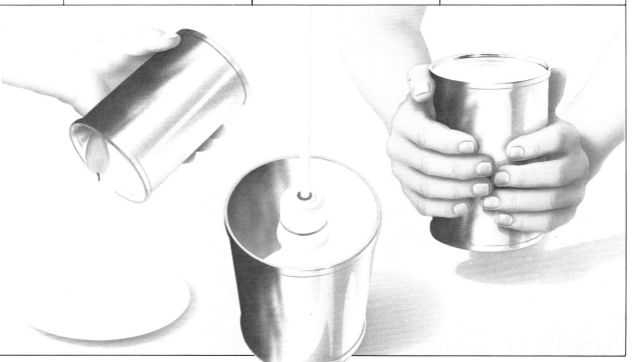

Take two similar plants with regular-shaped leaves. Cover one leaf with black paper on both sides and cover a leaf on the other plant with a clear plastic bag. After one week, remove the coverings and you will find that the leaf covered in black is pale and unhealthy, while the other is normal. The second leaf acted as a control, proving that it was the lack of light which affected the now-unhealthy leaf, and not the fact that it was covered.

atmosphere and turn them into sugar and oxygen. The light is absorbed by the green leaves, and used to supply energy to build up the sugar that is essential for the growing plant.

Even creatures living in the dark depend indirectly on light. Termites, for instance, avoid daylight, and survive by eating wood from the side of logs. But, without light, no trees would grow, and the termites would be left without food.

Several living things can glow in the dark. The best-known are the European and American beetles and larvae called fireflies or glow-worms; a glow-worm is shown far right. These creatures produce the light on the surface of their bodies by oxidizing special organic substances such as luciferin.

Some rocks give out a type of light called phosphorescence. On the right is a piece of calcium fluoride (fluorite). Although it shines, it is not hot like other forms of light. It is similar to luminous paints that glow in the dark. Such paints contain phosphorous compounds which can store electro-magnetic energy falling on them and use it to glow. They can store this energy for a long time, and a clock or watch coated with luminous paint (*above left*) will glow dimly even after years in the dark.

Listening is one of the most important ways of discovering what is going on in the world around you. When you think of all the sounds you hear in one day, from the patter of rain to the roar of jets overhead, you will realize that you can divide these sounds into two categories. There are those you like, which you usually call sounds, and those you dislike, which you usually call noise.

Expressive words are used to describe sounds and noises such as the 'bark' of a dog, the 'boom' of a cannon and the 'rustling' of leaves. By using your voice to produce these word-sounds, you make human communication simple.

Whenever you talk or listen, you are using sound. And all sounds, however different, are alike in one way – something is moving. When you speak, your vocal cords move. You can feel them by putting your fingers lightly in the vicinity of your Adam's apple. And when you ring a bell, put your finger on the metal and you will realize that the bell itself is vibrating.

You are able to hear that sound because the air itself passes sound from one place to another. This was proved as early as the 17th century by Robert Boyle, one of the greatest scientists of his day, and a friend and rival of the famous Sir Isaac Newton. Like many scientists in those days, Boyle was a wealthy nobleman who made scientific experiments his hobby.

He used one of the first air pumps ever built, which had already been the basis of important experiments to reveal the many properties of air (see pages 178–179). For his sound experiment, he put a bell into a glass globe and pumped out the air. As he watched and listened, he realized that the sound of the bell became fainter and fainter as the air was removed. Eventually it could not be heard at all. Then as he let air back into the globe, the sound of the bell gradually returned. In this simple way Boyle proved what many other scientists had failed to do,

that sound is definitely carried by air and that without air there can be no sound. Similarly, astronauts do not hear sounds in space, because there is no air to carry them to their ears.

Sound travels through air in the form of waves, and like all waves it takes time to make this journey. When a stone splashes into a pond, the waves do not reach the side of the pond immediately. The speed of these waves varies between small ripples and large ocean breakers. Light waves

impact take time to make the journey to your ears, although the light waves travel so fast that you see the action almost exactly as it happens.

You can make use of this knowledge to work out the location of a thunderstorm. As you saw on page 92, a flash of lightning is a huge electrical spark in the air. This spark suddenly heats the surrounding air, which expands, setting off a powerful sound wave which you hear as thunder. While

scientists first produced accurate measurements of the speed of sound by using cannons instead of thunder. They asked a colleague to fire a cannon some distance away and measured the time between the flash of the powder and the sound of the cannon firing. From this simple experiment, they deduced quite correctly that the speed of sound was about 335 m (1,100 ft) per second.

The French scientists working with the cannon (below) were appointed by a government commission of 1822. In the lower picture, the scientist holding the huge earphone is testing the speed of the sound of a bell rung underwater by a colleague working from another boat a measured distance away. This took place on Lake Geneva.

move at an impressive 298,050 km (186,281 miles) per second. Sound waves are slower, and travel at about 0.32 km ($\frac{1}{5}$ mile) a second.

You can test the difference in speed between light and sound waves. Watch a tennis match from a short distance away and you will see the players hitting the ball half a second or more before you hear the impact of the racquet on the ball. This is because the sound waves from that

the light waves reach you virtually immediately, the sound waves travel at a speed of about 1.6 km (1 mile) in five seconds. So you can find out how far away the storm is by counting the number of seconds between the lightning and the first clap of thunder, and dividing by five. A delay of 10 seconds, for instance, means the storm is only 3 km (2 miles) away.

This method was used as long ago as the 16th century. A group of Italian

Bell pump (above left) A reconstruction of the pump used by Boyle.
Sound experiments (above) An 1822 French experiment to find the speed of sound. A gun was fired, and the time lapse between flash and report noted. An 1826 experiment (right) to measure the speed of sound in water.
Locate the storm (right) Count the seconds between lightning and thunder clap; divide by five for an answer in miles.

HOW YOUR EAR WORKS

Your ear is a complicated organ which picks up sound waves and turns them into messages to your brain. The ear can hear sounds a hundred times fainter than a whisper, and survive noise a hundred times greater than thunder without damage.

You have two ears to help you locate the direction of a sound. Prove this by switching on the radio, covering your eyes, plugging one ear with cotton-wool and turning around a few times. You will find it difficult to decide where the sound is coming from.

The part of the ear outside the head is called the auricle. Its function is to collect the sound waves in the air. It seems that humans may once have been able to prick up their ears. There is a muscle behind our ears which still receives a message from the brain when we hear a sound. This muscle does not now move our ears, but doctors can put electrodes behind the ear to record the

impulse passed along the nerve from our brain to the muscle. It is the basis of a new and more accurate hearing test, which can be used on all patients, even new-born babies.

The main part of the ear is inside the skull, starting with the eardrum, a piece of skin stretched lightly across the inner end of the ear canal. This canal has wax and hairs to trap dirt that could harm your inner ear. Sound waves collected by the auricle hit the eardrum and make it vibrate. You can reproduce the way sound passes along the ear canal to cause vibration of the eardrum. Hold a cardboard tube against a balloon and make a noise into it. You can feel the balloon vibrating from the sound waves.

The eardrum is joined to a set of three small bones called the hammer, the anvil and the stirrup which pass the sound on to the inner ear. These bones are connected in such a way that they are able to increase the force of the

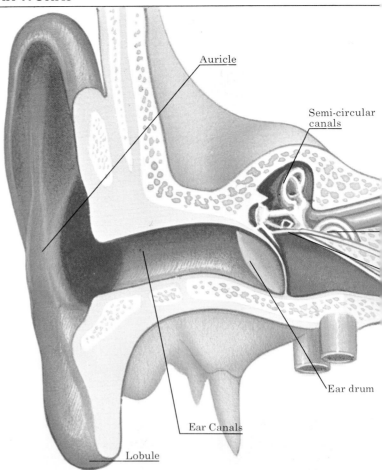

Auricle

Semi-circular canals

Ear drum

Ear Canals

Lobule

THE CAUSE OF SOUND

Every sound we hear is due to a vibration – a backward and forward movement that we can often feel and see. To see noise being made, spread a large piece of clear plastic over the top of a bowl. Pull it tight and keep it in position with a rubber band. Sprinkle some sugar on top of this simple drum. Hold a baking tray close to the drum and hit the tray hard with a wooden spoon. Watch the drum surface and you will see the sugar jump.

This happens because of the vibrations caused when you hit the baking tray with the spoon. The air carries the vibrations to your ears, so that you hear the noise. As we have seen, these disturbances are called sound waves, and behave very much like water waves.

When you throw a stone into a pond, you see small waves starting out from where the stone fell. These waves spread out steadily in circles, and, as they pass, anything floating on the water bobs up and down.

The waves pass motion from the stone to the floating object.

These waves show in slow motion what happens when you hear a sudden noise. A bang disturbs the air, and waves move out through the air in all directions. These sound waves pass some of the motion to your eardrum, so that you hear the sound.

As well as sudden noises, there is also steady sound. Dip a stick in and out of water at a regular rate. If you keep doing this, the whole surface of the water is covered with waves, spreading out from the end of the stick. A steady sound moves through the air on sound waves in much the same way. Both types of wave arise from something moving backward and forward at a steady rate, or vibrating. The number of vibrations in every second is called the frequency of the vibration.

To understand sound waves you have to know that all materials consist of minute particles, a

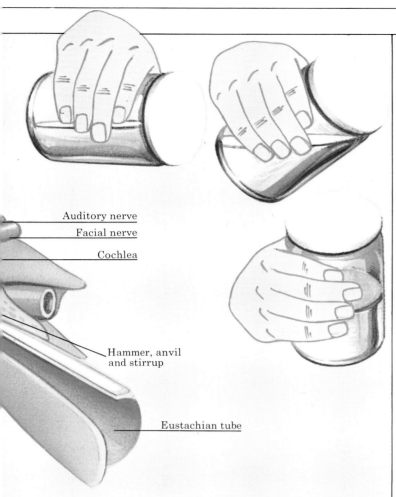

Auditory nerve
Facial nerve
Cochlea
Hammer, anvil and stirrup
Eustachian tube

sound waves many times. The Eustachian tube, which connects this part of the ear to the throat, balances the pressure of the air on both sides of the eardrum. This equilibrium can be upset by the sudden changes in pressure that you may experience while diving underwater, especially with an aqualung, or when you are in an aircraft that is rapidly losing height before landing. The Eustachian tube may then become blocked. To clear it you can try swallowing or waggling your jaw.

The main part of the inner ear, the cochlea, is shaped like a snail shell. It is filled with a liquid, and is lined with many nerve cells, designed to receive sound vibrations. When the eardrum vibrates, the vibrations are in turn passed along the hammer, the anvil and then the stirrup. This last bone is set into the cochlea, so the vibrations cause the liquid in the cochlea to move and sweep over the nerve cells, which send a message about the sound to the brain, along the auditory nerve.

This liquid in the inner ear plays an important part in balance (see also page 59). It always stays level when you move. You can see how it behaves (left) by taking a glass jar and half filling it with water. Add a few drops of food colouring so that you can see it move easily. Then hold it in many positions. It always stays level – just like the liquid in your cochlea. When you change the position of the jar, you will see that the water sloshes around, before it settles. In the same way, the liquid in the cochlea moves around when you move.

The behaviour of this liquid also explains why you feel dizzy. When you spin round and round the liquid in your inner ear whirls round too. But when you stop, it keeps going for a while. The whirling liquid sends a message to your brain saying that you are still spinning. This confuses your brain, and you feel dizzy.

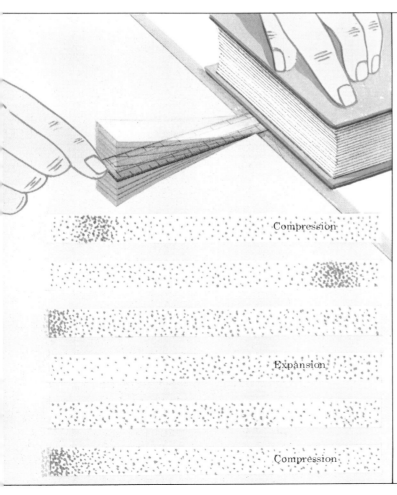

Compression
Expansion
Compression

million times too small to be seen. These molecules, as they are called, are never still. They move around constantly, bumping into each other. A sound wave occurs when the molecules in the air make extra movements, caused by a vibration. To visualize what happens, do the following experiment with a ruler.

Use a heavy book to hold down the end of the ruler on a table, so that most of the ruler projects over the edge (left). Hold the book in position and pull the other end of the ruler down and let it go. It makes a low twang as it vibrates. As the end of the ruler moves up, it pushes on the air molecules above it and they are squeezed closer together. This is called a compression. As these molecules relax, they push the air molecules next to them. In this way the compression is moved on quickly through the air.

In the meantime, the end of the ruler has started to move back down. It happens so fast that the molecules from the surrounding air do not have time to fill this space immediately, so this air contains fewer molecules. An area like this, where the molecules are thinned out, is called an expansion.

The expansion moves through the air after a compression, and makes the air near the ruler look rather like the illustration (below left). The compression is like the hump in a water wave and the expansion is like the hollow. A sound wave is normally drawn as a wavy curve with humps and hollows. This curve represents a very simple sound wave; many sounds are much more complicated. As a projectile cuts through the air for example, it produces two kinds of wave. First comes the bow wave created by the point of the shell or rocket, then the tail wave, behind which a vacuum is formed; air then rushes in to fill the gap, and a cone of sound is created.

The speed of sound

As a general rule, most liquids and solids transmit sound at a greater speed than air. You can test this yourself. Put your ear against a long metal fence and ask a friend to hit the fence with something like a hammer. You will hear the noise of the hammer hitting the metal fence before the sound reaches you through the air. That is why you can often hear the pounding noise of a train on the rails before you begin to hear the usual sounds of the approaching train. The steel rails carry sound 14 times faster than air. In the same way, sound travels faster through the ground than through air. American Indians, by putting an ear to the ground, were able to hear the sound of approaching horses or buffalo long before they could be heard in the normal way.

When you are swimming, you can test water's ability to transmit sound. Knock two rocks together in the air. Ask a friend to check how loud it sounds from 18 m (20 yd) away. Then do the same thing underwater. The sound of the rocks hitting each other will be louder when transmitted by water. You can make a string telephone, which shows how sound is conducted by solids. Take two empty cans or yoghurt pots and stretch a long string between them. Talk to a friend on the other end of the 'line' by speaking into the can, and he will hear your voice vibrations if he uses his own can as a receiver, placing it to his ear. The string conducts the speech vibrations faster than air, and voices seem louder using a string telephone than they would using just the voice and air alone. The ability of solids to transmit sound helps people with poor hearing, who can sometimes hear music by feeling vibrations.

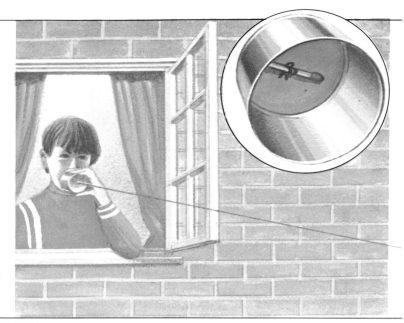

PITCH

The term pitch means the lowness or height of a sound, and is determined by the frequency of vibration, or the number of vibrations a second, of the sound waves reaching the ear. The more vibrations there are per second, the higher is the pitch. Conversely, the lower the frequency, the lower the pitch.

You can translate these patterns of sound into visual sets of wavelengths. The bottom drawing on the opposite page shows in effect how two different frequencies may be compared within a similar time-span. Sound frequencies are usually measured in thousands per second, and tests have shown that the human ear is most sensitive in the range between 2,000 and 5,000 cycles per second. Obviously it would not be practical to draw all the waves that a particular sound sets up, but the principle of waves per unit of time is the same.

The majority of sounds you hear come from things which stay in one place. But the situation is different if something moves quickly towards or away from you while it makes a sound. Then your ears can be confused and will not be able to judge the true pitch of the sound.

This happens when a police-car or ambulance speeds past you with its siren going. You notice that the pitch of the sound suddenly drops when the vehicle shoots by. You hear a sudden change in the sound, although in fact the noise which is given out by the siren is quite regular. The significant change that has taken place is not the speed of the vehicle or the frequency of the siren, but the direction from which the sound reaches your ear.

This effect is produced for the following reasons. Each sound wave that starts out is round, but because the siren is moving forward all the time, the centre of each circle is a little farther along the road than the last one. This makes the waves 'bunch up' in front and 'stretch out' at the rear. If you are standing ahead of the vehicle, the waves reaching you are crowded together, so that more than the normal number hit your ear each second. The pitch sounds higher than the true tone.

After the vehicle has passed, you hear the stretched-out sound waves. They hit your ear less often than normal, so that the sound you hear is lower in pitch. You notice the sudden drop in pitch just at the moment the vehicle passes, and the faster it is going, the greater the change.

This interesting effect of movement was first worked out over a century ago by an Austrian called Christian Doppler, and scientists now call it the Doppler effect. You can also notice the Doppler effect if you yourself are moving and the sound waves are coming from a stationary object.

Frequency
Test your understanding of frequency by trying this experiment. Take an old round baking tin and punch evenly spaced circular rows of holes in the bottom. Mount the baking tin on an electric hand drill. Start the drill spinning, then blow air through a narrow tube onto the various rows of holes. Listen to the sounds of varying pitch. A different note will be heard for each row of holes. You will notice too, that as the air is blown on to the rows containing more holes, the pitch rises. This is because the frequency increases as the number of holes increases.

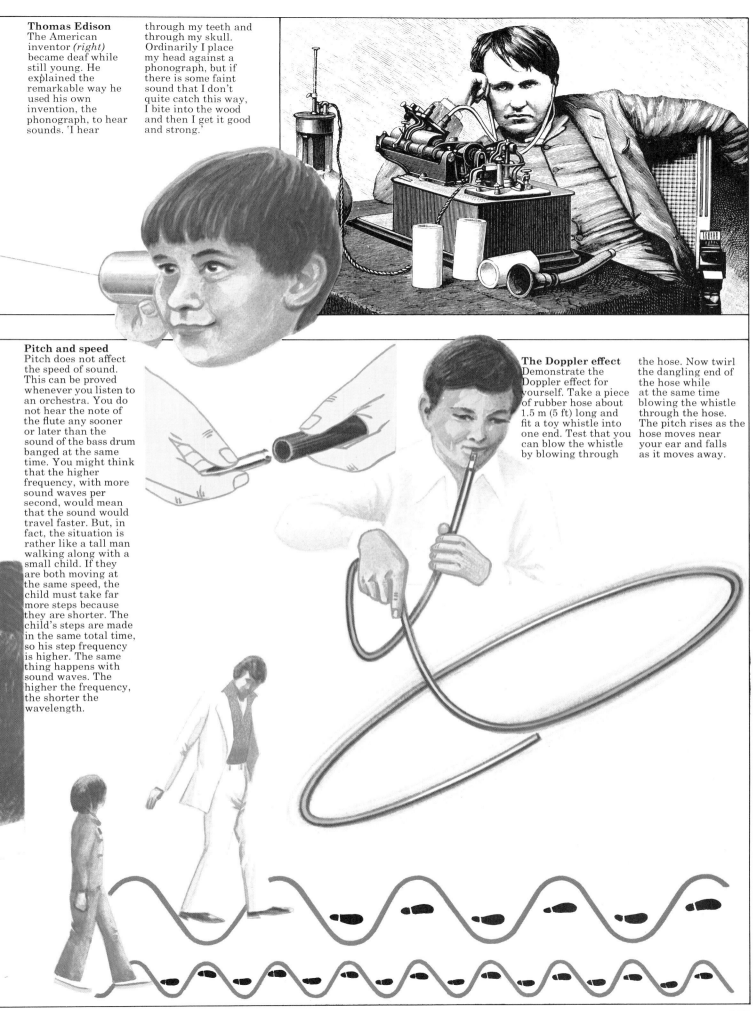

Thomas Edison
The American inventor *(right)* became deaf while still young. He explained the remarkable way he used his own invention, the phonograph, to hear sounds. 'I hear through my teeth and through my skull. Ordinarily I place my head against a phonograph, but if there is some faint sound that I don't quite catch this way, I bite into the wood and then I get it good and strong.'

Pitch and speed
Pitch does not affect the speed of sound. This can be proved whenever you listen to an orchestra. You do not hear the note of the flute any sooner or later than the sound of the bass drum banged at the same time. You might think that the higher frequency, with more sound waves per second, would mean that the sound would travel faster. But, in fact, the situation is rather like a tall man walking along with a small child. If they are both moving at the same speed, the child must take far more steps because they are shorter. The child's steps are made in the same total time, so his step frequency is higher. The same thing happens with sound waves. The higher the frequency, the shorter the wavelength.

The Doppler effect
Demonstrate the Doppler effect for yourself. Take a piece of rubber hose about 1.5 m (5 ft) long and fit a toy whistle into one end. Test that you can blow the whistle by blowing through the hose. Now twirl the dangling end of the hose while at the same time blowing the whistle through the hose. The pitch rises as the hose moves near your ear and falls as it moves away.

LOUDNESS

Another characteristic of sound is loudness, which means the pressure a sound imposes on the ear. Naturally, the closer you are to the source of a sound, the louder it will be. But all sound can be measured for loudness, or the intensity of the sound waves, using the unit called a decibel. Our table on the right shows measurements for various sounds.

The smallest difference in intensity that the human ear can pick up is a change of one decibel. Moving up from zero, or the point at which a sound can just be heard, which is called the threshold of hearing, the intensity level of a whisper is about 15 decibels. Normal talking is 50, busy traffic 70, and sound which becomes painful to our ears is above the 120-decibel range.

The problem of noise, whether at work, in discotheques or airports, is now being recognized. Exposure to constant loud noise can, in time, damage hearing, so safe levels are being set to protect us all. In Britain the recommended top limit for noise is 90 decibels. If that level is to be exceeded at work,

then employers have to provide protective gear for the people they wish to expose to it. This protection varies from earplugs (for noise up to 105 decibels), as worn in an engineering shop, to ear-muffs such as tractor drivers wear (up to 115 decibels), and helmets for exceptionally noisy jobs (above 115 decibels).

One place where no protection is offered is at rock concerts, where the waves of sound from the mountains of amplifiers can roar out at literally deafening levels. Rivalry among the bands to have

the most impressive sound system reached a point in the 1970s at which the musicians had to have their own special fold-back speakers so that they could actually hear what they were playing.

Echoes

At some time or other you will have been amused by hearing the echoes of your own voice reflected by a nearby hill, wall or cliff. This happens because the air disturbance caused by your voice is transmitted outwards until it reaches the hill. From there it bounces back again, so

that you hear the same disturbance that you created shortly before.

Just as light rays are reflected by a mirror, sound waves can be reflected by many surfaces. The smoother the reflecting surface, the less the waves are distorted, and therefore the 'better' the echo.

Indoors, the nearby walls reflect sound back so quickly that it blends with the original sound. You have to be some distance away from the reflecting surface to hear an echo. In fact, your ear can hear two sounds separately only if they come at least one-tenth of a second apart.

This means that, if you make a noise some distance from a hill, you will hear an echo only if the hill is far enough away for the sound to take one-tenth of a second or more to reach it and bounce back again. Since sound travels about 33 m (110 ft) in one-tenth of a second, you should be at least 17 m (55 ft) from the hill.

Echoes can be used to determine the distances between you and large reflecting surfaces. In foggy

Sound	Decibels
Space rocket at lift-off	140–190
Jet aircraft on take-off	110–140
Thunder	90–110
Railway train	65–90
Loud conversation	50–65
Quiet conversation	20–50
Rustling of leaves	0–10

Reflected sound

Take two very long stiff card tubes, an alarm clock and a piece of smooth card about 30 cm (12 in) square. Angle the tubes so that the ends are about 5 cm (2 in) apart. Position the card about 5 cm (2 in) from the tube ends. Place the clock at the other end of one tube and ask a friend to listen to the end of the second tube. The ticks of the clock will be heard, although the tubes are not connected. The sound travels along one tube, bounces against the card and is reflected into the other tube. Try covering the card with crumpled paper and see if this affects the quality of the sound.

Sonar

Reflecting sound waves are also used by the navies of the world in an instrument called Sonar – from the words *sound navigation and ranging*. It is a delicate device which tells its operator when ships are near, and is vital to submarine crews who must stay submerged for long periods, hiding from enemy ships. Sonar involves beaming high-frequency sound waves so that solid objects in their path will reflect the waves back to their source, where they are detected on sonar equipment. Because the speed of sound in water is known, the sonar operator only has to measure the time it took for the waves to make the journey from his own ship to the target and back. The distance from the target is then known. A sonar echo does make a sound, a kind of 'pinging' noise, and the operator has to be trained to tell the differences among various water sounds – for example between a submarine and a whale. One problem with sonar is that its transmissions are also detectable, like those of wireless and radar, so that the hunter can become the hunted.

weather, a ship sounds its horn if it seems likely that rocky cliffs or icebergs are nearby. The echo of the horn's sound tells the ship's captain if he is getting too close for safety.

The depths of the ocean can be charted using echoes. Short sound waves are sent out from a ship by means of an oscillator, and are bounced off the ocean bottom. The time taken for these waves to return is registered by an instrument called a fathometer, and a depth is registered. When a number of such readings have been gathered, charts of the ocean floor can be drawn.

Multiple echoes

In some circumstances, particularly in mountainous areas, there are so many reflecting surfaces that several echoes come back one after another, getting fainter all the time. The sound waves are bouncing around between neighbouring or nearly parallel surfaces.

There is an old joke about a trapper who lived in a log cabin in a spot famous for its echo. He needed no alarm clock to get him up in the morning, because last thing at night, he shouted out of the window, 'Time to get up' – and eight hours later the echo came back and woke him up. You could try to work out how far away the reflecting surface would have to be to make this story true.

There are some famous multiple-sound echoes. Amazing echoes can be produced in Mammoth Cave,

Kentucky, USA, which is 91 m (300 ft) below the Earth's surface. And in one old Italian castle, near Milan, a 40-fold echo can be heard. When a guide in the Baptistery at Pisa sings a few quick notes in succession, the echoes combine and can be heard for seconds afterwards. Curved walls in St Paul's Cathedral, London and the Capitol in Washington, DC reflect sound. They are called 'whispering galleries', because whispers can be heard a long way away, reflected along the curved surfaces.

Indoor sound

A person speaking at an ordinary level outside will be heard for only a short distance. This is because sound waves get weaker as they move out from their starting point. At a distance of 6 m (20 ft), for example, they are only 25 per cent as strong as at 3 m (10 ft) and at 12 m (40 ft), they are only 6.25 per cent as strong.

But the sound will be louder if there is a wall behind the person who is talking, because sound waves that would be lost are thrown back to the listeners, boosting the sound that comes directly to them. With four walls and a roof the speaker should be heard easily, if the room is built properly. This, however, is not as easy as it would seem.

Ever since churches, halls and theatres have been built, there have been problems with muffled sound – 'dead' spots where sound can be hardly heard at all, and other areas

where it seems unusually loud.

It was not until early this century that the behaviour of sound waves indoors began to be understood. The term, acoustics, from the Greek for hearing, is the science of sound waves, particularly sound waves indoors. In designing and constructing buildings, notably auditoriums or broadcasting studios, there are two major problems – reverberation and interference.

Reverberation is the repeated reflection of sound waves from smooth surfaces in an enclosed space. It is a resounding process, like a series of echoes. When you are listening to music in your own living-room, sound bounces around from various objects in the room. However, the surrounding surfaces absorb enough of this sound. This means that each new sound does not have to compete with the slowly dying reverberations of the sounds that came before, as it would in an empty, steel-enclosed room.

Interference is an effect produced by combinations of sound waves that reinforce, cancel, or in some way interfere with each other. Acoustical engineers know that the human ear needs about one-tenth of a second between two sounds if it is to recognize that there are two sounds instead of just one.

In large rooms like auditoriums, separate echoes coming back from a far wall sometimes arrive at the ear in time to cause confusion with the sounds

being made by the person on stage. These reflections have to be reduced by soundproofing.

Good absorbers of sound are porous materials like felt, carpet or special fibre wall tiles. Scientists can work out exactly how much absorbent material to put into a room to make the reflected sound die away as quickly or as slowly as desired.

Many musicians dislike working in a room where the sound fades too quickly because it muffles their playing. But speakers usually prefer a hall of this kind, because it is difficult for an audience to follow a speech when one syllable runs into the next. If one auditorium has to be used for both music and talks, average acoustics have to be agreed on. Scientists then work out how to design the hall to achieve the correct effect. They are able to regulate the exact fading-away time for sound by the amount of absorbent material used in the construction of the hall.

The famous Royal Albert Hall in London was built long before the science of acoustics was understood. But in the early days it was perfect for concerts. As time went on, however, people complained about the sound quality. Tests showed that sound was taking longer to fade away. Eventually it was discovered why this was so. Fashions of dress had changed, and the audiences no longer wore such long, bulky clothes, which had helped to absorb the sound. Special wall coverings had to be put up to solve this problem. Soundproofing is not the complete answer to producing good sound. An auditorium has to be built in a certain shape. Architects have learned to avoid having curved surfaces in places where they can beam the reflected waves down into the audience.

Imagine that you are looking down into an auditorium, watching the movement of sound waves. The first picture on the right shows what you would see after the speaker had made his first sound. The sound waves have spread out in all directions, but have not yet reached the last rows of seats.

The second picture shows a slightly later stage. Some of the original waves have already reached the walls and have been reflected. They are reflected many times before they fade. In the meantime new sounds are coming from the platform, so that the room is filled with complicated criss-crossing waves.

Scientists test for sound quality by using tanks of water built in the same shape as the auditorium they are planning to construct. Then they check in advance how the sound waves will behave by starting ripples in the water in the area where the stage will be, and watching how they spread. You can simulate a 'theatre tank' at home by carrying out the ripple test shown on the right.

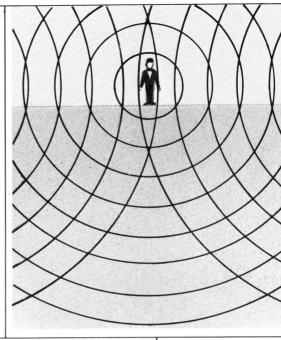

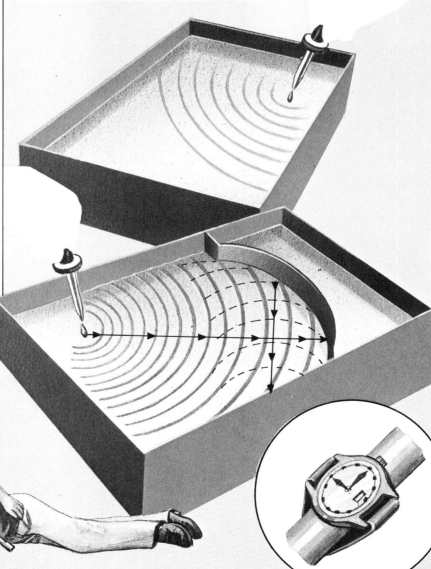

Ripple experiments

Take an oblong baking tray, let drops of water fall into the pan, and watch how the ripples are reflected from the sides again and again. You can even bend a strip of thin metal, forming the sort of outline found in many theatres, stand it in the pan and see how it affects the ripples. These ripple experiments may show up 'hot spots' where the sound waves gather after reflection. These are usually caused by curved areas of wall and ceiling. Instead of continuing to spread out, sound waves reflected from a curve will come together. You can test this by placing two open umbrellas about 6 m (20 ft) apart. Line up their handles in a straight line. Fasten a watch to the middle of one of the handles and put your ear to the same place on the other umbrella. You will hear the ticking clearly, reflected from the far umbrella.

RESONANCE

An object resonates when it is made to vibrate by another sounding body which has a frequency of free vibration either exactly the same or almost the same as its own. One way of understanding resonance is to imagine you are pushing someone on a swing. Every time the swing starts to move away from you, you give it an extra push. If the swing moves backwards and forwards once a second, you could say that its frequency of free vibration is one cycle a second. At the same time you are giving the swing exactly one push each second. If you gave more or fewer pushes, you might stop the swing's action altogether.

Your pushes exactly correspond with the frequency of the swing's vibration. Put another way, you could say that your pushes are in resonance with the swing's vibration.

Resonance can also be disruptive. This is why soldiers marching across a bridge have to break step, to prevent energy being stored up while the bridge is resonating which could suddenly collapse the entire structure.

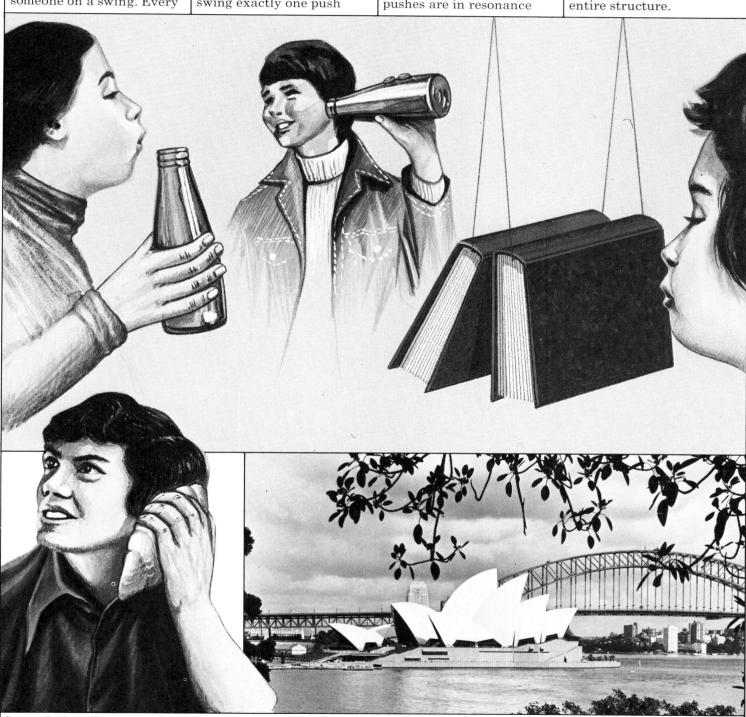

Sympathetic milk bottles and other experiments
Use two milk bottles of the same size and shape to demonstrate the principle of resonance. Ask a friend to hold one to his ear, then stand about 1 metre (1 yd) away and blow sharply across the top of the other bottle until you produce a sound. The air column in your friend's bottle will pick up similar vibrations, so that he will hear a faint note produced by resonance. Another way to demonstrate the principle is to suspend a heavy book by two long cords and blow on it. If your puffs are timed carefully to coincide with the book's natural period of vibration, it can soon be made to swing.

Finally, put a sea shell to your ear and hear 'the sound of the sea'. This is caused by resonance. In a big shell the sea will roar with a deep bass voice, while a small shell produces a higher noise. This is because the air within any enclosed space of moderate size vibrates more easily at one definite pitch than another. The bigger the space, the lower the pitch, and vice versa. The air around you is full of a mixture of sounds of different pitch.

When you put the shell to your ear, you hear an amplification of any sound that corresponds to the shell's natural pitch. Above is the Sydney Opera House. Its acoustic vibrations were put to the severest tests.

159

Anything that can produce one or more different sounds or tones can be called a musical instrument. The first musical instrument was probably a hollow log, hit by a stick. This was followed by horns of animals, hollowed out and fitted with hollow reeds. Then someone tried stretching thin strips of animal hide between two pegs in a board. The strips made an attractive twanging sound when they were plucked. Some basic early types are shown in the drawing below. You will notice that most are percussion instruments – the kind that make their sounds through being hit.

Musicians soon learned that some combinations of notes sound more pleasant than others. You can find out more about this by making a simple, one-stringed instrument. Slip an press the band down with your finger and pluck each side. The pitch is much higher. This is because you have changed the length of the vibrating part of the string. The shorter the vibrating string, the higher the tone.

Press down the rubber string exactly in its middle, and pluck either half.

String music

Musical instruments which produce sound by using vibrating strings are called stringed instruments. Although the Egyptians were using a form of harp nearly 5,000 years ago, the scientific facts about vibrating strings were not discovered until about 300 years ago.

Simple musical instruments
(far left) The marimba, an African type of xylophone.
(centre) Early examples of percussion instruments – castanets and drum; stringed instrument – lyre; wind instrument – shell trumpet.
(left) African drum of the Ashanti tribe.
(right) An African shell trumpet is blown as a call to war.

ordinary rubber band around a book and put two pencils under the loop, one near each end *(opposite)*.

If you pluck the stretched band near the middle it will give a note of a definite pitch. Now

Compare the tone with that of the whole string and you will realize that it is an octave higher. A string half as long vibrates twice as fast. If one note is an octave higher than another, its frequency is double.

PIPE MUSIC

When you blow across the top of an empty bottle you can produce a sound with a definite pitch. The bottle is acting like a simple wind instrument. The trumpet, flute and organ pipe all work in the same way. A wind instrument is a long tube, with one end open so that you can blow air into it. The other end can be open too, as with the flute, or it can be closed, as it is in some kinds of organs.

Imagine what happens in a closed pipe first. When you blow air across the opening, it makes a compression move down the tube at the speed of sound. Because the sides of the pipe prevent it spreading, it weakens very little, and at the end wall it is reflected back, acting like the waves on the rope of the previous experiment.

When it reaches the mouth of the pipe it is free to expand, and this expansion then travels down the tube and back to the opening. If it is still strong enough, the expansion sucks air into the pipe from outside to form a compression. So expansions and compressions move up and down the tube, forcing the stream of air from your lips to vibrate, and sound waves of a definite frequency are produced.

The length of pipe in wind instruments controls the notes. If the pipe is short, the compressions and expansions occur very quickly, causing fast vibration and a high-pitched sound. A longer pipe produces a lower pitch. You can see how pitch and length are related by comparing members of the clarinet or saxophone family.

Just as a vibrating string can produce more than one tone, depending on how it divides into loops, so a pipe can vibrate in its fundamental or in one of the overtones.

Wind instruments The player of the flute or clarinet produces different notes by covering and uncovering the small holes along the side of the instrument. This action shortens and lengthens the vibrating length of the tube. It is easy to demonstrate this if you fill about 10 glass bottles, all exactly the same size, with graduated amounts of water, as shown above. Blow across the mouths of the bottles to produce breathy musical notes. Those containing little water make low notes, but as the air columns get shorter in the bottles containing more water, the pitch of the notes will rise.

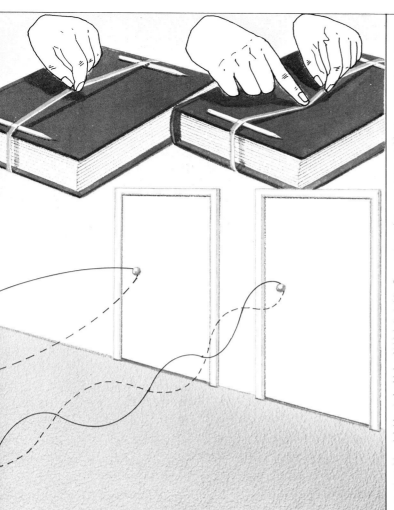

Galileo, the famous Italian scientist, was the first to find out how the vibration of a string depends on the size of the string and how tightly it is stretched.

The weight and thickness of a string affect frequency too. The lower-toned strings of the piano are wound all along their length with soft wire to make them heavier. Otherwise the only way to get these low tones would be to use longer strings, and the piano would then be considerably larger.

A violinist produces different tones from each string, after changing the length by pressing the string down at different points. Only the part that is rubbed by the bow vibrates. Watch a violinist as he plays, and you will notice that he produces the higher tones by pressing or 'stopping' the string close in, making the vibrating part short.

A string can also be made to vibrate in two or three equal parts even without 'stopping' it anywhere along its length.

You can prove this with your own experiment. Use a piece of rubber tubing or heavy clothes-line, about 6 m (20 ft) long, and tie it to a door-knob. Holding the other end in your hand, stretch it fairly tightly and move your hand up and down slowly. At first, humps or waves pass along the rope and back again. But after a while you will find that the rope will move up and down as a single unit.

If the rope was a violin string, it would now be producing the lowest note possible, called the fundamental. Now, taking care to move the rope up and down only, move your hand faster.

With practice you can make the rope vibrate in two, three or even four sections. These are called overtones. When a violin string vibrates in two sections, the frequency is just twice as great, giving a tone that is an octave higher than the fundamental. Three loops means three times the fundamental frequency, and so on.

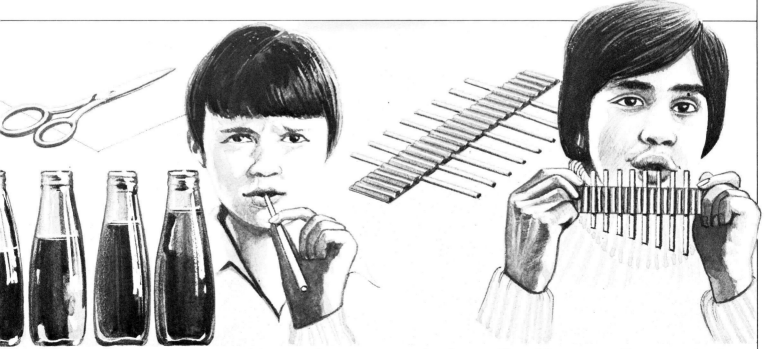

A humming flute
Here is how to make a humming flute.
Take a square piece of paper and snip off one corner from it. Then make two notches in the opposite corner. Now roll the paper from one untouched corner to the other so that it is just a little thicker than a drinking-straw. Push the cut-off corner back into the opening and blow through the tube. The paper corner vibrates with a deep humming sound.

Pipes of Pan
Take a strip of corrugated cardboard and push eight drinking straws through alternate openings of the cardboard, as shown above. Blow across the tops of the straws. You can tune them by cutting them successively shorter, to create notes of different pitch. Provided you make your cuts in an even gradation, you should then be able to get a complete octave.

As the chemist Paul Karrer wrote, 'Three-quarters of the Earth's surface is covered with water, and three-quarters of the bodies of plants and animals are filled with it.' A truer figure for the water area on Earth would be 70 per cent, but the regions covered are so vast that there is a case for wondering why the place in which we live is not called the planet Water.

The real nature of water was not fully understood until the late 18th century. Early scientists were so struck by its weight and strength that they declared that it consisted of only one indivisible substance. It was Henry Cavendish who began the process of breaking down the elements in water when he heated hydrogen ('combustible air') with oxygen in a closed test tube. This produced an amount of water that weighed exactly the same as the component gases. The

French scientist Lavoisier took these experiments further, and established that water is composed of a single oxygen atom and two hydrogen atoms.

While water is easily formed by joining oxygen and hydrogen atoms, it is extremely resilient and hard to break up once it is formed. Even if it is heated to 3,000°C, which is double the melting point of steel, only about 25% of the water molecules will split up again. Water has a number of curious properties that derive from the make-up of the water molecule. It exerts a remarkable solvent effect on many other chemical molecules, which

has made it a welcome slave in science laboratories.

Water is also unusual in that it is less dense when it is frozen. Logically, you would think that ice was denser than liquid water, but the truth is the other way round. Icebergs sit on or near the surface of water,

THE SCIENCE OF WATER

not on the ocean bed. This is fortunate, because if lakes and seas froze from the bed upwards, far greater areas of the world's waterways would freeze up, seriously affecting marine life, commercial shipping, and in fact the whole ecological balance. As it is, a surface layer of ice quickly forms when the air temperature drops below freezing point, and this layer protects the deeper waters. The dissolved salts in sea water also help to keep the waters denser and liquid at temperatures below 0°C.

The density of water, as compared with that of air, explains why man has taken so long to discover ways of staying underwater for long

periods. On land, the atmosphere exerts a pressure on our bodies which scientists measure as 1 bar. Below water the pressure increases rapidly, and exerts a crushing force on the hollow parts of the body: the cheeks, lungs, intestines, etc. Even at a depth of 1 metre, our lungs can hardly expand to take in enough air through a breathing tube. Already the pressure has dropped to 0.1 bar, and this process continues, reaching 30 bar at 300 metres. For that reason, the story of the intrepid Alexander the Great being lowered into the ocean in a transparent barrel for several days and nights, must be regarded as a fairy tale.

A crude early diving apparatus was Halley's bell of 1690, which was supplied by air lowered to it in barrels. A few years later an English carpenter called John Lethbridge constructed a 'diving engine' which was a forerunner of the

Cavendish's experiments *(opposite)* This eudiometer was used by Henry Cavendish (1731–1810) in his efforts to break down the elements of water.

Iceberg *(below)* These great bodies are ample proof that ice is less dense than water. If it were not, the iceberg would sink instead of sitting on or near the surface.

Halley's diving bell *(right)* In 1690 Sir Edmund Halley invented a diving-bell system capable of sustaining three men underwater. Two sat in the bell while a third worked outside it on the main aim of the mission, eg recovering treasure from a sunken wreck. The outside man obtained his air through a breathing tube joined to the bell. Fresh barrels of air were lowered from the boat and connected by tube to the bell. The base of the bell was left open so that the air in the bell took up the pressure of the water outside.

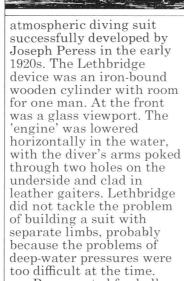

Jim Jarratt, and it is now worn all over the world by divers working on offshore oil and gas exploration. Today's diving methods and suits are so sophisticated that trained divers can work for worthwhile periods at depths in excess of 300 m.

The solo diver needs weights to make him sink to the required depth. Diving machines, like the submarine and submersible, work on the principle of letting water in to increase their weight so that they sink. To make them rise again, their tanks are emptied to the point where buoyancy exceeds gravity, and they go up through the water.

atmospheric diving suit successfully developed by Joseph Peress in the early 1920s. The Lethbridge device was an iron-bound wooden cylinder with room for one man. At the front was a glass viewport. The 'engine' was lowered horizontally in the water, with the diver's arms poked through two holes on the underside and clad in leather gaiters. Lethbridge did not tackle the problem of building a suit with separate limbs, probably because the problems of deep-water pressures were too difficult at the time.

Peress opted for ball-and-socket joints for the limbs, incorporating also a fluid 'cushion' between each ball and socket. This effectively withstood the fierce water pressure that otherwise would have jammed the ball in the socket and made the joint immovable. The suit became known as 'Jim', after Peress's chief mechanic

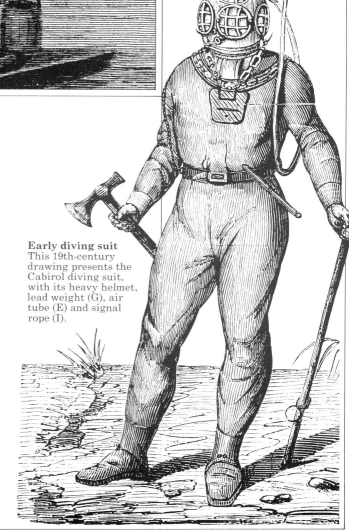

Early diving suit
This 19th-century drawing presents the Cabirol diving suit, with its heavy helmet, lead weight (G), air tube (E) and signal rope (I).

THE SURFACE OF WATER

The surface area of water and other liquids behaves very differently from the interior. The molecules at the surface are not in the same state of all-round mutual attraction as they have fellow molecules only on one side. So the bond between the molecules of the surface layer is increased, making it act rather like a light skin. Bubbles inside a liquid often froth at the surface without escaping, because of this 'skin'.

This surface tension, as it is called, is very powerful. For example, it can support the weight of insects; some are known for the ease with which they run across ponds (see the pond skater, right). Using a fine, hollow hook, the larva of the mosquito hangs onto the surface of the water to breathe. To combat malaria, substances are spread across the surface of pools so that the surface tension of the water is affected. The mosquitoes cannot breathe successfully and they, and malaria, are wiped out.

The strength of surface tension
There are many ways of demonstrating the strength of surface tension, ie water's 'skin'. First, fill a dry glass almost to the top with water, making sure none runs down the sides. Then put the glass into a shallow dish and fill the rest of the glass with an eye-dropper until the water level is well above the rim. The surface tension will allow the water to stand approximately 3 mm ($\frac{1}{8}$ in) above the top of the glass if it is kept quite still.

Extra proof can be obtained by doing a trick with a floating needle. Place a piece of tissue-paper underneath a needle and put both onto the surface of the water. Within a few minutes the air will be driven out of the paper and water will replace it.

The paper will sink to the bottom of the glass, leaving the needle floating on the surface.
Bubbles are a perfect illustration of the strength of a thin liquid film. You can make your own bubbles with solutions of soap or detergent, and when you pop them you will be surprised how small the quantity of liquid is that formed the spherical film. Rain-drops are also pulled into near-spherical shapes in the air. The sea is usually covered by waves and ripples, but surface tension, like an elastic skin, tends to limit their freedom and flatten them out. During rescues in high seas, oil is sometimes poured on the water to increase this effect and make the waves less violent (see photograph above).

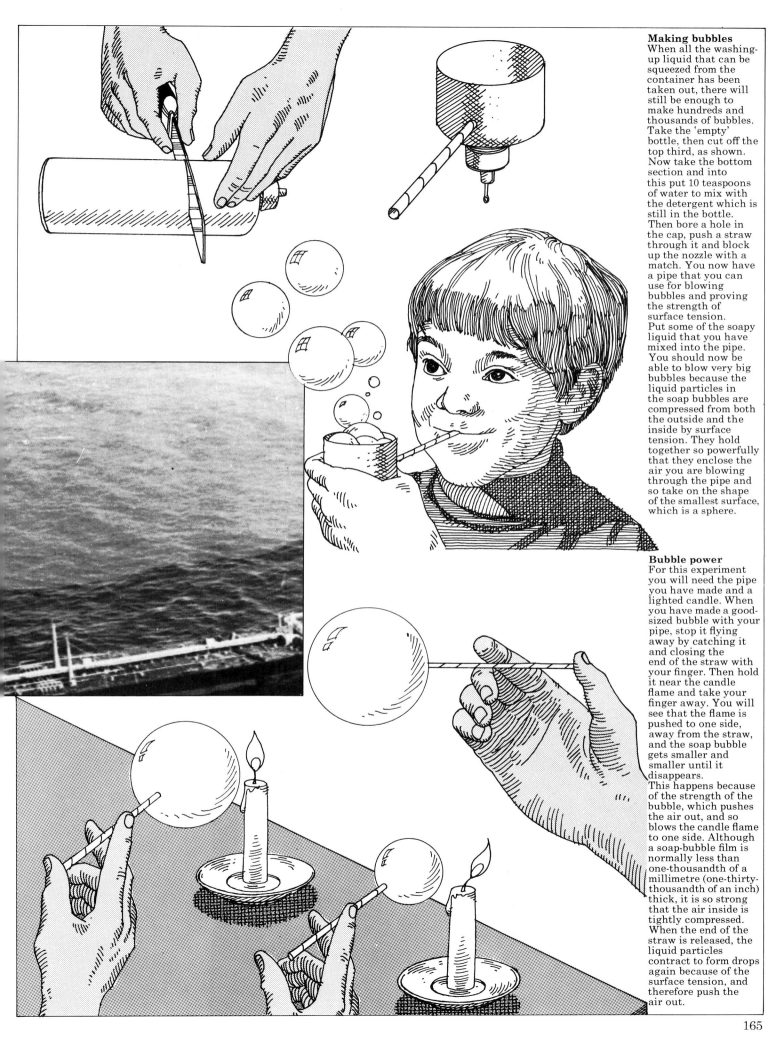

Making bubbles

When all the washing-up liquid that can be squeezed from the container has been taken out, there will still be enough to make hundreds and thousands of bubbles. Take the 'empty' bottle, then cut off the top third, as shown. Now take the bottom section and into this put 10 teaspoons of water to mix with the detergent which is still in the bottle. Then bore a hole in the cap, push a straw through it and block up the nozzle with a match. You now have a pipe that you can use for blowing bubbles and proving the strength of surface tension.

Put some of the soapy liquid that you have mixed into the pipe. You should now be able to blow very big bubbles because the liquid particles in the soap bubbles are compressed from both the outside and the inside by surface tension. They hold together so powerfully that they enclose the air you are blowing through the pipe and so take on the shape of the smallest surface, which is a sphere.

Bubble power

For this experiment you will need the pipe you have made and a lighted candle. When you have made a good-sized bubble with your pipe, stop it flying away by catching it and closing the end of the straw with your finger. Then hold it near the candle flame and take your finger away. You will see that the flame is pushed to one side, away from the straw, and the soap bubble gets smaller and smaller until it disappears.

This happens because of the strength of the bubble, which pushes the air out, and so blows the candle flame to one side. Although a soap-bubble film is normally less than one-thousandth of a millimetre (one-thirty-thousandth of an inch) thick, it is so strong that the air inside is tightly compressed. When the end of the straw is released, the liquid particles contract to form drops again because of the surface tension, and therefore push the air out.

165

Water can be wetter

Plain water can behave in an annoyingly 'dry' way. Try to colour feathers in water dye, for example, and the dye will roll off. Spray insecticide on your roses and you will see how the solution collects stubbornly in drops instead of wetting the leaves uniformly. And when you try to clean textiles, metals or glass with water mixtures, the water often refuses to wet the dirt.

The explanation for this is surface tension. If the surface coming into contact with water has sufficient attraction for water to break this tension, the surface will become wet. But if the surface is oily or in some way water-repellent, the water will roll off.

For centuries people have tried to make water wetter by finding methods of lowering the surface tension. Ordinary soap was one of the first materials used, and now synthetic wetting agents have been found which are added to special detergents and soapless shampoos.

To demonstrate how wetting agents work, sprinkle a little powdered sulphur onto the surface of a glass of water (see the illustration below). The sulphur is heavier than water but it is prevented from sinking by the water's surface tension. The plain water refuses to 'wet' it. Now add a few drops of detergent. The surface tension is reduced and the sulphur particles fall like snow to the bottom of the glass.

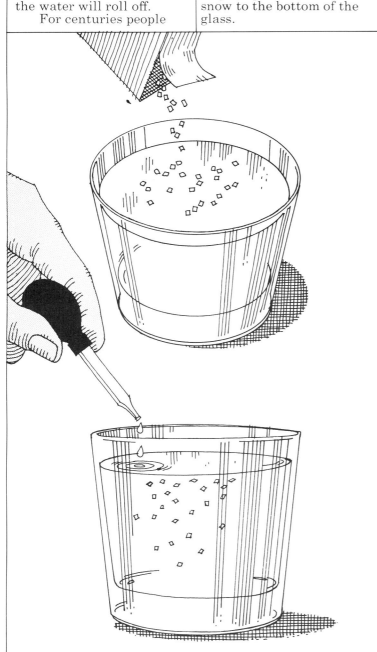

Soap and sugar in water

Soap and sugar behave very differently in water. Take a wooden spill, break it into small pieces and float them on the surface of a dish of water. Then put a cube of sugar in the water and the pieces will travel towards it. Sugar is obviously not magnetic but it is porous and so draws the water into itself, creating a current and causing the spills to move. Take the sugar out and repeat the experiment, putting a small cube of soap into the centre of the bowl. Some of the soap will go into solution, weakening the surface tension radiating from the spot where the soap is touching the water. The spills are very quickly forced away from the soap.

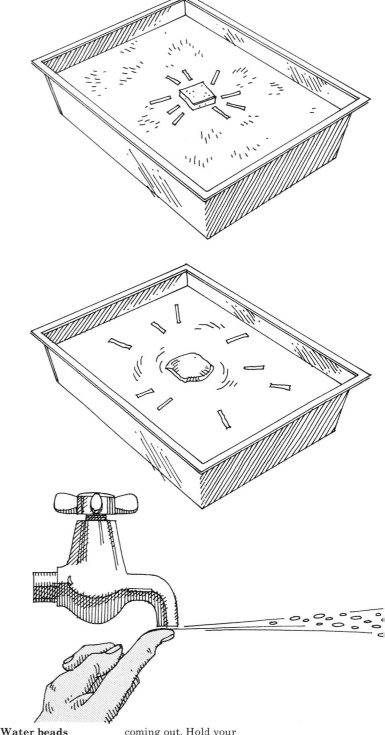

Water beads

Here is an experiment which demonstrates the surface tension of water by making a fine jet of water look like a string of glass beads. Turn a tap on so that you have a fine stream of water coming out. Hold your finger about 5 cm (2 in) from the tap. Then bring your finger closer to the tap until the water is so strongly obstructed that it separates into tiny droplets, or 'water beads'.

Rope trick

You can perform a rope trick using the above principle. Knot a piece of string into a circle and float it on top of the water. Dab the end of a match with soap or washing-up liquid and dip it into the middle of the irregularly shaped loop. The loop will immediately become circular, because the soap penetrates between the water particles, which were held together like a skin by surface tension. In this way the 'water skin' is weakened and breaks, and the liquid particles, which are made to move, push against the string loop with equal force along its entire length. The loop becomes rigid and is forced out into a circular shape.

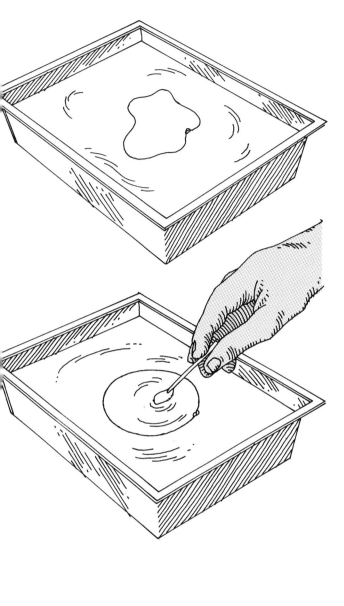

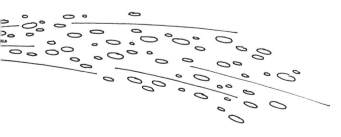

A watertight sieve

Surface tension also explains how you can make a watertight sieve. Fill a glass bottle with water and fix a piece of wire gauze on the top with a rubber band. With your hand over the top, turn the bottle upside down. Now if you take your hand away quickly no water will escape through the gauze. The reason for this is that water, because of its surface tension, surrounds itself with a 'skin' where it comes into contact with air. This happens so efficiently at each opening in the wire gauze that the water cannot flow out. In the same way, rain cannot get through the fine holes in tent material.

A camphor boat
This boat can be made to demonstrate surface tension. You will need a small piece of camphor, an aluminium milk bottle top, a used matchstick and coloured paper for the sail. First clean a bottle top well so that it is free from grease. Smooth out the foil and cut it into a boat shape. Make a V-shaped stern and put a piece of camphor in it. Glue on your stick to make the mast and attach a sail. Fill a clean bowl with water. Your boat will move magically across the water. The camphor slowly dissolves, making camphor solution, which has a lower surface tension than plain water. The pull of the water in front of the boat is greater than the pull of the camphor solution behind, so the boat moves forwards.

Tireless dancers
You can use the same principle to make something far more elaborate, which you can call your tireless dancers. Stick four needles into a cork disc to form a cross shape. On the end of each fit a piece of cork to which you have fastened a small piece of camphor (as in the drawing). Fit your cut-out figures onto the disc and drop the whole thing into a bowl of water. It will spin round for about three days. Although you will know that the reason lies in the surface tension, others may marvel at your perpetual-motion machine.

BUOYANCY

Archimedes became famous for his principle that a body placed in a fluid loses as much of its weight as is equal to the weight of the displaced fluid.

His discovery followed a problem put to him by the ruler of Sicily, who suspected that his new gold crown had some silver mixed with the gold. Archimedes was asked to show that the jeweller was being dishonest, without damaging the crown. This was a difficult problem and for a long time he was unable to find a way of solving it.

Then an idea came to him while he was having a bath. He saw that the water level rose as his body went under. It also seemed to him that his body lost weight in the water. He realized that his idea would enable him to solve the problem, and he is said to have jumped out of his bath and rushed naked through the streets of Syracuse shouting 'Eureka! Eureka!' meaning 'I have found it!'

He had found a way of determining the density of solids by measuring their change in weight when put into water. He could compare the density of the crown with that of pure gold.

Any object immersed in a liquid loses weight. When you are swimming in a river or the sea, pick up a large stone: you will be surprised how light it feels. The same stone will feel heavier out of the water. Demonstrate this if you have a spring balance, or if you can borrow one. Attach a stone to the balance and note its weight. Hang the stone in water and note the weight again. This time you will find that the weight has dropped.

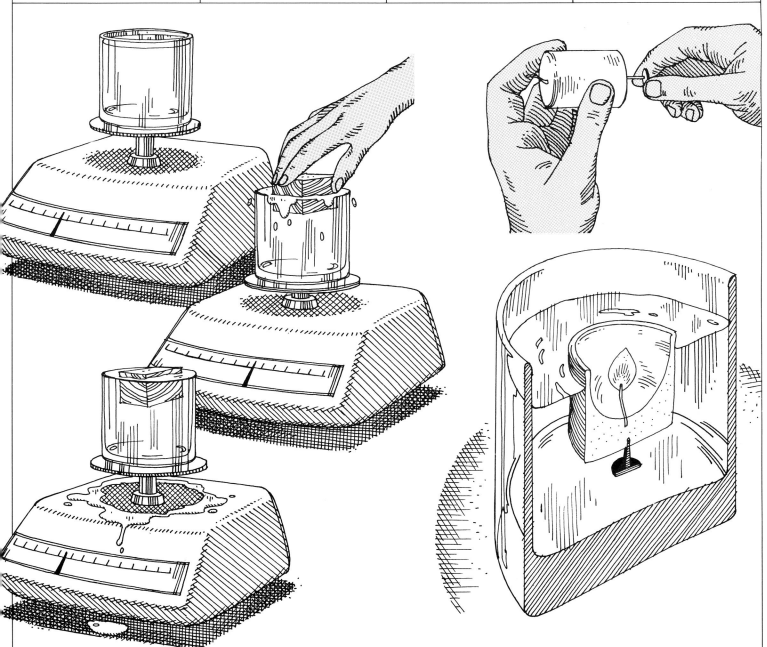

Weight loss in water
The loss of weight in a liquid is apparent when an object floats. Fill a wide glass jar with water to the top and weigh it. Then put a piece of wood on the water, which will make some of the water spill out. Weigh the jar again and you will find that despite the addition of the wood, the jar weighs the same. The water which spilt out of the jar weighs exactly the same as the piece of wood. This simple experiment is a way of confirming Archimedes' discovery that a body immersed in a liquid loses as much weight as the weight of liquid displaced by it. This apparent loss is called buoyancy.

A water candle
Archimedes' principle can be used to make a safe, long-burning candle which you can use in the garden in the evening. To make the candle float with its wick just above the water level, increase the weight by sticking a nail in the base. Try different nails until the candle floats as shown here. Light the candle. It will not go out once it reaches the water level but will go on burning under the surface. The water cools the candle so that its outer layer does not reach its melting point and the flame hollows out a deep funnel, leaving a thin wall of wax which stops the water from putting it out.

Dancing mothballs

Add some vinegar and bicarbonate of soda to a large glass jar of water. Colour several mothballs with crayon so that you will see them more clearly, and then toss them in the water. They will soon start to dance up and down. Because they are heavier than water, they sink. But the reaction between the bicarbonate of soda and vinegar produces carbon dioxide which collects in bubbles on the mothballs, increasing their buoyancy and lifting them to the surface. There, the bubbles of gas escape, the balls become heavy again and sink to the bottom of the jar, where the whole process is repeated.

Yellow submarine

Cut a small boat shape out of fresh lemon peel and decorate it, using a ballpoint pen. Place your boat in a large cylindrical jar full of water. Cover the top with a flexible plastic cap or make a tight-fitting rubber diaphragm with an old balloon. When this is pressed and released the boat rises and falls. Tiny holes in the porous lemon peel make the boat float. But the pressure on the diaphragm is transmitted through the water, compressing the bubbles in the peel so that their buoyancy is less and the boat sinks. Over 300 years ago a French philosopher called René Descartes made a more scientific version of this called a 'Cartesian diver' or 'bottle imp'. Make your own by inverting a small unstoppered bottle in a tall jar of water. Let just enough water into the small bottle so that it barely floats in the upside-down position. Cover the rim of the tall jar with your hand and press your palm into the jar. The bottle will sink until you release your hand, when it will rise again. It works because air can be compressed easily, but water cannot. Pressure on the water of the tall jar squeezes air out of the diving bottle, letting extra water in. So the bottle loses buoyancy and sinks. Submarines also dive by letting in water, and rise by expelling it.

Hot water rises

Buoyancy explains why we can have hot water in an upstairs bathroom even though the boiler is situated downstairs. The fact that hot water rises so easily is of great help to heating engineers installing hot-water systems and central heating into houses. The experiment on the left shows clearly how easily hot water rises. Fill a small bottle with hot water which you have coloured with ink. Lower it carefully into a much larger glass jar containing cold water. You will see a coloured cloud spreading like a volcano from the small bottle up to the surface of the cold water.

The reason for this is that hot water takes up a greater volume than cold because the space between the water particles is increased on heating. It is therefore lighter and experiences buoyancy. After a time the warm and cold water will have mixed thoroughly, so that the ink colours the water evenly. You can even make coloured hot water rise from one bottle into another. Take two wide-rimmed bottles of the same size. Fill one with cold water and cover the top with a square of card. Then fill the other bottle with hot water, coloured with ink. Make sure both bottles are filled right to the top, then, holding the card over the top, turn the bottle of cold water upside down with great care and place it exactly on top of the bottle containing hot water. When both bottles are quite steady, carefully slip out the card from between them. As you watch, the coloured hot water will rise into the top bottle and the cold water fall into the lower bottle.

DENSITY

We usually compare the density of liquids with the density of water, using the term specific gravity. The instrument used for this is called a hydrometer. The simplest type of hydrometer is a uniform rod, weighted at one end so that it floats in an upright position. The greater the density of the liquid, the higher the rod floats. It is marked with a scale, so readings for different liquids can be compared.

Density is important to any boat, submarine, barge or ship, and to make sure that cargo ships do not carry a load that would press the hull too far down in the water, they have to carry a mark called the Plimsoll line.

But because salt water is denser than fresh water, and cold water is denser than warm water, a ship will float in different positions depending on whether it is in the Indian Ocean or the North Atlantic, out in the sea or on a river. So one Plimsoll line is not enough, and several levels are marked on a ship to cover all the conditions that the vessel is likely to encounter (see below).

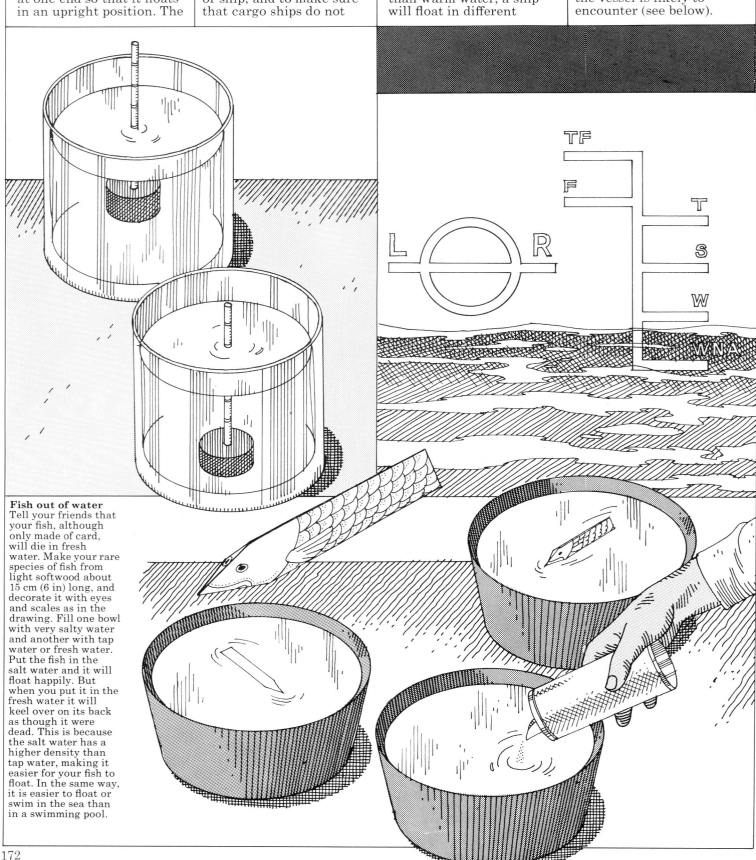

Fish out of water
Tell your friends that your fish, although only made of card, will die in fresh water. Make your rare species of fish from light softwood about 15 cm (6 in) long, and decorate it with eyes and scales as in the drawing. Fill one bowl with very salty water and another with tap water or fresh water. Put the fish in the salt water and it will float happily. But when you put it in the fresh water it will keel over on its back as though it were dead. This is because the salt water has a higher density than tap water, making it easier for your fish to float. In the same way, it is easier to float or swim in the sea than in a swimming pool.

Sink-or-swim eggs
Find three glass jars, two the same size and the third about twice as big. Put tap water in one of the small jars and the same amount of strong salt solution in the second. Drop an egg in the tap water and it will sink. Then put the egg into the salt solution and because of the higher density it will float.

Now pour tap water and salt solution in equal quantities into the large jar. If you balance the mixture carefully you can produce a liquid of exactly the same density as the egg. A state of equilibrium is reached and the egg will remain suspended midway in the liquid.

Then if you add some tap water the egg will sink, add salt water and it will rise. So you can make the egg bob up and down like a crazy submarine.

Floating liquids
You can fill a glass with five different liquids and keep them all separate if each one has a different density. Take a cone-shaped glass and make four paper replicas, folding their tips at right-angles and snipping off the ends to form a pinhole. First pour strong, sweet coffee in the bottom of the glass, then fill one of the paper cornets with water and allow it to dribble out slowly against the inside of the glass. When that has settled, use the next cone to pour wine into the glass. Then pour in a layer of oil and finally a layer of surgical spirit, allowing each layer to settle.

Coffee layer

Coffee plus water

Coffee plus water, plus wine

Add a fourth layer of oil

Top up with surgical spirit

173

CAPILLARY ACTION

If you stand a fine glass tube in water with an open end under the surface, you will notice that the water climbs by pulling itself up at the point of contact with the glass. In a very fine tube the level reached is higher than in a thicker one. This ability to climb up fine tubes is called capillary action.

We see many examples of this in everyday life. The way water creeps into the fine spaces of the threads of a towel is one example. The ways blotting paper soaks up ink, molten wax creeps up the wick of a candle, and oil climbs to feed the flame of a lamp, are others.

Thanks to capillary action, water is able to find its way through soil, supplying the roots of plants and trees with the moisture and nourishment they need. The spaces between soil particles act as fine capillary tubes. The same force helps the upward movement of sap to the leaves.

Making chromatograms
This is another way of separating out the different colours in inks and other coloured liquids that

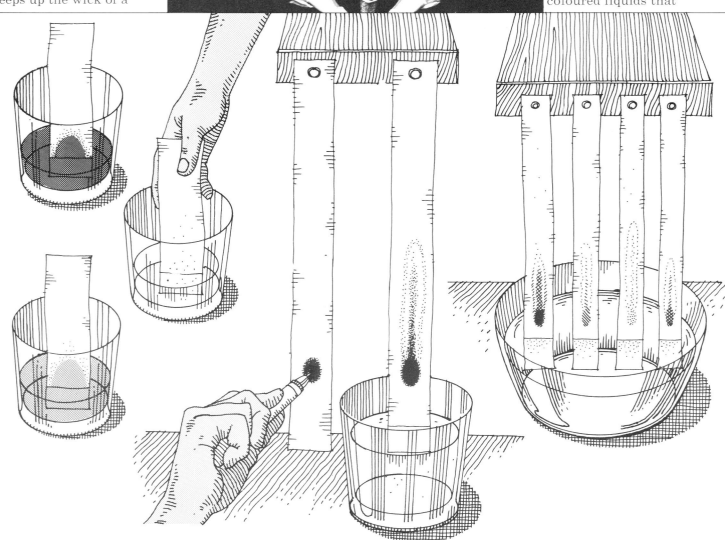

Capillarity in chemistry
Capillarity is used by chemists to separate a mixture of materials. There are very many tiny openings in blotting paper, for example, so that liquids can move up through them. When some substances are dissolved in water, they travel more slowly than others up

the paper. Mixtures of materials can be separated because the faster-moving materials leave the others behind. You can do your own experiments using different inks and strips of blotting paper. Inks are made up of mixtures of many pigments which move at different speeds. First, take three

small glasses with about 2½ cm (1 in) of water in each. Put a few drops of red ink in one and a few drops of blue ink in another and leave the third clear water. Put the end of a piece of blotting paper, about 15 by 4 cm (6 by 1½ in) in each. Compare how quickly the liquids climb up the blotting paper.

Then, using a 45 cm (18 in) length of blotting paper, make a small blot of black ink from a felt-tipped pen near the bottom of the paper, about 5 cm (2 in) from the end. Suspend the strip above a dish of water. Put the end of the paper with the blot into the water, so that the water does not touch or cover the

blot. You will see that the water will move up the blotting paper and will soon reach the black spot that you made. When this happens, the ink will separate into different colours, which then move up at different speeds. The green and yellow colours, for example, move faster than the navy blue. Using

capillarity you have separated the pigments that make up the black ink. Take the paper out and let it dry before the water reaches the top of the strip.
Using four strips and a large bowl of water, you can try different inks and let their colours race against each other as they separate.

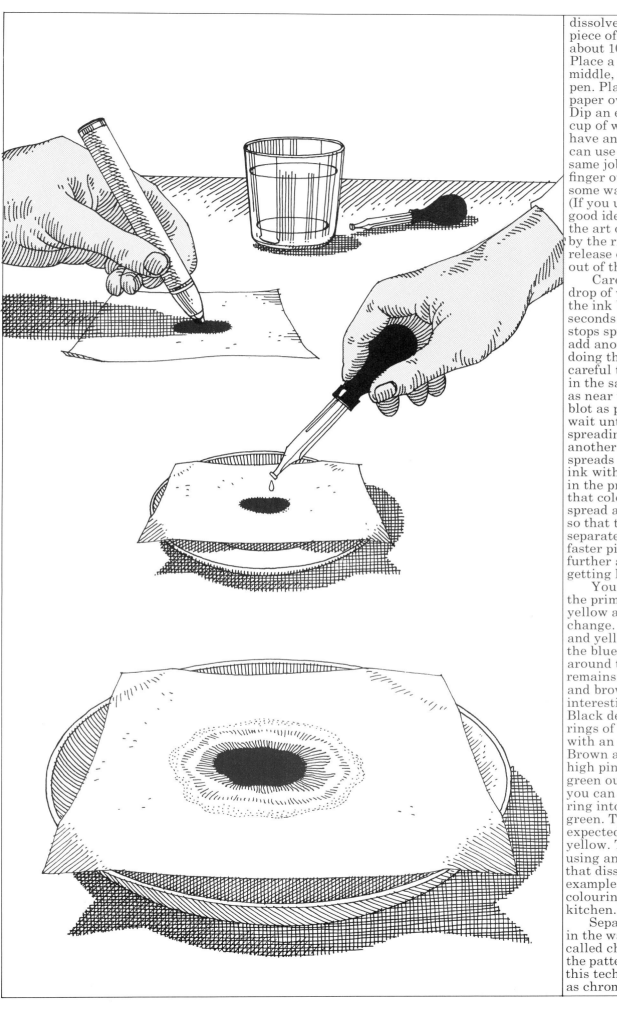

dissolve in water. Cut a piece of blotting paper about 10 cm (4 in) square. Place a blob of ink in the middle, using a felt-tipped pen. Place the blotting paper over an old saucer. Dip an eye-dropper into a cup of water. If you do not have an eye-dropper you can use a straw to do the same job, putting your finger over the top to trap some water in the straw. (If you use a straw, it is a good idea first to practise the art of lifting your finger by the right amount to release one drop at a time out of the straw.)

Carefully allow one drop of water to drip onto the ink blot. Wait a few seconds until the water stops spreading and then add another drop. Keep doing this, being very careful to let the drops fall in the same place each time, as near the middle of the blot as possible. Always wait until the water stops spreading before adding another drop. As the water spreads out, it takes the ink with it. You will see, as in the previous experiment, that coloured materials spread at different speeds, so that they become separated out, with the faster pigments travelling further and the slower ones getting left behind.

You will also find that the primary colours – red, yellow and blue – do not change. But while the red and yellow spread outwards, the blue does not; the halo around the blue blot remains colourless. Black and brown are particularly interesting colours to try. Black develops successive rings of various colours, with an outer ring of blue. Brown at first reveals a high pink content, with a green outer ring. See if you can separate this outer ring into the components of green. These, as might be expected, are blue and yellow. Try this experiment using any coloured liquids that dissolve in water. One example is the food colouring used in the kitchen.

Separating out things in the way shown here is called chromatography, and the patterns you make using this technique are known as chromatograms.

In the 17th century, Otto von Guericke, the mayor of Magdeburg in Germany, carried out some of the first experiments with air pressure. In one famous experiment he fitted tightly together two hollow, bronze bowls, called hemispheres, and removed all the air from inside with an air pump. Von Guericke showed that two teams of horses could not pull the hemispheres apart until the combined strength of 30 horses was used. Yet when he let the air back into the closed hemispheres, they could be separated with the slightest touch.

THE SCIENCE OF THE ATMOSPHERE

did his famous experiment with mercury in a tube – the principle of the barometer – and made the first effective instrument to measure air pressure.

If you have access to mercury, you can repeat his experiment and make a home-made mercury barometer at the same time.

air pressure rises and falls.

In 1648 the French scientist Blaise Pascal had one of Torricelli's mercury barometers carried up the famous 1,524 m (5,000 ft) Puy-de-Dôme mountain in France, because he suspected that air pressure would decrease at great heights. The higher the

barometer' usually tells us that storms or snow are coming, while a rising barometer means good weather. Weather bureaux use a barograph to record these changes. This is a barometer with a pen for an indicator that keeps a permanent record of air pressure changes.

Also in the 17th century, an English chemist, Robert Boyle, noticed how elastic air

Power of a vacuum
(*left*) Von Guericke's demonstration of the power of a vacuum, using Magdeburg hemispheres and two teams of horses. Illustration from his *Experimenta Nova*, Amsterdam, 1672.

Height of liquid
Torricelli's demonstration (1643) showed that the height of a column of liquid is governed by atmospheric pressure. Water rises to 10 m (33 ft), but mercury, which is about $13\frac{1}{2}$ times denser, rises to only 73 cm (29 in), as is seen in the second illustration (*opposite below*).

The first man to measure air pressure successfully was Evangelista Torricelli, in 1643. He was a pupil of Galileo, and for years had wondered why an ordinary pump could not raise water in a pipe higher than 10 m (33 ft). Galileo died before he could find out, leaving the problem for his pupil to solve.

Torricelli decided that it must be the weight of the air on the water inside the pump, which caused the water to rise 10 m (33 ft) and no more. So he investigated how the pressure of the atmosphere acted on other liquids, because working with a 10-m (33 ft) tube of water was inconvenient. He

Take a heavy glass tube about 90 cm (35 in) long and closed at one end. Fill the tube with mercury and seal it with your finger at the open end. Turn it upside down and put it in a dish of mercury, removing your finger as you do so.

Watch the mercury and see it drop slightly, creating a vacuum which is still called the Torricellian vacuum. Measure the column of mercury; at sea-level it is always about 76 cm (30 in) high, held at that height in the tube by air pressure pushing down on the mercury in the dish. A more sophisticated version with a scale is used as a mercury barometer today, accurately showing when

barometer was taken up the mountain, the lower the mercury dropped in the tube. At the very top, the column had dropped 7.5 cm (3 in) to 68.5 cm (27 in), because there was much less air pressing down on the mercury.

A barometer will fall to about 38 cm (15 in) at an altitude of 5,486 m (18,000 ft), while 32 km (20 miles) above the earth it will only register about 1 cm ($\frac{1}{2}$ in). An aneroid barometer has no liquid in it. A development of the aneroid barometer is the altimeter which records an aircraft's altitude above sea-level.

Air-pressure changes act as signposts for predicting weather. A 'falling

could be, calling it 'the spring of the air'. In a famous experiment he first realized how air could be compressed by pouring mercury into a U-shaped tube, closed at one end. Air trapped in the closed end was squeezed so that it occupied a smaller space.

He went on to discover his own Boyle's Law. If air is enclosed in a bottle, the molecules of air strike the inside of the bottle with a push of ordinary air pressure, that is about 101,325 newtons per square metre (15 lb per sq in) of the bottle. His law states that if the same amount of air is forced into a bottle half the

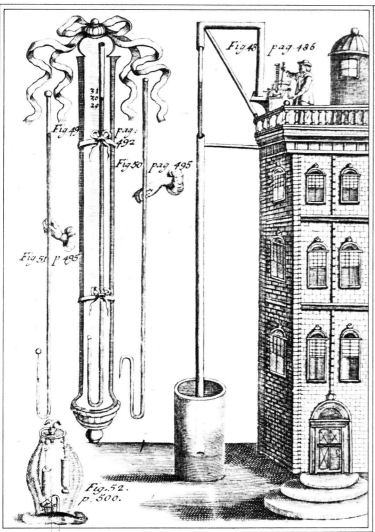

size, the air pressure of the molecules is doubled. And if that same air were forced into a bottle one-tenth the size of the original, there would be 10 times as much pressure.

This is why compressed air can be so powerful in paint sprays, pneumatic drills, sand-blasters and deep-sea diving equipment.

Boyle was also interested in the part played by air in burning and breathing. One of his followers, the English physician John Mayow, first came near to the secret of air by watching the process of combustion. He isolated air under a pear-shaped glass jar, placed upside down in a bowl of water. A candle burning in the jar went out after a short time, while the water in the jar rose slightly. He concluded that part of the air had obviously been used up by the burning candle, and that the remaining air was no use for combustion.

His experiments with mice produced the same results, and so he realized that part of the air, necessary for both burning and breathing, had been removed. What was left, which only later was given the name nitrogen, seemed to have precisely the opposite effect.

But it was not until the late 18th century that scientists like Joseph Priestley were able to analyse air accurately, destroying completely the old concept of air as a single element. Chemists became fascinated by gases as a result of this research.

In 1774 Priestley made an announcement that he had broken new ground in chemistry. He had isolated oxygen after heating mercuric oxide, and found that it had reviving properties. 'Up to now only two mice and I have had the advantage of breathing it,' he said early in his research.

Lavoisier took this work further in his famous Paris laboratory. He carried out some of the most detailed experiments of that time. He looked at the decomposition and recomposition of air, proving that oxygen made up about one-fifth of the atmosphere, with nitrogen making up most of the rest. He also proved that respiration was a burning process, just as Mayow had thought.

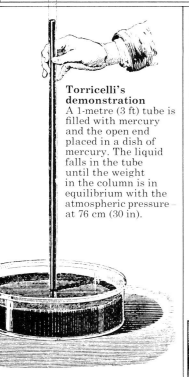

Torricelli's demonstration
A 1-metre (3 ft) tube is filled with mercury and the open end placed in a dish of mercury. The liquid falls in the tube until the weight in the column is in equilibrium with the atmospheric pressure at 76 cm (30 in).

Boyle's experiments
(above) Robert Boyle's experiments on the 'spring of the air'. He found that no matter how energetically he pumped, he could not raise water above a height of 10 m (33 ft).

Experiments with air
(below) Some of Priestley's apparatus from his *Experiments and Observations on Different Kinds of Air*, London, 1774–77.

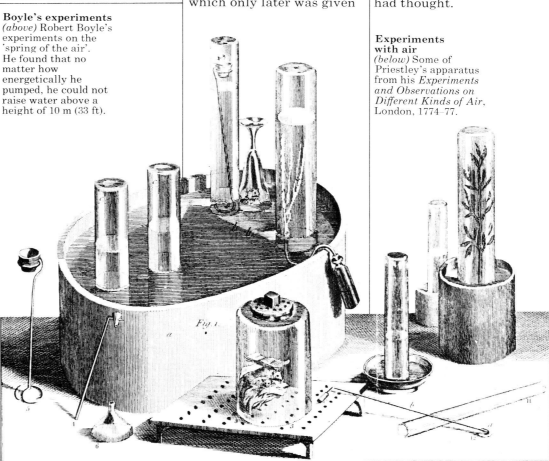

Air is real

On these pages are some simple experiments that prove the existence of air.

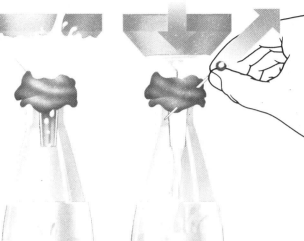

Air in a bottle

Place a funnel with not too wide a spout into the neck of a bottle, about two-thirds full of water. Seal the funnel into the neck with modelling clay and pour in some water. It will either not run into the bottle at all, or only in small spurts. Now make a hole in the clay with a pin and water passes into the bottle. Without the hole, the air in the bottle prevented water from entering. The water only enters the bottle if the air can escape through the pinhole.

Air is everywhere

You cannot see air, but it fills nearly every space. When you describe a glass or a box as empty, it is, in fact, full of air. Air is a mixture of gases which you cannot feel, except when you breathe in and out or when the wind blows directly at you.

Although air feels insubstantial, there is a thick layer of air round the Earth, which pushes on everything around us. At sea-level, air presses down with a force of about 101,325 newtons per square metre (15 lb per sq in).

Room for air

Submerge a glass in a bowl of water so that it fills. Hold it upside down with one hand, and with the other push a second glass, top first, into the water. Tilt this glass under the first, so that the air inside it bubbles up into the first glass. This air drives out the water in the first glass. Simultaneously, the second glass fills with water. This experiment proves that the water must make room for the air. This is why, when you pour liquid from a sealed tin, you must make *two* holes – one for the liquid to come out, and the other for the air to enter so that it can take its place.

The weight of air

Prove again that air is heavy. Hang a 60 cm (2 ft) stick from a piece of string tied tightly to the middle of the stick. Slide the string along until the stick hangs exactly level. Blow up two balloons to the same size and tie one to each end of the stick. Slide the balloons to make the stick level. Now prick one balloon with a pin; as it bursts the air escapes and the other balloon will weigh more, because it contains air. The end of the stick holding the inflated balloon goes down. If the second balloon is burst, the stick becomes level again.

Hanging water

Fill a glass to the rim and lay a postcard on it. Supporting the card with one hand, turn the glass upside down. Remove your hand and the pressure of air will keep the card in place.

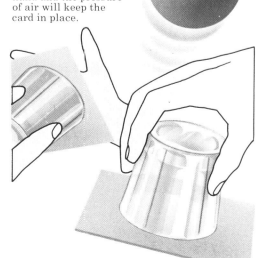

Air is heavy

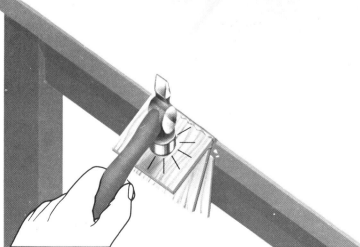

You can prove that air is heavy as follows. Put a thin piece of wood, about 8 cm (3 in) wide by 60 cm (2 ft) long, on a table, so that about 10 cm (4 in) of the end projects over the edge. Then spread two double sheets of newspaper over the wood resting on the table, carefully smoothing them down so that they hug the wood and table closely. Now hit the wood with a hammer. Do it quickly and the wood snaps instead of throwing the paper towards the ceiling. The air is unable to get under the paper fast enough to balance the air above it. The air pressing down on the paper is heavy, so the wood breaks.

Can crushing

If you can borrow an air pump, you can easily demonstrate the great crushing power of air pressure. Gradually remove the air from an empty oil can. When all, or nearly all, the air has been removed, the empty space is called a vacuum. When a vacuum has been achieved, the can will slowly collapse due to the air pushing in on it from the outside. You can do a similar experiment at home without an air pump. Put about 13 mm ($\frac{1}{2}$ in) of water in an oil can and boil it for several minutes. As soon as the steam subsides, put a stopper or screw cap on the can. As it cools, the steam inside condenses to form a partial vacuum. The air at reduced pressure

inside cannot compete with the greater pressure of the atmosphere outside. Finally the can collapses, crushed by air pressing on it. The same thing could happen to a badly-built big building,

if it were airtight and all the air were removed from inside it. If your body was not made up of incompressible liquids and solids, with air filling the spaces between them, you also would be crushed

by the external pressure of the atmosphere. But some internal organs, eg the lungs and intestines, are hollow, and divers cannot withstand the pressures under water unless they breathe pressurized gas.

Hold up a stool by air

Those suction pads that hold hooks to walls depend upon atmospheric pressure. When you press them against a smooth surface, air is forced out from under them. The atmospheric pressure then pushes them against the wall. Perfectly flat surfaces can also be held together by air

pressure. To show this, tie a string to a flat sink stopper, or any suction pad, wet the underside, and press it against the smooth top of a stool or small table. You will find that you can lift the piece of furniture because the air forces it against the stopper. You can do the same with half a radish and a plate.

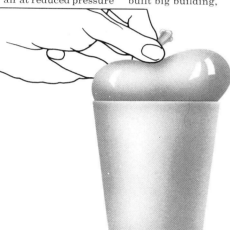

Compressed air experiment

Put an empty balloon inside a plastic beaker, and, keeping it inside, blow it up and squeeze the neck so that the air cannot come out. When you

lift the balloon you will find that the beaker comes with it. But then let the air out of the balloon very gradually and watch when the beaker falls off. The beaker was lifted

up with the balloon because the air in the balloon was pressing outwards against the sides of the beaker. The more you blow or compress air inside the balloon the more it presses outwards.

When you are pumping up your bicycle tyre you are compressing air inside it. The more air you pump in, the more strongly the air pushes outwards and the harder the tyre becomes.

Bottle barometer

Fix a straw with modelling clay on top of a piece of rubber balloon stretched over the mouth of a glass bottle. The end of the straw will move as the air pressure varies with the weather. You can make a scale to check changes more accurately.
In fine weather, when the air pressure is high, the rubber will be pressed inwards, and the end of the pointer will rise. It will fall with the air pressure, because the pressure on the rubber will be reduced. (This simple barometer will only work well if it is kept at a constant temperature, because the air in the bottle will expand if heated.)

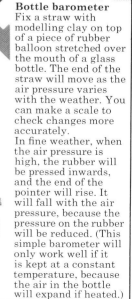

THE IMPORTANCE OF AIR

Without air, we could not make fires; most sounds would not reach our ears, and plants could not grow. Without air, there would be no water, and the Earth's surface would be as oceanless as the Moon's. It would be impossible for humans and all animals to live if there was no air to breathe.

The protective blanket of air surrounding Earth acts like a glass greenhouse roof, lessening the extremes of heat and cold between night and day, and summer and winter. It does this by trapping the heat of the Sun's rays so that it escapes more slowly into space. The Moon, which has no blanket of air around it, suffers from severe changes in temperature. During the great heat of the lunar day, temperatures can reach the boiling point of water, but at night they can drop as low as minus 130°C (minus 650°F).

The air also shelters the Earth from a steady rain of rock pieces from outer space. Many millions of these pieces are scattered throughout the solar system, some as big as boulders. They are travelling at very high speed when they hit the layer of air around the Earth, where they become red-hot and normally burn themselves up. Occasionally they survive and land on Earth, as meteorites. It was not accepted until the early 19th century that such material could fall from the sky, and the Sacred Stone at Mecca is in fact a meteorite. The largest one known fell in prehistoric times at Hoba West, SW Africa; it weighs 60 t.

Air's ingredients

We really live on one gigantic sphere, the Earth, and inside another much larger one. This is the vast layer of air completely surrounding the Earth, called the atmosphere. It reaches a height of about 1,126 km (700 miles) and then gradually merges into space.

This air is a mixture of colourless, invisible gases. Four-fifths of the air is a gas called nitrogen, which is essential for plant growth, while oxygen makes up most of the rest. There is also a small amount of carbon dioxide, which is one of the chemical compounds of the air, made up of one part carbon and two parts oxygen. We breathe out carbon dioxide, and plants use it in their food-making process. Carbon dioxide is also valuable in retaining the Earth's heat.

The air also contains small amounts of the inert gases neon, argon, xenon and krypton, called 'inert' because they do not combine with other elements. Although it is not really known how important they are in the air, neon is used in advertising signs, and argon in electric light bulbs.

Helium and hydrogen are very scarce in air, except at great heights. Being the lightest of all gases, they are used inside balloons and other lighter-than-air craft for lifting purposes. Ozone is a very active, pure form of oxygen, and it is the only gas in the air that has a smell.

Water vapour is present in air in varying quantities as a gas which has evaporated from lakes and rivers. Like carbon dioxide it is a chemical compound, and is composed of two parts hydrogen and one part oxygen. Water vapour is important because it forms clouds, which in turn produce the rain so essential for plant and animal life on the Earth. On a hot summer day, the air in an average room could contain as much as 1 kg (2 lb) of water vapour, that is about 1.5 l (2½ pt) in liquid form.

Dust is an important impurity in air, because it acts as a centre where moisture collects. Without dust, water vapour would not be able to condense into droplets, and there would be no clouds or rain. The amount of dust in the air obviously varies. Above mountains and the sea there may be only a few thousand particles per cubic centimetre (.06 cu in), while over polluted cities there can be five million or more.

Air contains oxygen
To prove that air is about one-fifth oxygen, all you need is a tall glass, a bowl of water and a small candle. Mount the candle on a cork float, light it and place it on top of the water in the bowl. Now hold the glass over the candle, with the mouth of the glass pushed down into the water. In a short time the candle will go out, which proves that the flame has used up all the oxygen in the air contained in the glass. Meanwhile, the water will have risen about one-fifth of the way up into the glass to replace the lost oxygen. The oxygen used forms carbon dioxide, which dissolves in water, leaving space for the water to occupy. If you repeated the experiment with larger glass jars, you would find that the candle burns longer because there is more air and therefore more oxygen to be used up.

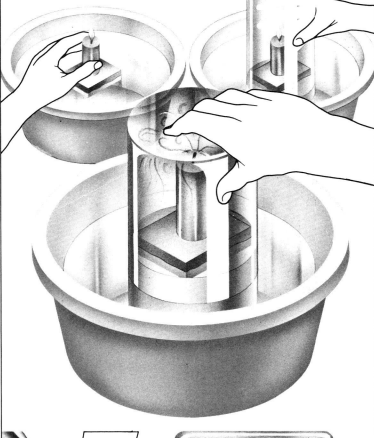

Rust experiment
It is also possible to use rusting iron to measure the amount of oxygen in the air. Wedge a wad of steel wool, moistened with vinegar to speed up the rust reaction, in the bottom of a tall glass. Then invert the glass in a dish of water. Make sure that the steel wool stays firmly in position up against the base of the glass. Slowly, the iron in the steel wool rusts, and as it does so you will find that it takes oxygen from the air, and water rises in the glass to take its place. Rust is a compound of iron, oxygen and water. In a matter of hours, the water will rise about one-fifth of the way up the glass.

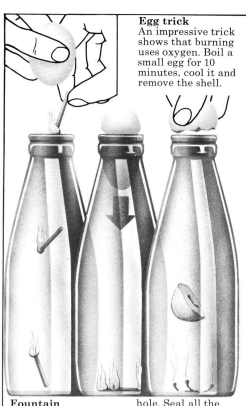

Egg trick

An impressive trick shows that burning uses oxygen. Boil a small egg for 10 minutes, cool it and remove the shell.

Place the egg in the neck of a bottle (the neck should be slightly smaller than the egg). The egg will stay in position with the air inside and outside the bottle pressing equally on it.

But now raise the egg and drop three lighted matches into the bottle. Replace the egg and gradually it squeezes through the bottle-neck. The burning matches use up oxygen from inside the bottle, and the air pressure decreases. The greater air pressure outside pushes the egg down. It will either go right into the bottle, or become so tightly wedged that it breaks if you try to pull it out.

Pumps

Air pressure is vital for working pumps, fountains and siphons. The common pump has been used by man for raising water for centuries.

In the cross-section view below, the workings of the pump are explained. First, the handle moves the piston up and the first valve opens. Then the pressure of the outside air forces water up into the cylinder. When the piston moves down, the second valve opens and the first valve shuts. Water is forced out through the spout when the piston is moved up for the second time.

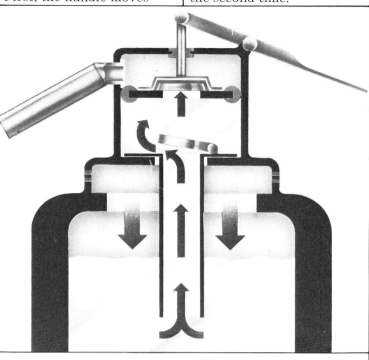

Fountain

Make two holes in the lid of a glass jar and push a plastic straw about 5 cm (2 in) through one of the holes. Join three straws together with sticking tape, and push through the second hole. Seal all the joints with warm modelling clay, and screw the lid to the jar, which should be about one-third full of water. Invert the fountain, letting the short straw dip into another jar filled with water. First the water pours from the upper jar through the long tube, resulting in lower air pressure inside the jar. Air outside tries to get in and pushes water up in a fountain into the top jar.

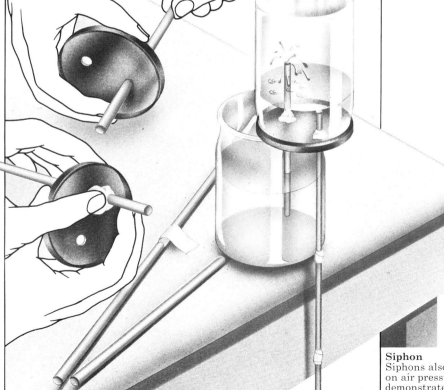

Siphon

Siphons also depend on air pressure. To demonstrate a siphon, half fill two glasses with water and connect them with a plastic or rubber tube, also filled with water. Now raise one glass above the other, and the water flows from the higher water level to the lower. Raise the other glass, and the water flows back until the level in both glasses is equal. When the water level in the two glasses is equal, the downward pressure of the water in the two legs of the tube is balanced, and opposes equally the upward force of air pressure. When one glass is lowered, the downward pressure in the leg on that side increases, because its water column is lengthened. Air pressure in the upper glass forces water to the lower glass.

181

AERODYNAMICS

When you spin a ball you involve a strange scientific law, called the Bernouilli effect. It was discovered by the famous Swiss mathematician, Daniel Bernouilli, over 200 years ago.

His law states that if the velocity of a fluid such as air or water is increased, the pressure inside that fluid is decreased. It seems unlikely that the pressure in a fast-flowing river can be less than the water pressure in a pond. But it is so, and the law is much easier to demonstrate than explain.

Increased velocity
Point an electric fan or fan heater upwards. Then turn it on and drop an inflated balloon into the air stream. Every time the balloon reaches the top of the stream. the higher pressure of the still air pushes it back. The static pressure, the pressure of one particle against another within the air, reduces when the velocity is increased. This principle can be confirmed by increasing the air velocity from your own lungs. Suspend two apples or table-tennis balls from long strings, about 5 cm (2 in) apart. Then blow as strongly as you can between them. The apples bump together, because your fast breath lowers the pressure between them. The apples are pushed together by normal air pressure on the outside. To show this even more effectively, make two paper flags on long pins and set them on a piece of wood about 5 cm (2 in) apart. Curve the flags inwards and blow between them with a straw. The harder you blow, the more the flags come together.

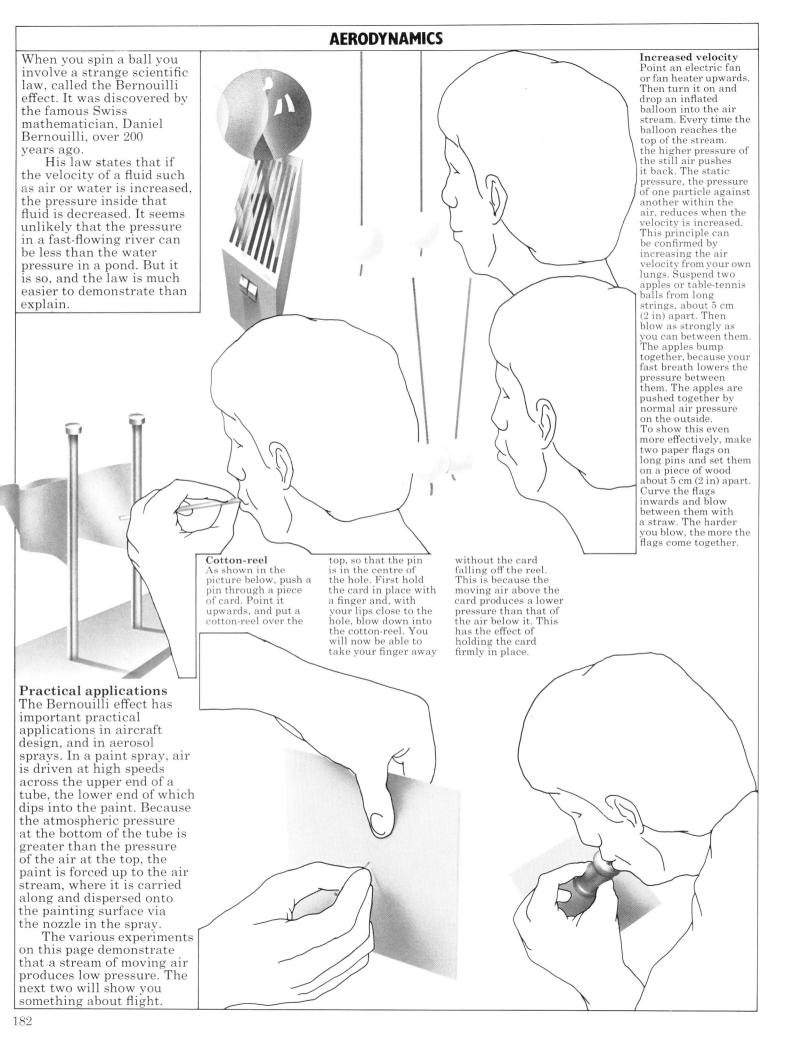

Cotton-reel
As shown in the picture below, push a pin through a piece of card. Point it upwards, and put a cotton-reel over the top, so that the pin is in the centre of the hole. First hold the card in place with a finger and, with your lips close to the hole, blow down into the cotton-reel. You will now be able to take your finger away without the card falling off the reel. This is because the moving air above the card produces a lower pressure than that of the air below it. This has the effect of holding the card firmly in place.

Practical applications
The Bernouilli effect has important practical applications in aircraft design, and in aerosol sprays. In a paint spray, air is driven at high speeds across the upper end of a tube, the lower end of which dips into the paint. Because the atmospheric pressure at the bottom of the tube is greater than the pressure of the air at the top, the paint is forced up to the air stream, where it is carried along and dispersed onto the painting surface via the nozzle in the spray.

The various experiments on this page demonstrate that a stream of moving air produces low pressure. The next two will show you something about flight.

Air lift

The 'lift' principle is what keeps aircraft in the air. It is the air streaming at breakneck speed over the *top* of their wings that gives them most of their *lift*. You can prove this by a simple experiment. Anchor one end of a strip of paper between the pages of a book. Now turn on an electric fan or fan heater, directing the air current over the top of the paper. The paper soon lifts and flutters out straight. The normal atmospheric pressure below the paper presses it upwards into the low-pressure, high-velocity air stream.

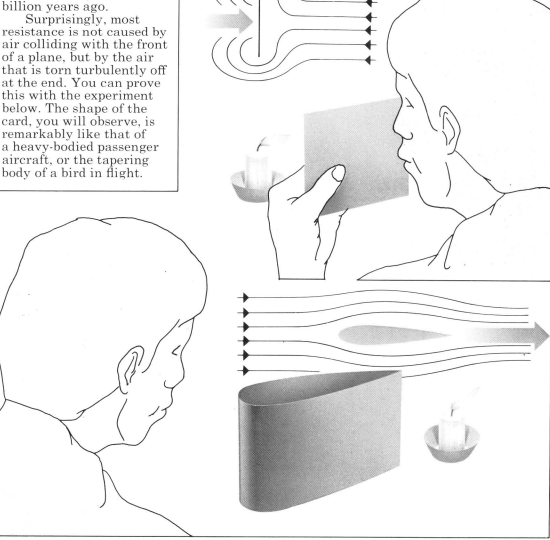

Lift and streamlining

When an airman refers to 'lift', he means that something heavier than air, whether a strip of paper, a bird or a jumbo jet, is lifted up when air moves past it. You will have seen birds staying quite still in the air, wings outstretched. They are using this lift, caused by different air pressures against their wings.

Even the men who designed the first aircraft did not know exactly what held them in the air. At first, lift was thought to be caused by a positive air pressure on the underside of the wing produced by the forward motion of the plane; or to be a mysterious suction produced above the wing as the air was torn away from it.

It was only after research that scientists realized that air was not being torn away from the upper surface of a plane wing, but that it clung closely to the wing surface. It was eventually discovered that the upward curve of the top of the wing surface forced the air to travel more quickly there than at the bottom. The reduced pressure on the upper surface, produced by this increased velocity, accounted for 75% of the plane's lift. The difference in pressure might be only 57–85 g (2–3 oz) per 6 cm² (1 sq in). But, multiplied by thousands of square centimetres, this gave a lift in tonnes.

Streamlining is also vital to aircraft design, because resistance to movement at high speeds can be enormous. This resistance could be reduced, designers found, if aircraft were so shaped that air could flow smoothly around them. The ideal shape turned out to be that of a blunt-nosed fish, a creature streamlined by nature a few billion years ago.

Surprisingly, most resistance is not caused by air colliding with the front of a plane, but by the air that is torn turbulently off at the end. You can prove this with the experiment below. The shape of the card, you will observe, is remarkably like that of a heavy-bodied passenger aircraft, or the tapering body of a bird in flight.

Air drag

Find a flat piece of card and hold it in front of a candle flame. Blow towards the candle as shown in the picture below. The flame will flutter towards you instead of blowing away, because the air was unable to flow smoothly around the flat card. It tumbled erratically past the flame creating currents and a partial vacuum. It is this disturbance at the rear of an aircraft which produces most of an aeroplane's drag If you try the same experiment with a teardrop-shaped card, your breath blows the candle steadily away from you.

You have now investigated two of the forces at work on an aircraft in flight, called *lift* and *drag*. There are also two others, *weight* and *thrust*. Gravity acts upon the weight of the aircraft, pulling it downwards. Lift, provided by air flowing past the wings, counteracts this and keeps the plane airborne. The air resists the aircraft passing through it, causing drag, so the engine must provide enough thrust to overcome this and drive the plane forward. When lift is equal to weight and thrust is equal to drag, then the aircraft is in equilibrium and achieves balanced flight at a constant airspeed.

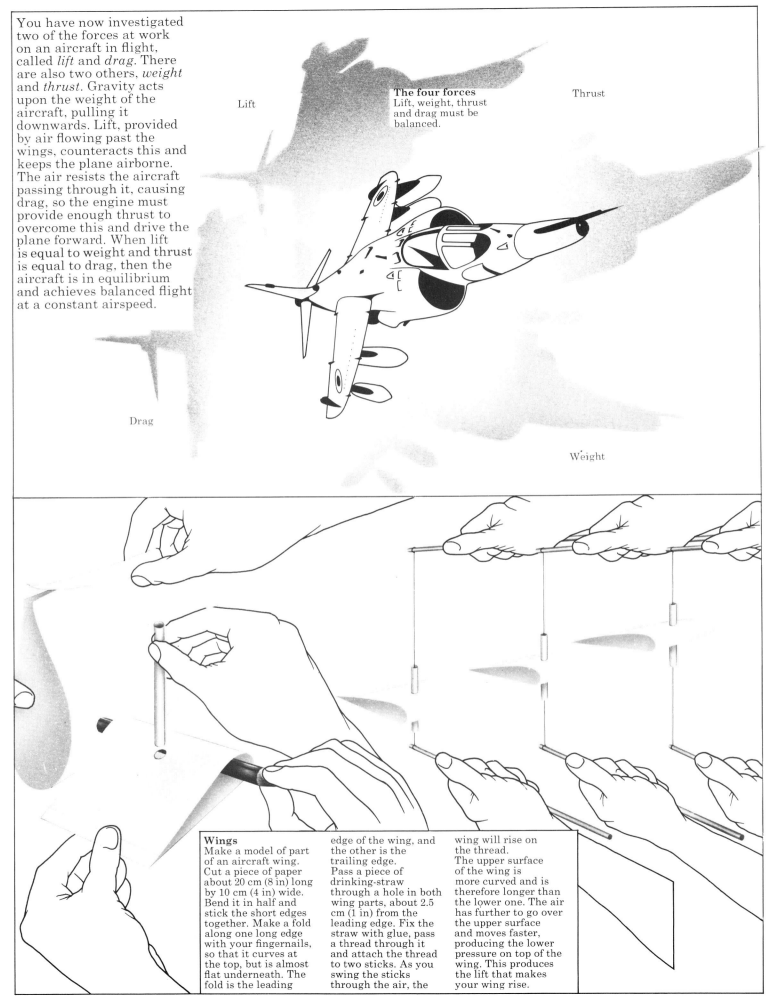

Lift

Drag

The four forces
Lift, weight, thrust and drag must be balanced.

Thrust

Weight

Wings
Make a model of part of an aircraft wing. Cut a piece of paper about 20 cm (8 in) long by 10 cm (4 in) wide. Bend it in half and stick the short edges together. Make a fold along one long edge with your fingernails, so that it curves at the top, but is almost flat underneath. The fold is the leading edge of the wing, and the other is the trailing edge. Pass a piece of drinking-straw through a hole in both wing parts, about 2.5 cm (1 in) from the leading edge. Fix the straw with glue, pass a thread through it and attach the thread to two sticks. As you swing the sticks through the air, the wing will rise on the thread. The upper surface of the wing is more curved and is therefore longer than the lower one. The air has further to go over the upper surface and moves faster, producing the lower pressure on top of the wing. This produces the lift that makes your wing rise.

184

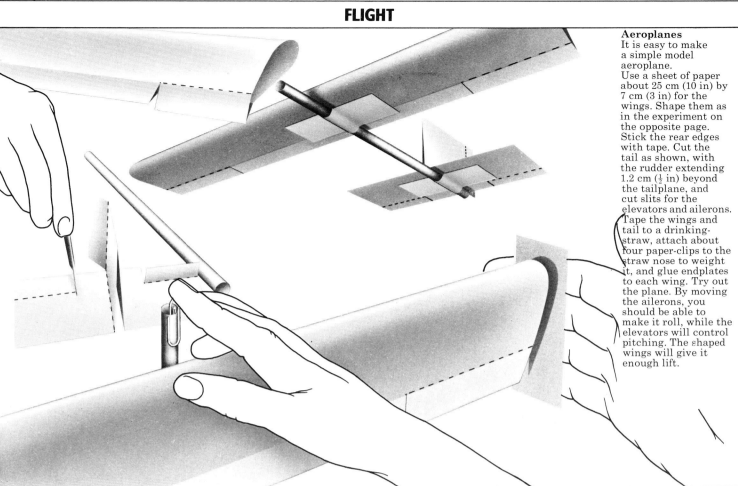

Aeroplanes
It is easy to make a simple model aeroplane.
Use a sheet of paper about 25 cm (10 in) by 7 cm (3 in) for the wings. Shape them as in the experiment on the opposite page. Stick the rear edges with tape. Cut the tail as shown, with the rudder extending 1.2 cm ($\frac{1}{2}$ in) beyond the tailplane, and cut slits for the elevators and ailerons. Tape the wings and tail to a drinking-straw, attach about four paper-clips to the straw nose to weight it, and glue endplates to each wing. Try out the plane. By moving the ailerons, you should be able to make it roll, while the elevators will control pitching. The shaped wings will give it enough lift.

Jet flight

It took a long time for the jet engine to be invented, considering that the principle on which it works was known in ancient Greece. An inventor called Hero developed a sphere that was turned by escaping steam. Two bent nozzles projected at opposite sides of a hollow sphere, mounted so that it could rotate. Steam from the nozzles pushed back on them, causing the ball to whirl round. The idea of using jet-propulsion for aircraft was first suggested in 1865, although the earliest planes were all propeller-driven. Twenty-five years after the Wright brothers' first flight, an English airman called Frank Whittle started work on the first jets. He began planning an engine in the late 1920s, when he was at the Royal Air Force College, at Cranwell. The Air Ministry rejected his designs, so everything had to wait until 1935 when a friend raised money to back him, and Power Jets Ltd was formed. The first working engine ran two years later, and by 1939 the company had a contract to build an engine for the experimental Gloster E28/39, nicknamed the 'Squirt' *(below left)*. The plane flew in May 1941, and was a forerunner of the Gloster Meteor, the Allies' only jet in World War II.

Jet flight is a practical application of Newton's famous Third Law of Motion, which states that for every action there is an equal and opposite reaction. Try it yourself by blowing up a balloon. While you hold the neck the air is trapped; when you let it go, the air rushes out. This action causes a reaction, so the balloon shoots forward in the opposite direction to the air.

You will have proved this law many times. When you jump quickly from a small boat to the shore, you push the boat backwards to propel yourself forwards. When a cork pops from a bottle, the expanding gases push downwards on the bottle with the same force that they hurl the cork into the air. A gun 'kicks' back for the same reason. The cork and bullet only move forward more dramatically than the bottle or gun because they are much lighter.

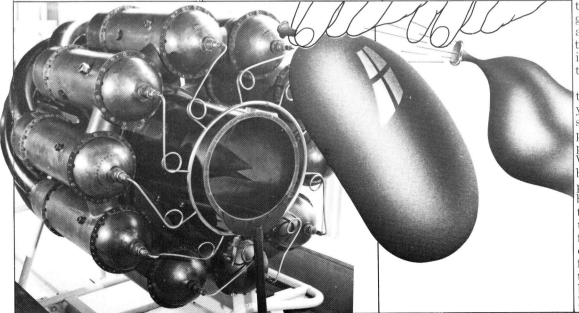

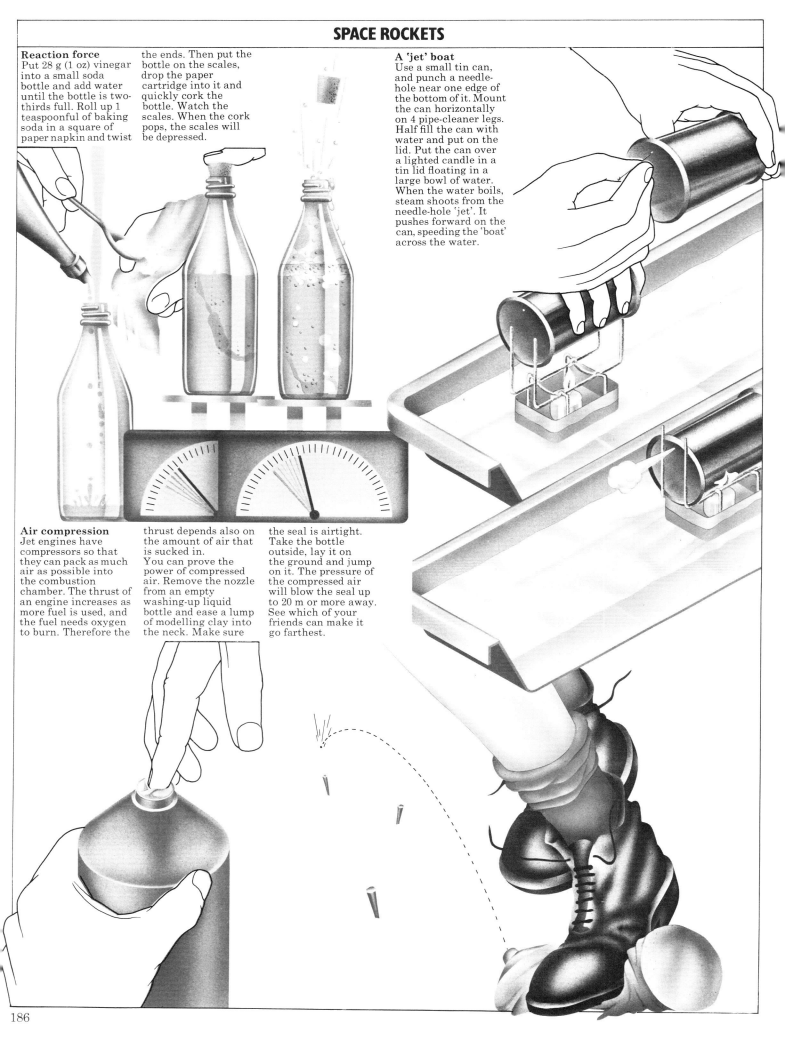

Reaction force
Put 28 g (1 oz) vinegar into a small soda bottle and add water until the bottle is two-thirds full. Roll up 1 teaspoonful of baking soda in a square of paper napkin and twist the ends. Then put the bottle on the scales, drop the paper cartridge into it and quickly cork the bottle. Watch the scales. When the cork pops, the scales will be depressed.

A 'jet' boat
Use a small tin can, and punch a needle-hole near one edge of the bottom of it. Mount the can horizontally on 4 pipe-cleaner legs. Half fill the can with water and put on the lid. Put the can over a lighted candle in a tin lid floating in a large bowl of water. When the water boils, steam shoots from the needle-hole 'jet'. It pushes forward on the can, speeding the 'boat' across the water.

Air compression
Jet engines have compressors so that they can pack as much air as possible into the combustion chamber. The thrust of an engine increases as more fuel is used, and the fuel needs oxygen to burn. Therefore the thrust depends also on the amount of air that is sucked in.
You can prove the power of compressed air. Remove the nozzle from an empty washing-up liquid bottle and ease a lump of modelling clay into the neck. Make sure the seal is airtight. Take the bottle outside, lay it on the ground and jump on it. The pressure of the compressed air will blow the seal up to 20 m or more away. See which of your friends can make it go farthest.

The air becomes thinner as we move away from the Earth's surface, and once in space the atmosphere ends and there is no air. A propellor-driven aeroplane cannot fly above a certain height, because the air is too thin for the propellor to bite into. There is also a height limit for jets above which there is not enough oxygen to burn the fuel. When the air is thin there is also the problem of reduced lift.

That is why scientists have had to look for other methods of travel at great heights in the sky. The ideal answer has been the rocket. Like a jet, a rocket moves by throwing out hot gases, but it takes in its own oxygen for combustion, rather than relying on oxygen in the atmosphere. Therefore a space rocket can burn its fuel and produce thrust when it has travelled beyond the atmosphere. And once in space, much less thrust is needed because there is no air to offer resistance.

When, in the initial stages of a space flight, all the rocket's propellant fuel has been transformed into gas, and thence into thrust, it has reached its maximum velocity. This can only then be increased by a multi-stage system. Each stage has its own supply of fuel, which takes over when the previous supply is exhausted and the spent

part of the rocket is mechanically separated. Now the mass of the vehicle is reduced, and the firing of the new propellant adds greater thrust. Final velocity – the ultimate speed in space – is reached when the last stage, which carries the payload, is detached and thrusts forward.

Compressed air rocket
You can make your own air rocket which uses compressed air. Make a hole in the cap of a plastic bottle, push a plastic straw through and seal the joints with modelling clay. This will act as your launching-pad. The basis of the rocket is a larger straw, which can slide easily over the plastic straw. Paper straws are often wider than the plastic type. Cut the straw down to 10 cm (4 in), decorate it if you wish – stick on four paper triangles to form a tail, and make a head at the other end with a little modelling clay. Push the plastic straw of the launching-pad into the rocket's straw, until it sticks lightly into the clay head. Then press hard on the plastic bottle. The air inside is compressed and when the pressure is great enough, the plastic straw will be freed from the clay head of the rocket. The released air will expand again and the rocket will shoot off to a distance of 9 m (10 yd) or more.

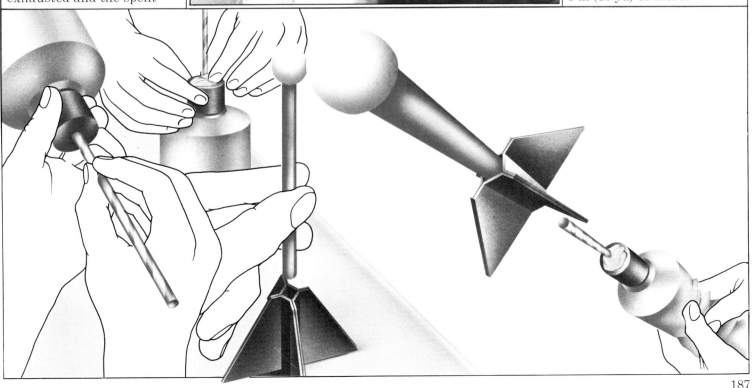

INDEX

**Page numbers in italics
refer to illustrations**

NOTES

ACKNOWLEDGMENTS

The author and publishers wish to thank the many individuals and organizations that provided advice and material for the book. They are grateful in particular to Robert Watkins for his invaluable comments on the text; to Tony Evans for his special photography, and to the artists whose work is a fundamental part of the whole. They are: Alan Austin, Frank Dickens, David Draper, Mike Lynn, David Pocknell, Tony Swift, John Thompson and Gerald Whitcomb.

Thanks are also extended to the following photographers and collections: Ann Ronan Picture Library; Science Museum, London; Royal Astronomical Society, London; Mansell Collection; Space Frontiers; Natural History Photographic Agency; Stephanie Colasanti; Paul Brierley; Popperfoto; South London Consortium for Local Authority Building Research and Development; Photo Research International; Meteorological Office, Bracknell; Ronald Sheridan; Mary Evans Picture Library; Camera Press; Jonathan Bayer; Keystone Press Agency; P Morris; New South Wales Government House, London; Picturepont.

PRINTED IN BELGIUM BY

proost
INTERNATIONAL BOOK PRODUCTION

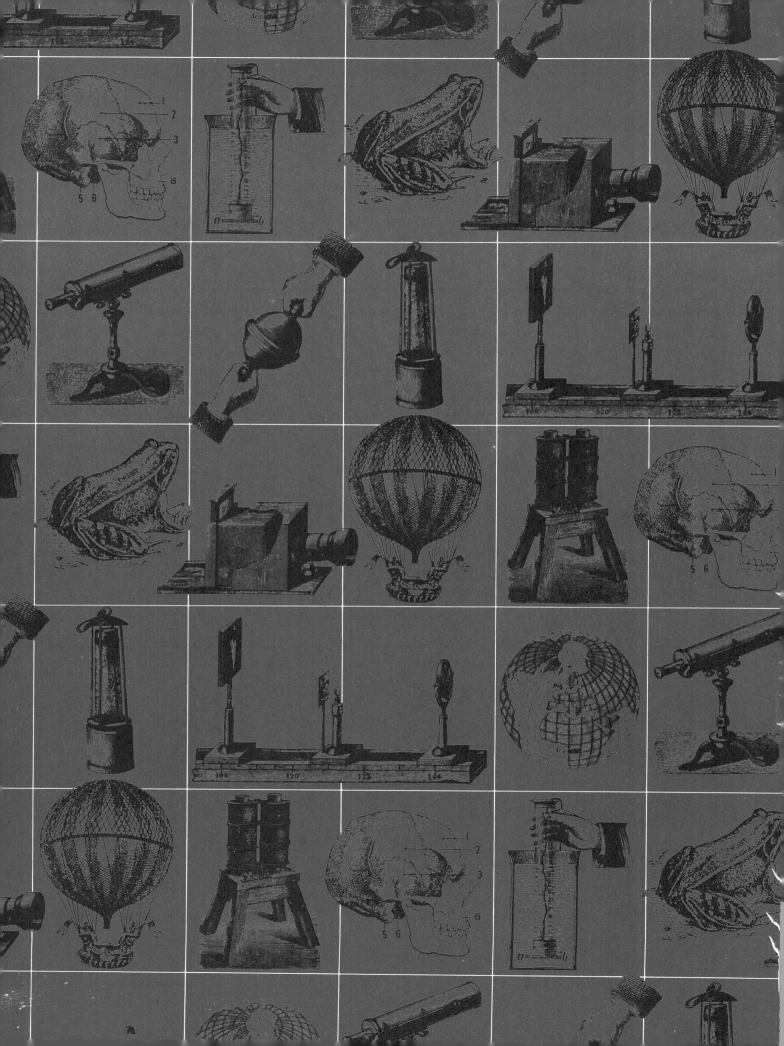